THIS BITCH OF A LIFE

CARLOS MOORE

Foreword by Gilberto Gil
Introduction by Margaret Busby

Lawrence Hill Books

Cover design: Jonathan Hahn
Cover photograph: © David Corio
Spine illustration: Vincent Gordon
Photo credits: Photographs © by individual photographers (André
Bernabé, Chico, Donald Cox, Bernard Matussière, Raymond
Sardaby) and Fela Kuti, Fela Kuti Collection

Published by Lawrence Hill Books
An imprint of Chicago Review Press, Incorporated
814 North Franklin Street
Chicago, Illinois 60610
ISBN: 978-1-55652-835-4
Printed in the United States of America
5 4 3 2

Contents

Foreword

Gilberto Gil

Rio de Janeiro, Brazil, August 18, 2008

Africa, with her many peoples and cultures, is where the tragi-comedy of the human race first fatefully presented itself, wearing a mask at once beautiful and horrendous. The Motherland, the cradle of civilization, acknowledged as the original birthplace of us all, where the body and soul of mankind sank earliest roots into the soil—Africa is, confoundingly, also the most reviled, wounded, and disinherited of continents. Africa, treasure trove of fabulous material and symbolic riches that throughout history have succored the rest of the world, is yet the terrain that witnesses the greatest hunger ever, for bread and for justice.

This is the scenario into which Fela Anikulapo-Kuti, Africa's most recent genius, emerged and struggled.

I was privileged to meet Fela in 1977 in his own musical kingdom, the Shrine, a club located in one of Lagos's lively working-class neighborhoods. It was during the Second Festival of Black and African Arts and Culture (FESTAC), and on that evening the great Stevie Wonder was also visiting.

Fela was the brilliant incarnation of Africa's tragic dimension. He was an authentic contemporary African hero whose genius was to make his scream heard in every corner of the globe. Through his art, his wisdom, his politics, his formidable vigor and love of life, he managed to rend the stubborn veil that marginalizes "Otherness." Deeply torn between the imperative of rejecting a legacy of subordination and the need to affirm a new libertarian future for his land and people, Fela ended up creating a body of work that is incomparable in terms of international popular music that expresses the cosmopolitan—and "cosmopolitical"—spirit of the second half of the twentieth century.

Fela was possessed by an apocalyptic vision, wherein he saw how tall were the walls that had to be broken down. Thus, he engaged in a messianic rebellion. He was enthralled by the haunting lamentations that emerged from the diaspora of uprooted black slaves, reminding him of his own outraged sense of deracination in his native Africa—a land increasingly usurped by neocolonial self-interest. He was divided between the *awareness* that a universal future for all mankind was inevitable and the *awareness* that there was danger in denying Africa its own place in that future. Therefore he determined to rescue, both for his own people and for the world, the wise traditions of tribal Africa, having in mind that we might one day constitute a global tribe.

Arming himself with a Saxon horn—a saxophone—Fela made music that harked back to days of yore, when his forebears were warriors and cattle herders. Yet putting into the balance his virtuoso improvisation, his poetic outbursts, he made everyone swing: in the Shrine, in the whole of Lagos, in every reservation, in every shantytown, in every township of the black planet.

Today, some time after his passing, we are at a juncture at which we recognize and acknowledge Fela's work. But we must confer another form of acknowledgment, one that goes beyond the careful, reverential attention that, increasingly, is afforded his music—an acknowledgment in a wider intellectual sense: one rooted in a careful analytical interpretation of what Fela and his work stood for.

This book is among those that are aiming to fulfill that mandate.

At a time when, all over the world, we are engaged in the huge and (who knows?) perhaps final effort to establish a viable humanist legacy for the generations still to come—in an era that I may call posthuman—it is indispensable to be able to rely on books that bestow on those efforts a true dimension of legacy.

We need books that will tell us, now and here, and that later on will also tell the builders of posthumankind, about those notable men and women of our recent past, such as Fela Anikulapo-Kuti.

We need to know who they were and what they were about and how they have enriched us.

Translated from the Portuguese by Tereza Burmeister

A Note from the Author

Originally published in France in 1982 as *Cette putain de vie (This Bitch of a Life)*, this book was born of a deep friendship with Fela and could not have been written in the first person without his unreserved trust. He never intruded in the work and allowed me full access to his personal files and domestic intimacy. I thank him; his senior wife, the late Remi Taylor; his cowives; and those members of his organization who assisted me in gathering the material for the book: J. K. Braimah, Mabinuori Kayode Idowu (aka ID), Durotimi Ikujenyo (aka Duro), and bandleader Lekan Animashaun. I am also grateful to Sandra Izsadore, Fela's long-time friend, for her generous assistance.

Writing the life story of someone else in the first person, then translating it into another language, are tricky and perilous tasks. I succeeded only thanks to Shawna Davis, who transcribed and edited the more than fifteen hours of tape-recorded interviews that served as the building blocks for the original version, then translated the manuscript into English. Her involvement was particularly important in the two opening chapters, "Abiku" and "Three Thousand Strokes," and she contributed the descriptive biographical presentations of all those interviewed, as well as the general introduction to chapter 19, "My Queens" (where for the first time Fela's wives expressed themselves). Without Shawna's rewriting and translation skills, and keen eye for the artistic, *Fela: This Bitch of a Life* would have been a much different and certainly less attractive book. My debt to her is immense.

Gratitude is also due to Nayede Thompson, who assisted Shawna with the transcription and early drafts. I am beholden to the late Ellen Wright—former literary agent and widow of Richard Wright—for having read the original manuscript and made pertinent suggestions, as did Marcia Lord, whose feedback was greatly valued.

In addition, I acknowledge the generous assistance of André

Bernabé, Heriberto Cuadrado Cogollo, and Donald Cox, whose photos, drawings, and newspaper collages helped create the proper mood for Fela's story.

This book owes a lot to Margaret Busby, who published the first English edition of the book in 1982. Befittingly, twenty-seven years later she has written the introduction to this new edition. I thank her dearly.

I am especially grateful to Gilberto Gil for undertaking to write the foreword and to Stevie Wonder, Hugh Masekela, Randy Weston, and Femi Kuti for their commentaries.

My literary agent, Janell Agyeman, and Lawrence Hill Books senior editor Susan Bradanini Betz worked hard toward the agreement that has finally made Fela's life story, told in his own words, available to the public once more, and for the first time in the United States.

Introduction

Margaret Busby

Fela Anikulapo-Kuti was a fearless maverick for whom music was a righteous and invincible weapon. His self-given second name, Anikulapo—which translates as "the one who carries death in his pouch"—spoke of indestructibility and resilience. It was an apt choice for the creator of an amazingly timeless body of work that for decades has transcended barriers of class and nationality, gathering ever more strength and devotees with the passing decades. Fela was indeed a man who seems always to have been destined for the almost-mythical status he has now claimed among music fans around the world.

When his life was cut short in 1997, after fifty-eight years lived to the extreme and beyond all predictable convention, countless individuals felt the loss. On the day of his funeral, the streets of Lagos were brought to a standstill, with more than a million people defying the Nigerian government ban on public gatherings that had been imposed by the military dictator General Sani Abacha. One hundred and fifty thousand mourners are reputed to have queued in Tafawa Balewa Square, in the heart of Lagos, to pay their last respects as they filed past the glass coffin, which was then carried by hearse through the extraordinary throng, the cavalcade taking seven hours to cover a mere twenty kilometers to reach the neighborhood of Ikeja, where Fela was to be laid to rest.

In the words of Fela's illustrious cousin, the Nobel Prize–winning writer Wole Soyinka, "Neither the police nor the military dared show its face on that day, and the uniformed exceptions only came to pay tribute. Quite openly, with no attempt whatsoever at disguising their identities, they stopped by his bier, saluted the stilled scourge of corrupt power, mimic culture and militarism. It was a much needed act of solidarity for us."[1]

More than a decade has passed since then, and recognition of Fela and of his significance is at an all-time high. The multinational entertainment group HMV ranked him as number 46 in a

9

list of the 100 most influential musicians of the twentieth century. His ongoing legacy has been confirmed not only in the rising individual musical careers of his two sons, Femi (who served a teenage apprenticeship with his father's band Egypt 80 before founding his own, the Positive Force) and Seun (inheritor of Egypt 80), but also in the plethora of commemorative events to honor him that have been mounted in major cities around the world and that continue to be planned. There have been birthday concerts played and tribute CDs produced, involving musicians as varied as Jorge Ben, Macy Gray, Manu Dibango, MeShell Ndegecello, Baaba Maal, Archie Shepp, and Taj Mahal, among others. From London to San Francisco there have been major exhibitions, including the 2003–2004 multimedia "Black President: The Art and Legacy of Fela Kuti" exhibition, curated by Trevor Schoonmaker for the New Museum of Contemporary Art in New York, which celebrated Fela through the response of an impressive variety of visual and other artists. The year 2008 brought exciting news of *Fela! A New Musical* bursting onto the Off-Broadway stage. Ethnomusicologist Michael Veal's scholarly work *Fela: Life and Times of an African* brought Fela to the attention of the academic community, and a groundbreaking film is in preparation by acclaimed director John Akomfrah. The momentum is indeed gathering for a whole new generation to be brought the message of Fela Kuti.

However, anyone who seeks the essence of the man himself can still do no better than reading the only book that can lay claim to being autobiographical, distilled from hours of conversation and close interaction between Fela and Carlos Moore. *Fela, Fela: This Bitch of a Life*, first published by Allison & Busby in London over a quarter century ago, has long been out of print, with rare secondhand copies changing ownership sometimes at hundreds of dollars, so it is gratifying that it is at last to enjoy currency again. Here can be found Fela's uncensored and uncompromising words and thoughts.

Twenty-five-plus years ago, when this book originally appeared, becoming the first biography ever (to my knowledge) of an African musician, Fela could accurately be described as controversy personified—African superstar, popular composer, singer-musician who had swept to international celebrity on a wave of scandal and flamboyance. He was "a living legend . . . Africa's most popular entertainer," said the *New Musical Express*. His volcanic performances and notoriously unconventional lifestyle brought him into constant conflict with the Nigerian authorities, while millions of ordinary people connected emotionally and physically with his

10

songs. Newspaper headlines played up his public image, his marriage to twenty-seven women, the brutal raid on his household, his arrest and acquittal on numerous charges.

By the accident of birth Fela (or Olufela Olusegun Oludotun Ransome-Kuti, as he was originally named) could have chosen to settle for the conformist existence and trappings of Nigeria's educated middle class, yet from the outset he instinctively rejected that option. He considered himself an *abiku*, a spirit child in the Yoruba tradition, who was reborn on October 15, 1938, in Abeokuta, the fourth of five children, coming into the world three years after his politically aware parents had suffered an infant bereavement. His mother Funmilayo was a pioneering feminist and campaigner in the anticolonial movement; his father, Reverend Israel Ransome-Kuti, was the first president of the Nigerian Union of Teachers.[2]

At the age of nineteen Fela was sent to London to study medicine but instead enrolled at Trinity College of Music, forming his Koola Lobitos band in 1961 with his school friend J. K. Braimah. In 1969 he traveled with the group to the United States, where he connected with Black Power militants and became increasingly politicized. Specifically, his meeting with Sandra Smith (currently Sandra Izsadore), a member of the Black Panthers, was a catalyst for everything that was to follow. Turned on to books on black history and politics, particularly Alex Haley's *The Autobiography of Malcolm X*, Fela began to demonstrate a new consciousness in his lyrics.

He returned to Nigeria, renamed the band Afrika 70, offloaded his "slave name" of Ransome, and set to championing the cause of the poor underclass and exposing the hypocrisy of the ruling elites, establishing his commune, the Kalakuta Republic, and his nightclub, the Afrika Shrine. The pidgin in which he wrote his lyrics, dealing wittily and provocatively with everything from gender relations to government corruption, made him accessible and hugely popular not only in Nigeria but in the rest of Africa, in line with the Nkrumahist Pan-Africanism he espoused, as well as bringing him to the attention of top musicians from the West. The genre he created, Afrobeat, is a heady, mesmerizing concoction with traditional African rhythmic roots but which also drew on various strands of contemporary black music—jazz, calypso, funk. It was a two-way process, and when James Brown and his musicians toured Nigeria in 1970 they took notice of what the rebellious young Nigerian was doing. He was making an indelible impact on master performers such as Gilberto Gil and Stevie

11

Wonder, Randy Weston, and Hugh Masekela. Paul McCartney, recording in Lagos in 1972, called Fela's group "the best band I've ever seen live. . . . When Fela and his band eventually began to play, after a long, crazy build-up, I just couldn't stop weeping with joy. It was a very moving experience."[3] (Fela did not return the compliment, reportedly berating the Beatle for trying to "steal black man's music.") Brian Eno of Roxy Music and David Byrne of Talking Heads are among those who could also testify to the fact that encountering Fela and his music had a way of changing people's lives forever.

The Nigerian establishment and the military regime responded with increasing violence both to Fela's counterculture lifestyle and to his naked condemnation of the military regime, notably in his 1977 hit "Zombie." His compound was attacked by hundreds of soldiers, who not only inflicted a fractured skull and other wounds on Fela but callously threw his octogenarian mother out of a window, leading to her death—an episode trenchantly marked in "Coffin for Head of State" and "Unknown Soldier." He founded an organization called Movement of the People, but his ambition to run for the presidency of Nigeria was thwarted by the authorities.

Fela adamantly disavowed conventional morals, and his unabashed, sacramental approach to sex awakened the media's prurient interest. It is rare to find any press consideration of his music that does not interpolate voyeuristic references to his domestic arrangements, and there is no denying that he was a gift to the tabloid media in thrall to the exoticism of black sexuality. This is not the place to debate in detail what the connection may be between Fela's polygyny and the misogyny he has been accused of (evidenced by songs such as "Mattress"), but it is worth mentioning a theory that has been advanced by DJ Rita Ray: that, far from exploiting the young women he took as wives—his "queens," many of whom speak out for themselves for the first time in this book—Fela was taking a progressive stance by conferring on his dancers the respectability of being married. Nonetheless, for a man who was so clear-sighted on certain political issues, he was not immune from embracing often dubious attitudes, be they sexist or homophobic. Now, as much as then, Fela has the capability to disturb and shock and confuse, as well as to inspire. Insofar as he was resistant to being made to feel there was anything shameful or immoral in the pursuit of sexual pleasure, he chose to believe he was simply interpreting and expressing what comes naturally for the typical African male, unfettered by Western-imposed religious teachings. Nor, it has to be said, were his views on women necessarily far removed from those that could have been found among many other black militants of the era.

As much as Fela was a man of principle, he was a man of contradiction. His lasting appeal is in the sum of all the parts. He was a composer, a protest singer, and a multi-instrumentalist—a visionary musician rather than a technical virtuoso. He was a rebel and a revolutionary and, at the same time, a kind of shaman. The infectious groove of his compositions is accompanied by razor-sharp social commentary, the shifts of gear and mood changes of each track sometimes extending for as long as thirty minutes. As the revolutionary philosopher and psychiatrist Frantz Fanon did long before him, Fela identified the ills afflicting postindependence Africa, saw that the new elites were not going to be the emancipators. In "Colonial Mentality" he accused:

You don be slave from before,
Dem don release you now
But you never release yourself.

In composition after composition, Fela mounted a sustained challenge to neocolonialism and was unafraid to name names when condemning the specific failings of those in authority in Nigeria. Little wonder that he was rewarded with their opprobrium. But that violent hostility of the ruling elite was the price Fela accepted he must pay for advocating people power.

"Fela loved to buck the system," his relative Wole Soyinka recognized. "His music, to many, was both salvation and echo of their anguish, frustrations and suppressed aggression. The black race was the beginning and end of knowledge and wisdom, his life mission, to effect a mental and physical liberation of the race."[4]

Fela: This Bitch of a Life is unique in being able to give us some truly remarkable insights into an acknowledged creative genius for whom even superlatives can seem inadequate.

Notes

1. Wole Soyinka, *You Must Set Forth at Dawn: A Memoir* (London: Methuen, in association with Bookcraft, 2007), 35.
2. Activism and public service are a Ransome-Kuti family hallmark. Fela's brothers were both respected doctors: Beko (1940–2006) helped form Nigeria's first human rights organization and in the 1990s was sentenced to life imprisonment at a military tribunal;

13

Koye (1927–2003) was professor of pediatrics at the University of Lagos and deputy director general of the World Health Organization. Their indefatigable sister Yemisi is a patron of the arts and currently executive director of the Nigeria Network of Non-Government Organisations.

3. Quoted in Peter Culshaw, "The Big Fela," *The Observer* (August 15, 2004).
4. Soyinka, *You Must Set Forth*, 33.

Discography

Discography of Fela Anikulapo-Kuti

1960s

Fela Ransome-Kuti and His Highlife Rakers
"Aigana" b/w "Fela's Special" (7" UK,
Melodisc 1532)

Fela Ransome-Kuti and His Highlife Rakers
"Highlife Rakers Calypso No.1" b/w
"Wa Ba Mi Jo Bosue" (7" UK, Melodisc
unissued)

The Highlife Jazz Band
"Onifere" (7" Nigeria, Phillips)

The Highlife Jazz Band
"Yeshe Yeshe" (7" Nigeria, Phillips)

The Highlife Jazz Band
"Mr. Who Are You" (7" Nigeria, Phillips)

Fela Ransome-Kuti and His Koola Lobitos
"Bonfo" b/w "Fere" (7" Nigeria, RK label RK1)

Fela Ransome-Kuti and His Koola Lobitos
"Onifere No. 2" b/w "Oyejo" (7" Nigeria,
RK label RK4)

Fela Ransome-Kuti and His Koola Lobitos
"Oloruka" b/w "Awo" (7" Nigeria, RK label
RK5)

Fela Ransome-Kuti Quintet
"Great Kids" b/w "Amaechi's Blues" (7"
Nigeria, Phillips West Africa Records
382734 PF [PF 734])

Fela Ransome-Kuti and His Koola Lobitos
"Yese" b/w "Egbin" (7" Nigeria, Parlophone
NPJ420—7XNPS1399/1400)

Fela Ransome-Kuti and His Koola Lobitos
"Ololufe" b/w "Araba's Delight"
(7" Nigeria, Parlophone
NPJ513—7XNPS1573/1574)

Fela Ransome-Kuti and His Koola Lobitos
"Wadele" (or "Wa Dele") b/w
"Laise" (7" Nigeria, Parlophone
NPJ514—7XNPS1575/1576)

Fela Ransome-Kuti and His Koola Lobitos
"Omuti Ti Se" (7" Nigeria)

Fela Ransome-Kuti and the Koola Lobitos
(1965, LP Nigeria, EMI PNL 1002)
[A] "Signature Tune" / "It's Highlife Time"
/ "Lagos Baby" / "Omuti" / "Ololufe" /
"Araba's Delight"
[B] "Wa Dele" / "Lai Se" / "Mi O Mo" /
"Obinrin Le" / "Omo Ejo"

Koola Lobitos featuring VC 7
"Orise" b/w "Eke" (7" Nigeria, Parlophone
NPJ533—7XNPS1613/1614)
Koola Lobitos featuring VC 7
"V. C. 7" b/w "I Know Your Feel-
ing" (7" Nigeria, Parlophone
NPJ534—7XNPS1615/1616)

Fela Ransome-Kuti Quintet
Title Unknown (LP Nigeria)
[A] "Great Kids" / "Lagos Baby" / "Lai Se"
/ "Wa Dele"
[B] "Mi O Mo" / "Ajo" / "Iya Mi Oshe O!" /
"Araba's Delight"

Fela Ransome-Kuti plays with The Koola Lobitos
"Mi O Fe" b/w "Fine, Fine Baby" (7" Nigeria, Parlophone PNE101)

Fela Ransome-Kuti plays with The Koola Lobitos
"Die Die" b/w "Kusimilaya" (7" Nigeria, Parlophone PNE102)

Fela Ransome-Kuti and His Koola Lobitos
"Fire" b/w "Oni Machini" (7" Nigeria, Parlophone PNE103)

Fela Ransome-Kuti and His Koola Lobitos
Title Unknown (LP Nigeria)
[A] "Ololufe" / "Ayawa Ni" / "Onidodo" / "Yese" / "Araba's Delight"
[B] "Abiara" / "Onijibiti" / "Madele" / "Orun" / "Ojo"

Fela Ransome-Kuti and His Koola Lobitos
Afro Beat on Stage: Recorded Live at the Afro Spot (10" LP Nigeria, Phillips/Polydor PLP001)
[A] "Everyday I Got My Blues" / "Moti Gborokan" / "Waka Waka"
[B] "Ako" / "Ororuka" / "Lai Se"

Fela Ransome-Kuti and His Koola Lobitos
"Onidodo" b/w "Alagbara" (7" Nigeria, Phillips West Africa Records PF383 620)

Fela Ransome-Kuti and His Koola Lobitos
"Abiara" b/w "Ajo" (7" Nigeria, Phillips West Africa Records PF383 622)

Fela Ransome-Kuti and His Koola Lobitos
"Waka Waka" b/w "Se E Tunde" (7" Nigeria, Phillips West Africa Records PF383 802)

Fela Ransome-Kuti and His Koola Lobitos
"My Baby Don Love Me" b/w "Home Cooking" (7" Nigeria, Phillips WA425004)

Fela Ransome-Kuti and His Koola Lobitos
Voice of America Sessions
"Ironu" / "Magbe Yenwa" / "Iro" / "Ojo (Part 1)" / "Ojo (Part 2)" / "Oyejo" / "Igba L'aiye"

Fela Ransome-Kuti and The Nigeria 70
"Viva Nigeria" b/w "Witchcraft" (1969, 7" Nigeria, The Duke Records DUK-001)

Fela Ransome-Kuti and The Nigeria 70
"Lover" b/w "Wayo" (1969, 7" Nigeria, The Duke Records DUK-002)

Fela Ransome-Kuti and The Nigeria 70
"Ako" b/w "Ladies Frustration" (1969, 7" Nigeria, The Duke Records DUK-005)

Fela Ransome-Kuti and His Africa 70
Fela Fela Fela (LP Nigeria, EMI HMV HNLX5033)
[A] "My Lady's Frustration" / "Viva Nigeria" / "Obe (Stew)" / "Ako" / "Witchcraft"
[B] "Wayo" / "Lover" / "Funky Horn" / "Eko" / "This Is Sad"

1970s

Fela Ransome-Kuti and The Nigeria 70
Fela's London Scene (1970, LP Nigeria, EMI HNLX5200; LP USA (1983), Editions Makossa M2399)
[A] "J'ehin-J'ehin" / "Egbe Mi O"
[B] "Who're You" / "Buy Africa" / "Fight to Finish"

Fela Ransome-Kuti and The Africa 70
"Blackman's Cry" b/w "Beautiful Dancer" (1970, 7" Nigeria, EMI HMV HNP526; 7" France, Pathe Marconi 2C006-80777)

Fela Ransome-Kuti and The Nigeria 70
"Jeun K'oku (Chop & Quench) Part I" b/w "Jeun K'oku (Chop & Quench) Part II" (1971, 7" Nigeria, EMI HMV HNS1016; Ghana, EMI HMV HNS1016; France 1970-1971; Pathe Marconi 2C006-80776)

Fela Ransome-Kuti and His Africa 70
"Na Fight-O! (Part 1)" b/w "Na Fight-O! (Part 2)" (7" Nigeria, EMI HMV HNS1049)

Fela Ransome-Kuti and His Africa 70
"Who're You? (Part 1)" b/w "Who're You? (Part 2)" (1971, 7" Nigeria, EMI HMV HNS1058; Ghana, EMI HMV HNS1058)

Fela Ransome-Kuti and His Africa 70
"Jeun K'oku (Instrumental version, Part 1)"
b/w "Jeun K'oku (Instrumental version, Part
2)" (1971, 7" Nigeria, EMI HMV HNS1075)

Fela Ransome-Kuti and His Africa 70
"Don't Gag Me (Part 1") b/w "Don't Gag
Me (Part 2)" (7" Nigeria, Jon200; Ghana,
Jon200)

Fela Ransome-Kuti and The Africa 70
Why Black Man Dey Suffer (1971, LP Nige-
ria, African Songs AS0001)
[A] "Why Black Man Dey Suffer"
[B] "Ikoyi Mentality Versus Mushin
Mentality"

Fela Ransome-Kuti and His Africa 70
The Best of Fela (1971, LP Nigeria, EMI
HMV HNLX5043)
[A] "Beautiful Dancer" / "Jeun Ko Ku
(Chop and Quench) (Part1 & Part 2)" /
"Black Man's Cry"
[B] "Na Fight O (Part1 & Part 2)" / "Who're
You?"

Fela Ransome-Kuti and The Africa 70
Na Poi (1971, LP Nigeria, EMI HMV
HNLX 5070)
[A] "Na Poi (Part 1)"
[B] "Na Poi (Part 2)" / "You No Go Die
Unless You Wan Die"

Fela Ransome-Kuti and The Africa 70
"Alujon-Jon-Ki-Jon (Part 1)" b/w "Alu-
jon-Jon-Ki-Jon (Part 2)" (7" Ghana, HMV
HNS1119)

Fela Ransome-Kuti and The Nigeria 70
"Beggar's Song (Orin Alagbe) (Part 1)" b/w
"Beggar's Song (Orin Alagbe) (Part 2)" (7"
Nigeria, HMV HNS1237)

Fela Ransome-Kuti and The Nigeria 70
"Shenshema (Part 1)" b/w "Shenshema (Part
2)" (1971, 7" Nigeria, HMV HNS1299)

Fela Ransome-Kuti and The Nigeria 70
"Monday Morning (Part 1)" b/w "Mon-
day Morning (Part 2)" (7" Nigeria, HMV
HNS1322)

Fela Ransome-Kuti and The Nigeria 70
"Fogo-Fogo (Part 1)" b/w "Fogo-Fogo (Part
2)" (7" Ghana, HMV HNS1472)

Fela Ransome-Kuti and The Africa 70
"Ariya (Part 1)" b/w "Ariya (Part 2)" (7"
Nigeria, HMV HNS1531)

Fela Ransome-Kuti and The Africa 70
"Going In and Coming Out (Part 1)" b/w
"Going In and Coming Out (Part 2)" (7"
Nigeria, EMI(s) 062N)

Fela Ransome-Kuti and The Africa 70
*The Best of Fela Volume 2: Fela's Budget
Special* (LP Nigeria, EMI HNLX 5081)
[A] "Monday Morning in Lagos" / "Shensh-
ema" / "Don't Gag Me"
[B] "Beggar's Song" / "Alu-Jon-Jon-Ki-Jon"
/ "Chop & Quench (Instrumental)"

Fela Ransome-Kuti and The Africa 70
Open and Close (1971, LP Nigeria, EMI
HNLX5090; LP France (1975), Pathe Mar-
coni 062-81957)
[A] "Open and Close" / "Swegbe and Pako"
[B] "Gbagada Gbagada Gbogodo Gbogodo"

Fela Ransome-Kuti The Africa 70 (with
Ginger Baker)
Live! (1971, LP UK, Regal Zonophone
SLRZ1023)
[A] "Let's Start" / "Black Man's Cry"
[B] "Ye Ye De Smell" / "Egbe Mi O (Carry
Me, I Want to Die)"

Fela Ransome-Kuti and His Nigeria 70
"Chop and Quench" b/w "Egbe Mi O" (7"
UK, Regal Zonophone RZ3052)

Ginger Baker with Fela Ransome-Kuti
(voice over, keyboard)
Stratavarious (1972, LP UK, Polydor 2383
133; LP USA, Atco SD7013)
[A] "Ariwo" / "Tiwa"
[B] "Something Nice" / "Juju" / "Blood
Brothers 69" / "Coda"

Fela Ransome-Kuti and His Nigeria 70
"Let's Start" b/w "Egbe Mi O" (7" France,
Pathe Marconi 2C006-80995)

Fela Ransome-Kuti and The Africa 70
"Egbe Mi O" b/w "Chop & Quench" (1972,
7" Ghana, Stateside GSS0029)

Fela Ransome-Kuti and The Africa 70
Shakara (1972, LP Nigeria, EMI 008N;
1974, LP USA, Editions Makossa EM2305;
1974LP France Pathe Marconi 062 82718;
1975, LP UK, Creole CRLP501)
[A] "Shakara Oloje"
[B] "Lady"

Fela Ransome-Kuti and The Africa 70
Music of Fela / Roforofo Fight (1972, LP
Nigeria, Jofabro Nigeria JILP001; 1975,
LP USA, Editions Makossa EM2307 and
EM2309; 1976, LP France, Pathe Marconi
062-82132/3)
[A] "Roforofo Fight"
[B] "Trouble Sleep Yanga Wake Am
[C] "Question Jam Answer"
[D] "Go Slow"

Fela Ransome-Kuti and The Africa 70
Afrodisiac (1973, LP Nigeria, EMI 062;
1972, LP UK, Regal Zonophone/EMI
SLRZ1034; 1975, LP France, Pathe Marconi
062 81290)
[A] "Alu Jon Jonki Jon" / "Chop and
Quench"
[B] "Eko Ile" / "Je'n Wi Temi"

Fela Ransome-Kuti and The Africa 70
Gentleman (1973, LP Nigeria, EMI NEMI
0009; 1975, LP France, Pathe Marconi 2C
062 81960; 1979, LP UK, Creole CRLP502;
1983, LP USA, Makossa M2398)
[A] "Gentleman"
[B] "Fefe Naa Efe" / "Igbe (Na Shit)"

Fela Ransome-Kuti and The Africa 70
Alagbon Close (1974, LP Nigeria, Jofabro
Nigeria JILP1002; 1975, LP USA, Editions
Makossa EM2313; 1976, LP France, Pathe
Marconi 062-82135)
[A] "Alagbon Close"
[B] "I No Get Eye for Back"

Fela Ransome-Kuti and The Africa 70
He Miss Road (1975, LP Nigeria, EMI

006N; LP France, Pathe Marconi 052 81958
1984, LP UK, rereleased on Sterns 3008)
[A] "He Miss Road" / "Monday Morning in
Lagos"
[B] "He No Possible"

Fela Ransome-Kuti and The Africa 70
Expensive Shit (1975, LP Nigeria, Sound-
work Shop SWS1001; LP USA, Editions
Makossa EM2315)
[A] "Expensive Shit"
[B] "Water No Get Enemy"

Fela Ransome-Kuti and The Africa 70
Noise for Vendor Mouth (1975, LP Nigeria,
Afrobeat ABRO11)
[A] "Noise for Vendor Mouth"
[B] "Mattress"

Fela Ransome-Kuti and The Africa 70
Everything Scatter (1975, LP Nigeria, Coco-
nut PMLP1000; 1976, LP France, Phillips
9286-434;1977, LP UK, Creole CRLP509)
[A] "Everything Scatter"
[B] "Who No Know Go Know"

Fela Ransome-Kuti and The Africa 70
Confusion (1975, LP Nigeria, EMI
NEMI0004; LP France, Pathe Marconi
062-81959)
[A] "Confusion" (Instrumental)
[B] "Confusion" (Vocal)

Tony Allen and The Africa 70 with Fela
Ransome-Kuti (tenor sax, piano, arr., prod.)
Jealousy (1975, LP Nigeria, Sound Work-
shop 1004)
[A] "Jealousy"
[B] "Hustler"

Fela Ransome-Kuti and The Africa 70
Kalakuta Show (LP Nigeria, EMI; LP
Nigeria, Kalakuta KR 01; 1976, LP USA,
Editions Makossa M2320; 1976, LP France,
Pathe Marconi 062-82134)
[A] "Kalakuta Show"
[B] "Don't Meke Garnan Garnan"

Fela Ransome-Kuti and The Africa 70
No Bread (1976, LP Nigeria, Soundwork

Shop SWS1003; 1982, LP USA, Editions
Makossa EM2382)
[A] "No Bread"
[B] "Unnecessary Begging"

Fela Anikulapo-Kuti and The Africa 70
Ikoyi Blindness (1976, LP Nigeria, Africa
Music AMILP001)
[A] "Ikoyi Blindness"
[B] "Gba Mi Leti Ki N'dolowo"

Fela Anikulapo-Kuti and The Africa 70
Yellow Fever (1976, LP Nigeria, Decca
Afrodisia DWAPS2004)
[A] "Yellow Fever"
[B] "Napoi 75"

Fela Anikulapo-Kuti and The Africa 70
Upside Down (1976, LP Nigeria, Decca
Afrodisia DWAPS2005; 1985, LP USA,
Celluloid CELL 6123; 1990, CD USA,
CELD6123)
[A] "Upside Down"
[B] "Go Slow"

Fela Anikulapo-Kuti and The Africa 70
Before I Jump Like Monkey Give Me Banana
(1976, LP Nigeria, Coconut PMLP1001)
[A] "Monkey Banana"
[B] "Sense Wiseness"

Fela Anikulapo-Kuti and The Africa 70
Again, Excuse O (1976, LP Nigeria, Coco-
nut PMLP1002)
[A] "Excuse-O"
[B] "Mr Grammatology-Lisationalism Is
the Boss"

Fela Anikulapo-Kuti and The Africa 70
Zombie (1976, LP Nigeria, Coconut
PMLP1003; 1977, LP UK, Creole
CRLP511)
[A] "Zombie"
[B] "Mr Follow Follow"

Fela Anikulapo-Kuti and The Africa 70
Zombie (1977, LP USA; Mercury
SRM-1-3709)
[A] "Zombie"
[B] "Monkey Banana" / "Everything
Scatter"

Fela Ransome-Kuti
Fela Ransome-Kuti Vol. 1 & 2 (1977, LP
France; EMI/Pathe Marconi 2C 15983/4)
[A] "Shakara (Oloje)" / "Chop & Quench"
[B] "Let's Start" / "Black Man's Cry
[C] "Lady" / "Je'nwi Temi (Don't Gag Me)"
[D] "Alu Jo Jonki Jon" / "Egbe Mi O (Carry
Me I Want to Die)"

The Basa-Basa Soundz
The Basa-Basa Soundz (1976, LP Nigeria,
Decca Afrodisia DWAPS 2016)
[A] "Dr Solotsu" / "Nye Tao Ame" / "Tinapa
Minana" / "Aziza"
[B] "Lakuma" / "Yayaa" / "Nature" /
"Amal"

Fela Anikulapo-Kuti and The Africa 70
J.J.D. (1977, LP Nigeria, Decca Afrodisia
DWAPS2023)
[A] "J.J.D."(Instrumental)
[B] "J.J.D." (Vocal)

Fela Anikulapo-Kuti and The Africa 70
Sorrow, Tears and Blood (1977, LP Nigeria,
Decca Afrodisia DWAPS2025; recorded but
unreleased)
[A] "Sorrow, Tears, and Blood"
[B] "Colonial Mentality"

Fela Anikulapo-Kuti and The Africa 70
Opposite People (1977, LP Nigeria, Decca
Afrodisia DWAPS2026)
[A] "Opposite People"
[B] "Equalisation of Trouser and Pant"

Tunde Williams plays with The Africa 70
with Fela Anikulapo-Kuti (tenor sax, piano,
prod.)
Mr. Big Mouth (1977, LP Nigeria, Decca
Afrodisia DWAPS2030)
[A] "Mr. Big Mouth"
[B] "The Beginning"

Fela Anikulapo-Kuti and The Africa 70
Stalemate (1977, LP Nigeria, Decca Afrodi-
sia DWAPS2033)
[A] "Stalemate"
[B] "African Message (Don't Worry About
My Mouth-O)"

Fela Anikulapo-Kuti and The Africa 70
Fear Not for Man (1977, LP Nigeria, Decca
Afrodisia DWAPS2035)
[A] "Fear Not for Man"
[B] "Palm-Wine Sound"

Fela Anikulapo-Kuti and The Africa 70
Why Black Man Dey Suffer (1977, LP Nige-
ria, Decca Afrodisia DWAPS2036; recorded
but unreleased.)
[A] "Why Black Man Dey Suffer"
[B] "Male"

Fela Anikulapo-Kuti and The Africa 70
Observation No Crime (1977, LP Nigeria,
Decca Afrodisia DWAPS2037; recorded but
unreleased.)
[A] "Observation No Crime"
[B] "Lady"

Fela Anikulapo-Kuti and The Africa 70
I Go Shout Plenty (1977, LP Nigeria, Decca
Afrodisia DWAPS2038; recorded but
unreleased.)
[A] "I Go Shout Plenty"
[B] "Frustration of My Lady"

Fela Anikulapo-Kuti and The Africa 70
No Agreement (1977, LP Nigeria, Decca
Afrodisia DWAPS2039; LP France, Barclay
829 682-1; 1985, LP USA, Celluloid CELL
6122)
[A] "No Agreement"
[B] "Dog Eat Dog"

Tony Allen and The Africa 70 with Fela
Anikulapo-Kuti (tenor sax, piano, co-prod.)
Progress (1977, LP Nigeria, Coconut
PMLP1004)
[A] "Progress"
[B] "Afro Disco Beat"

Fela Anikulapo-Kuti and The Africa 70
Sorrow, Tears and Blood (1977, LP Nigeria,
Kalakuta KK001-A)
[A] "Sorrow, Tears, and Blood"
[B] "Colonial Mentality"

Fela Anikulapo-Kuti and The Africa 70
Shuffering and Shmiling (1977, LP Nigeria,
Coconut PMLP1005; 1985, LP USA, Cel-
luloid CELL 6117)

[A] "Shuffering and Shmiling"
(Instrumental)
[B] "Shuffering and Shmiling" (Vocal)

Fela Anikulapo-Kuti and The Africa 70
Shuffering and Shmiling (1978, LP France,
Barclay 829 710-1)
[A] "Shuffering and Shmiling"
[B] "Perambulator"

Tony Allen and The Africa 70 with Fela
Anikulapo-Kuti (coproducer)
No Accommodation for Lagos (1979, LP
Nigeria, Phonogram POLP035)
[A] "No Accommodation for Lagos"
[B] "African Message"

Fela Anikulapo-Kuti and The Africa 70
Unknown Soldier (1979, LP Nigeria, Phon-
odisk Skylark SKLP003A; 1982, LP USA,
Uno Melodic UM 0002)
[A] "Unknown Soldier" (Instrumental)
[B] "Unknown Soldier" (Vocal)

Fela Anikulapo-Kuti and Africa 70
V.I.P.-Vagabons in Power (1979, LP Nigeria,
Jofabro/Kalakuta KILP001)
[A] "V.I.P." (Instrumental)
[B] "V.I.P." (Vocal)

Fela Anikulapo-Kuti and The Africa 70
"I.T.T.-International Thief Thief" (1979, LP
Nigeria, Kalakuta no suffix)
[A] "I.T.T." (Instrumental)
[B] "I.T.T." (Vocal)

1980s

Fela Anikulapo-Kuti and The Africa 70
Authority Stealing (1980, LP Nigeria, Kala-
kuta no suffix)
[A] "Authority Stealing" (Instrumental)
[B] "Authority Stealing" (Vocal)

Fela Anikulapo-Kuti and The Africa 70 with
Roy Ayers
Music of Many Colors (1980, LP Nigeria,
Phonodisk PHD003; 1986, LP USA, Cellu-
loid CELL 6125)
[A] "Africa - Center of the World"
[B] "Blacks Got to Be Free"

Fela Anikulapo-Kuti and The Africa 70
Coffin for Head of State (1981, LP Nigeria,
Kalakuta KALP003)
[A] "Coffin for Head of State"
(Instrumental)
[B] "Coffin for Head of State" (Vocal)

Black-President(1981, LP UK, Arista
SPART 1167)
[A] "Sorrow Tears and Blood" / "Colonial
Mentality"
[B] "I.T.T. (International Thief Thief)"

Fela Anikulapo-Kuti and The Egypt 80
Original Sufferhead (1981, LP Nigeria,
Lagos International 2; LP UK, Arista
SPART1177)
[A] "Original Sufferhead"
[B] "Power Show"

Fela Anikulapo-Kuti and The Africa 70
(1981, 7" USA, Arista 408)
"Sorrow Tears and Blood" b/w "Colonial
Mentality"

Fela Anikulapo-Kuti and The Egypt 80
Perambulator (1983, LP Nigeria, Lagos
International LIR6)
[A] "Perambulator"
[B] "Frustration"

Fela Kuti (1983, 7" UK, EMI EMIDJ5441)
"Lady (Part 1)" b/w "Lady (Part 2)"

Fela Kuti
"Lady" b/w "Unknown Soldier" (1983, 12"
45 UK, EM 12 EMI 5441)

Fela Anikulapo-Kuti and The Egypt 80
Live in Amsterdam - Music Is the Weapon
(1984, LP UK, EMI FELA2401293; 1986,
LP Nigeria, Polygram PH2000 and PH2002)
[A] "Movement of the People Political
Statement Number I (Part 1)"
[B] "Movement of the People Political
Statement Number I (Part 2)"
[C] "Gimme Shit I Give You Shit"
[D] "Custom Check Point"

Fela Anikulapo Kuti
M. O. P. (Movement of People) (1984, 12"
France, EMI/Pathee Marconi SP1249)

[A] "M. O. P. (Movement of People)" (Club
Version)
[B] "M. O. P. (Movement of People)"
(Radio Version)

Fela Anikulapo Kuti
M. O. P. (1984, 12" 45, EMI PSLP 379,
promotional disc)
[A] "M. O. P." (Short Version, Stereo) / "M.
O. P." (Long Version, Stereo)
[B] "M. O. P." (Short Version, Mono) / "M.
O. P." (Long Version, Mono)

Fela Anikulapo-Kuti and The Egypt 80
Army Arrangement (1985, LP USA, Cellu-
loid CELL6115)
[A] "Army Arrangement" (Instrumental)
[B] "Army Arrangement" (Vocal)

Fela Anikulapo-Kuti and The Egypt 80
Army Arrangement (1985, LP UK, Yaba
- Celluloid CEL6109; LP USA, Celluloid
CELL 6109)
[A] "Army Arrangement"
[B] "Cross Exmination" / "Government
Chicken Boy"

Fela Anikulapo-Kuti and The Egypt 80
Army Arrangement (1985, LP Nigeria, Kala-
kuta K007)
[A] "Army Arrangement" (Instrumental)
[B] "Army Arrangement" (Vocal)

Fela Anikulapo-Kuti
Mr. Follow Follow (1986, LP USA, Cellu-
loid CELL 6124)
[A] "Mr. Follow Follow"
[B] "Who No Know Go Know"

Fela Anikulapo-Kuti and The Egypt 80
Teacher Don't Teach Me Nonsense (1986,
LP Nigeria, Polygram PH2004)
[A] "Teacher Don't Teach Me Nonsense"
(Instrumental)
[B] "Teacher Don't Teach Me Nonsense"
(Vocal)

Fela Anikulapo-Kuti and The Egypt 80
Teacher Don't Teach Me Nonsense (1986,
LP France, Barclay 831325-1/ 831-362-1,
831-362-2)

[A] "Teacher Don't Teach Me Nonsense" (Instrumental)
[B] "Teacher Don't Teach Me Nonsense" (Vocal)
[C] "Look And Laugh" (Instrumental)
[D] "Look And Laugh" (Vocal)

Fela Anikulapo-Kuti and The Egypt 80
Look And Laugh (1986, 7" France, Barclay 6837 900 / 45T.PROMO)
[A] "Look And Laugh" (Vocal)
[B] "Look And Laugh" (Instrumental)

Fela Anikulapo-Kuti and The Africa 70
I Go Shout Plenty (1986, LP Nigeria, Decca-Afrodisia DWAPS2251)
[A] "I Go Shout Plenty"
[B] "Why Black Man Dey Suffer"

Fela Anikulapo-Kuti and The Africa 70
Fela In Concert (1986, Video View Video NTSC1305)
"Movement of the People Political Statement Number 1" / "Army Arrangement" / "Power Show" (Instrumental)

Fela Anikulapo-Kuti and The Africa 70
Jenwi Temi (Don't Gag Me) (1987, LP Nigeria, Philips PH 2005)
[A] "Lady" / "Jenwi Temi"
[B] "Alu Jo Jonki Jon" / "Egbe Mi O"

Oluko Imo with Fela Anikulapo-Kuti (tenor sax, prod.)
Oduduwa (1988, LP Nigeria, Arigidi 01-7)
[A] "Oduduwa"
[B] "Were Oju Le"

Fela Anikulapo-Kuti and The Egypt 80
Teacher Don't Teach Me Nonsense (1988, Video Hendring Video HEN2090)

Fela Anikulapo-Kuti and The Egypt 80
Fela Live (1988, Video Hendring Video HEN2091)

Fela Anikulapo-Kuti and The Egypt 80
Beasts of No Nation (1989, LP Nigeria, Kalakuta K008)
[A] "Beasts of No Nation" (Instrumental)
[B] "Beasts of No Nation" (Vocal)

Fela Anikulapo-Kuti and The Egypt 80
Beasts of No Nation (1989, LP UK Eurobound/Yaba JU-UDR360153; CD USA, Shanachie 43070)
[A] "Beasts of No Nation"
[B] "Just Like That"

Fela Anikulapo-Kuti and The Egypt 80
Overtake Don Overtake Overtake (1989, LP Nigeria, Kalakuta K009; CD USA, Shanachie 43078)
[A] "Overtake Don Overtake Overtake" (Instrumental)
[B] "Overtake Don Overtake Overtake" (Vocal)

1990s

Fela Anikulapo-Kuti and The Egypt 80
Confusion Break Bones (1990, LP Nigeria, Kalakuta K010)
[A] "Confusion Break Bones" (Instrumental)
[B] "Confusion Break Bones" (Vocal)

Fela Anikulapo-Kuti and The Egypt 80
Just Like That (1990, LP Nigeria, Kalakuta K011)
[A] "Just Like That"
[B] "Movement of The People Political Statement Number 1"

Fela Anikulapo-Kuti
Original Sufferhead (1991, CD USA, Shanachie 44010)
"Original Sufferhead" / "Sorrow Tears and Blood" / "Colonial Mentality" / "I.T.T."

Fela Anikulapo-Kuti and The Egypt 80
Fela Live (1991, Video USA, Shanachie 101)
"Confusion Break Bones" / "Teacher Don't Teach Me Nonsense"

Fela Anikulapo-Kuti and The Egypt 80
Underground System (1992, LP Nigeria, Kalakuta KALP013; CD UK, Sterns STCD1043)
[A] "Underground System"
[B] "Pansa Pansa"

Fela Anikulapo-Kuti
Black Man's Cry (1992, CD USA, Shanachie 44013)
"Zombie" / "Shuffering & Shmiling" / "No Agreement" / "Shakara" / "Black Man's Cry" / "Lady"

Fela Ransome-Kuti and The Nigeria 70
The '69 Los Angeles Sessions (1993, CD UK, Stern's STCD3005)
"My Lady Frustration" / "Viva Nigeria" / "Obe" / "Ako" / "Witchcraft" / "Wayo" / "Lover" / "Funky Horn" / "Eko" / "This Is Sad"

2000s

Fela Anikulapo-Kuti and The Africa 70
Zombie (2001, CD France, Barclay 549 383-2)
"Mistake"

Fela Ransome-Kuti and The Africa 70 with Ginger Baker - Live! (2001, CD France, Barclay 549 380-2)
Ginger Baker and Tonny Allen, "Drum Solo"

Roforofo Fight / CD Singles (2001, CD France, Barclay 549 380-2)
"Shenshema" / "Ariya"

Fela Anikulapo-Kuti and The Egypt 80
Army Arrangement (2001, CD France, Barclay 549 381-2)
[A] "Army Arrangement"
[B] "Government Chicken Boy"

Fela Kuti mixed by Chief Xcel
The Underground Spiritual Game (2004, CD USA, Quannum QP 048; CD France, Barclay 98118045)

Fela Ransome-Kuti and The Nigeria 70
Afro Baby / The Evolution of the Afro-Sound in Nigeria 1970–1979 (2004, CD UK, Sound Way SNDWCD002)
"Fogo-Fogo"

Fela Ransome-Kuti and His Koola Lobitos
Highlife-Jazz and Afro-Soul (1963–1969) (2005, CD Japan; P-Vine PCD-18511/3)

[Disc 1] "Bonfo" / "Fere" / "Onifere No. 2" / "Oyejo" / "Oloruka" / "Awo" / "Great Kids" / "Amaechi's Blues" / "Yese" / "Egbin" / "Orise" / "Eke" / "V.C. 7" / "I Know Your Feeling"
[Disc 2] "Signature Tune" / "It's Highlife Time" / "Lagos Baby" / "Omuti" / "Ololufe" / "Araba's Delight" / "Wa Dele" / "Lai Se" / "Mi O Mo" / "Obinrin Lo" / "Omo Ejo"
[Disc 3] "Everyday I Got My Blues" / "Moti Gborokan" / "Waka Waka" / "Ako" / "Ororuka" / "Lai Se" / "Onidodo" / "Alagbara" / "Ajo" / "Abiara" / "Se E Tunde" / "Waka Waka" / "My Baby Don Love Me" / "Home Cooking"

Fela and His Koola Lobitos
Complete Works of Fela Anikulapo Kuti (2007, CD Nigeria, Evergreen Musical Company)
Fela and His Koola Lobitos
[1] "Everyday I Got My Blues" / "Ololufe Mi" / "Fere" / "Yese" / "Omuti" / "Omo Ejo" / "Oloruka" / "Abiara" / "Ako" / "Home Cooking" / "Great Kids"
[2] "Highlife Time" / "Ekuro La Labaku" / "Mi O Mo" / "Viva Nigeria" / "Lagos Baby" / "Alagbara" / "Opuro O Se O (Home Cooking)" / "Wayo (2nd Version)" / "Obe" / "Eko" / "Funky Horn"
[3] "Oyejo" / "Onidodo" / "Se E Tun De" / "Araba's Delight" / "Obinrin Le" / "Yabons Ke Lele" / "Waka Waka" / "Eke" / "My Baby Don't Love Me" / "Orise" / "V.C.7" / "I Know Your Feeling" / "This Is Sad"
[4] "Fere" / "Bonfo" / "Wa Dele" / "Awo" / "Egbin" / "My Dog and Cat" / "Yabomisa" / "Ajo" / "Mo Ti Gboro Kan" / "Lai Se" / "Amaechi's Blues"
Fela Anikulapo Kuti
[5] "Jeun Ko Ku" / "Buy Africa" / "Fefe Naa Efe" / "Open and Close" / "Who Are You"
[6] "Trouble Sleep Yanga Wake Am" / "Teacher Don't Teach Me Nonsense"
[7] "Yellow Fever" / "Water No Get Enemy" / "Army Arrangement"
[8] "Unknown Soldier" / "Rofo Rofo Fight" / "Mistake: Live in Berlin"
[9] "Colonial Mentality" / Look and Laugh"
[10] "Na Poi 1 and 2" / "Vagabonds in Power"

[11] "Coffin for Head of State" / "You No Go Die" / "Noise for Vendor Mouth"
[12] "Sorrow, Tears, and Blood" / "Rere Run (Everything Scatter)" / "Alagbon Close"
[13] "Authority Stealing" / "Shakara" / "Stalemate"
[14] "I.T.T." / "Kalakuta Show 1"
[15] "Na Poi '75" / "Just Like That" / "Black Man's Cry"
[16] "Why Black Man De Suffer" / "I No Get Eye for Back" / "Ikoyi Mentality versus Mushin Mentality"
[17] "Overtake Don Overtake Overtake" (Vocals) / "No Agreement"
[18] "No Bread" / "Na Fight O" / "I No Be Gentleman"
[19] "Jehin Jehin" / "Jenwi Temi (Don't Gag Me)" / "Fogo Fogo" / "Monkey Banana"
[20] "Yeye De Smell" / "Question Jam Answer" / "Original Suffer Head"
[21] "Confusion Break Bones (C.B.B.)" / "Government Chicken Boy"
[22] "Equalization of Trouser and Pant" / "J.J.D."
[23] "Te Je Je" / "Unnecessary Begging" / "Pansa Pansa"
[24] "Go Slow" / "He No Possible" / "Beautiful Dancer"
[25] "Opposite People" / "Egbe Mi O" (with Ginger Baker) / "Shenshema"
[26] "Sense Wiseness" / "Going In and Going Out" / "Excuse O" / "Instrumental"
[27] "Upside Down" / "Mr. Follow Follow" / "Palmwine Sound"
[28] "Beasts of No Nation" / "Fight to Finish" / "Igbe" / "He Miss Road"
[29] "Expensive Shit" / "Mr. Gramaticalogy: Lisationalism Is the Boss"
[30] "Beggars' Song" / "Ariya" / "Eko Ile" / "Jeun Koku" (Instrumental) / "Gba Mi Leti Ki N'Dolowo"
[31] "Monday Morning" / "Fear Not for Man" / "Confusion 1"
[32] "I Go Shout Plenty" / "Dog Eat Dog" / "Alujonjon Ki Jon"
[33] "Suegbe and Pako" / "Who No Know Go Know" /"Gbagada Gbogodo"
[34] "Lady" / "Let's Start" / "Underground System"
[35] "Zombie" / "M.O.P. (1)"

[36] "Africa Centre of the World" / "Mattress" / "Don't Worry About My Mouth"
[37] "Power Show" / "Param Bulator" / "Custom Check Point"
[38] "M.O.P. (2)" / "Ikoyi Blindness" / "Cross Examination"
[39] "Shuffering and Shmiling / "Give Me Shit, I Give You Shit"
[40] "2000 Blacks" / "Stranger (Alhaji Alhaji)"

According to Michael Veal and Olajide Bello, the following songs were often performed, but not recorded.

"Ojo Ton Su"
"Football Government"
"O. A. U."
"Nigerian Natural Grass"
"Music Against Second Slavery"
"Big Blind Country"
"Chop and Clean Mouth Like Nothing Happen"
"Country of Pain"
"Government of Crooks"
"Akunakuna, Senior Brother of Parabulator"
"Condom Stalawagy and Scatter"
"Clear Road for Jaga Jaga"
"Bamaiyi"
"Cock Dance"
"Sisi Me-o"

Special thanks to Yoshiki Fukasawa, Michael E. Veal, Ray Templeton, Deen Ipaye, Dr. John H. Cowley, John Beadle, T. Ajayi Thomas, Olajide Bello, Greg Villanova, Carter van Pelt, Steve Mereu, Carlo C. Brander, Miles Cleret, Michael Kieffer, Paul Heck, Duncan Brooker, Andrew Symington , Kazuya Ogiwara, and Patrick Mund.

Compiled by Toshiya Endo
(http://biochem.chem.nagoya-u.ac.jp/~endo/EAFela.html)

Carlos & Fela
Photo: Chico

1

Abiku

The Twice-Born

After three years of waiting, my mother and father really wanted a baby. But it wasn't me they wanted. No, man! No! They wanted any fucking baby.

You know, the meek, quiet type. Well-mannered. Yes-Sir this. Yes-Sir that. They didn't want a motherfucker like me, man! Well, here I am now. I came. In spite of them. In spite of everything. I was born twice, man!

The first time I was born was in 1935. What I experienced twice I have no recollection of. Nothing! Zero! That's one of our limitations, man, not knowing where we come from. Anyway, when I was born my father wanted to imitate his own father. They were both Protestant reverends. So to make some white man happy, my father asked this German missionary to . . . name me. Can you imagine that, man? A white man naming an African child! In Africa, man, where names are taken so seriously. There's even a special "naming ceremony" each time a child is born. Without that, it's said that a child can't really enter the world of the living. And just to make some white missionary happy, my own father. . . . Oh, no, man! Nooooooh!

You know what that motherfucker named me? Hildegart! Yes, man. Hildegart! Oooooooooh, man! That's how much I wasn't wanted. Me, who was supposed to come and talk about Blackism and Africanism, the plight of my people. Me, who was to try and do something to change that! Oh, man. I felt that name like a wound. My father had rejected me. And my mother too. The one whose very womb had born me. Here I was, tied hand and foot, being handed over to the executioner!

Bear the name of conquerors? Or reject this first arrival in the world? The *orishas* they heard me. And they spared me. Two weeks after my first birth, my soul left my body for the world of spirits. What çan I say? I wasn't Hildegart! Shit, man! It wasn't for white man to give me name. So it's because of a name that I've already known death. Maybe that's why a name is a matter of life or death, more for me than anybody else. What can I say about parents who wanted this motherfucking compromise? It's only recently I've begun asking myself questions about them, their past. You see, till now I've been so busy with the whole African problem I rarely ever looked at my own ancestors because the other thing was more important. But things are beginning to fall into place.

Both on my mother's and father's side, my ancestors came from Ilesha in Yorubaland. My father was the Right Reverend Israel Oludotun Ransome-Kuti. His middle name, Oludotun, means "The Great Being Is Always Right". I think my father was convinced that he, too, was always right. In any case, that's the impression he made. Oh, he could be so hard with his children! There was Dolu,[1] my sister, the eldest of all; then Koye,[2] then me; and lastly, my younger brother Beko.[3] The only person who could call my father by his nickname – "Daudu" (The Good Teacher) – was my mother. We had to call him *Sir.* Yeh! That's how it was! That's what they call respect, man!

I don't know much about my father's maternal side except that they all came from Ilesha. But on his paternal side, I know quite a lot about my grandfather, Reverend Canon J.J. Ransome-Kuti. He was the one who was a missionary in Abeokuta. He died young, at sixty-something. My grandfather became a legend. He was one of the big pioneers of the Yoruba Christian Church. He was a musician and composed religious hymns. The man was so talented. The missionaries fully exploited his talent too. They took him to England to do some recordings in London. One of those who took him there was named *Ransome.* You follow me, man? They took him around London and had him record something like twenty-five records – 78rpms – with the label EMI. That was in 1925.

1. Oluwadolupo Ransome-Kuti: presently head nurse in private hospitals in Lagos.
2. Olikoye Ransome-Kuti: pediatrician and medical professor at the University of Lagos.
3. Bekololari Ransome-Kuti: surgeon in one of the largest hospitals in Lagos, and Secretary General of the Nigerian Medical Association.

At the time, his songs were so popular in Nigeria. Religious songs, you know. But very Africanized. Even now his tunes are used for folksongs and things like that. Ah, Canon J.J., he was some man! He was so Christian that the traditionalists in Abeokuta almost killed him. Man, even after a hundred years of Christian penetration in Yorubaland, the people continued to resist. They were against the missionaries. So you know what had to happen to as fervent a missionary as my grandfather. One day, he was attacked. They had wanted to kill him, but he didn't die. They just left him there, thinking he was dead. But he was not dead. My grandfather was motherfucking strong, man!

Now, where was I in the story? Oh, yes. After leaving England, the missionaries then took my grandfather to Jerusalem. You know what for? So he could kiss the ground where Christ had walked. Imagine that! Now when they showed him Jesus Christ's tomb, he was so devout he jumped in and wanted to go to sleep right there. But that's not all, man! Once he got back to Nigeria, the missionary named Ransome thought he would honour my grandfather by giving him the name Ransome. So they put Ransome between his name to make it Ransome-Kuti. That's how my family got the name Ransome, man!

My grandfather, though, wasn't even born into a Christian family. His father – that's my great-grandfather whose name I haven't yet found out – was an authentic traditionalist who resisted to his very last breath the spread of Christianity in Yorubaland. But in spite of that, he was unable to keep his own son out of the hands of the missionaries, man. Remember that then, around 1800, the only schools where you could learn to read and write were missionary schools. These *oyinbo* schools didn't mean shit to my great-grandfather: "The white man gives out his medicine at the same time as his poison." I can almost hear him cry out, man, the day when his wife announced that his own son would be going from then on to one of those schools! "The white man is only here to steal our sheer butter!" My grandfather would never forget those words, however Christian he became afterwards. And they were handed down from father to son and only got to me when I was already big.

On my mother's side, things are still a bit unclear. I know though that on her father's side I am a descendant of a slave. You know that till around the middle of the nine-teenth century the slave trade across the Atlantic was still going on, making ravages everywhere in Yorubaland and also among the Ibos, Calabaris and other peoples who lived along the coasts and in the interior – what's called Nigeria today. Again this fucking matter of a name, man! Nigeria! Who ever heard of such a name before 1906? No joke, man. It was the wife of a colonial governor who pulled it out of her head or out of a hat. I swear! In any case, my mother's father was a freed slave. He was captured as a small boy in Ilesha – probably seven or eight years old at the time – and was taken as a slave to Sierra Leone. The British decided to give this freedom thing just in time to keep my mother's father from being shipped off to the plantations of the West Indies or the south of the United States. That was in 1834.*

Once free, many of the slaves in Sierra Leone who still remembered their country of birth wanted to return. My grandfather was one of those. He was among the Egba from Yorubaland who left Sierra Leone around 1838 – on foot – to return home. I think it must have taken them *years* of walking before they got to Lagos. Two thousand kilometres on foot! Imagine that! My grandfather walked . . . and walked . . . and walked, man. The funny part of the story is that just as he was getting near to Ilesha, about one hundred and fifty kilometres away, my grandfather got tired. So he stopped and settled in Abeokuta and stayed there.

You see, my grandfather was just a child when he was captured. He grew up in slavery. He didn't know his ancestors. He didn't even know his real African name. He had to accept Christianity. That's how he acquired Thomas. That's the name the missionaries of Sierra Leone imposed on him. Becoming in turn one of those staunch Christians himself, he ended up building a church. He had only one wife whose name was Adejonwo, which means "We Are All Looking Up To The Crown". Today I interpret the word "crown" as meaning *tradition*. For, in spite of her conversion to Christianity, my maternal grandmother

---

* At the time, the colony of Sierra Leone actually served as an embarkation port from where the slaves captured all along the coast were either destined to the Americas or the West Indies.

continued worshipping Oshùn, the goddess of rivers and ravines. She was a descendant of that family which worships Oshùn. That was the kind of woman who gave birth, in 1900, to my mother Funmilayo* Thomas. Imagine that, man, today I could have been named Fela Ransome-Thomas!

* "Give Me Happiness."

Fela's father, Reverend I.O. Ransome-Kuti ("Daudu")
Photo: West African Photo House, Abeokuta

2

Three Thousand Strokes

On 15 October 1938, I was born a second time in a hospital somewhere in Abeokuta. Abeokuta? Terrible, man. A planless town. Desolate. The only people you saw in the streets were tax collectors and soldiers. There was the reservation where the white man lived – called "Ibara" – and then the town. Finish. Abeokuta was the deadest town you ever saw. Nothing happened. There were occasional Yoruba ceremonies, but we children were discouraged from being interested in such things. Our family was Christian and those things, we were taught, were "pagan".

The people of Abeokuta had pride because, as they recounted, "Abeokuta was never colonized." I once heard an elder say: "Let the Englishman tell about the Adubi War. He wanted to make a road from Lagos to Abeokuta. One man only fought the whole English army. Many soldiers were sent, but they all died-o." I swear, man! It's true. They could not take Abeokuta. The British had to sign a Protectorate Agreement. So Abeokuta was a protectorate because of the 1914 War of Adubi. This is not mythology, man. This is fact. Historical facts that aren't taught in school.

Where did they take me after my birth? Maybe to the Abeokuta Grammar School where my parents were living then. The school was owned by them. Some students who came from far away would board at the school. But all that is very blurred in my mind! It was a big school with well-tended flower gardens. In time, the Ransome-Kuti family compound was referred to as a "village" because it was self-dependent. There was the school, with its chapel, my parents' large house and a garage too for the one family car. Yes, man, my parents had a car. Then, there was a huge courtyard where countless day-to-day activities went on. We grew our own food and raised lots of goats, chickens and other small livestock. There was everything one needed in the Ransome-Kuti compound. But at home I

35

was never free. That much I remember very clearly, man.

My father, Reverend I.O. Ransome-Kuti, was Principal of the Abeokuta Grammar School and for a while of the Grammar School of Ijebu-Ode, several kilometres away. He was also the first President of the Nigerian Union of Teachers. There was something curious about him though. Unlike other clergymen, he was never a pastor of any church parish. He was mainly concerned with teaching. He preached sermons very rarely; probably only during school functions. What he did do was invite other reverends to preach in the school chapel. I think that my father must have seen there was something wrong in the Nigerian education system, in Nigerian politics and Nigerian social life. Maybe he didn't understand what it was exactly. But in any case, he transformed Abeokuta Grammar School into a forum, a forum of teaching, a forum of learning.

My father was so strict, man. He believed in discipline. He also taught music at school. And probably got his musical aptitude from his father who was also a composer. When it came to his music lessons he was even more strict. He wouldn't hesitate to use his *atori* (cane) to whip the back of his students. I was among his best students in music but that didn't keep me from getting beaten with the *atori*. He was so strict during our lessons that we were all afraid. If anyone got out of line, he would get his *nyash* (ass) beat severely. Mark you, he would whip your *nyash*, then say: "Straighten up your knees!" And if you didn't straighten them, you would get even more severely beaten.

My father was so strange! He was strict, but he was also interesting because he was always jovial. Reverend I.O. Ransome-Kuti liked flowers and he had the most neatly kept flower gardens you can think of around the school compound. He wouldn't allow goats to graze or to come around there and he always had us students chase them away. He was generally in good humour, except when you went against his laid-down principles.

If you offended him while he was beating you, you would get beaten with three times as much force. I always wondered how a man who looked so jovial could be so fucking cold when he would flog you. The students were terrified of him. Whenever they heard the words, *"Oga mbo"* – meaning, "The Principal is coming" – there was a stampede. The whole place would become pandemonium-o, with everyone trying to find their own place to avoid the beatings. My father used to believe and say, "Those who walk crookedly are either rogues or men of dubious character." So if you walked crookedly in front of him you would get the shit beaten out of you. That's for sure.

My mother wasn't any better than my father. Ummmmmmmmmmmm!!! She beat the hell outta me, man. My mother was the most wicked mother ever seen in life when it came to beating. Oh-la-la! Every time, I would say, "This is the end of me." Oh, how she would beat me! She beat me with sticks. Different kinds of sticks . . . small, big, medium. She doesn't think about it twice. She'd say, "Bend over. Touch your toes." And with my *nyash* up in the air, she would beat my ass like a man. Five strokes. Twelve. Twenty-four. Thirty. She is something else! Well, you see, I couldn't reconcile her love for me and the beating. I couldn't reconcile it. I understood it later on, but not then. My parents themselves were confused. Confused about education and how to bring us up. They were really into the white man's education. So if you ask me who was worse – my father or my mother, I couldn't say. . . . They were both bad. My mother would kick my ass and my father would kick my ass. You know what I mean? They were both kicking ass, man. Left, right and centre.

I'm telling you, man. The beatings that I, Fela, alone received amounted to no less than three thousand strokes. After my father died I started thinking about it. I began counting all the beatings I could remember. And I counted . . . *three thousand!* Three thousand, I'm telling you. Between my mother and father combined I got three thousand strokes between the ages of nine and seventeen. That's without counting the beatings I got from my teachers. I'm not kidding, man. My teachers too. Oh, yes, they kicked my ass almost every day, man! There's no week I didn't get ass-kicking. Ask my brothers. Ask anybody who was with me at school at that time. The education they brought was to kick the boys, kick their asses. They thought the white man was right, you know.

What I liked about my father is that he kicked *everybody's* ass. One day, he even kicked a white man's ass. It was a British education officer who made the rounds inspecting schools. My father's school was built by our people in Abeokuta, not by the British government. So my father never allowed any British to come and inspect *his* school. When this inspector came, my father told him he couldn't inspect the school, but the man insisted. My father said: "This is MY school!" And he grabbed his *atori* and flogged him out – *flam, flam, flam!* Oh, man, I dug him for that!

The Reverend I.O. Ransome-Kuti did not like the military either. He wasn't into politics, but in his own way he would also clash occasionally with the military colonial government of his day. One day, for instance, he was passing through the premises of the military settlement of Abeokuta with his hat on. A Nigerian soldier ordered him to remove his hat. "Why?" asked my father.

And you know what that fucking soldier answered?

"Don't you see you're walking past the British flag?"

When my father still refused to obey the order, the soldier tried forcing the hat off his head with a bayonet. My father resisted and received a bayonet stab in the face, near the eye. He almost lost an eye from the injury. Ah, but the British authorities heard about that, and how! My father complained bitterly and made a big fuss over it to the colonial authorities. In the end, the soldiers' barracks – which were then at Itesi, near Sacred Heart Hospital – were removed from the heart of town where this incident occurred and moved to the fringes of town, in Lafenwa. And they're still there today. The British military and their Nigerian lackeys were kicked out of town because of my father's protest. As a child, though, I never knew about that terrible incident. That stupid soldier was capable of *killing* my father, man! It wasn't until 1974, after the first police raid on my house, that my mother told me the story.

"That's what they did to your father, too," she said. "They cut his face with a bayonet, almost took out his eye, in front of Sacred Heart Hospital. . . ."

When I was small I felt nothing about the British colonial soldiers I used to see around. They just seemed a part of the scenery. I never felt anything towards them. I thought it was the right thing that was happening. I was born into it. It never occurred to me to ask why they were there. My parents never brought it up. All they would talk about to us children was religion, man.

Sad? Happy? Indifferent? What did I feel in my childhood? I couldn't say if I was happy or unhappy. It was a confused life for me. Things I wanted to do I couldn't do then. I had to do what my parents told me to do. What did I want? I wanted to be free, go out with my friends, but my parents wouldn't let me. They had this English colonized mentality, you see. Luckily, I found some solace in the companionship of my sister and brothers. At the beginning I was closer to my younger brother Beko, because we're about the same age. But then my elder brother Koye was very friendly and we became close too. We were all close. Maybe because we all feared our parents. Even today, as far as I'm concerned I'm close to all of them. We have our squabbles but we're all close. We only differ ideologically.

They live in their own world and have their own material-istic quarrels. Quarrels about how my sister behaves, about the family property in Abeokuta and things like that. I don't get involved. Actually I don't discuss particularly with them. I refuse to get into squabbles over things like heritage, property, etc. If things come in, just pass it to me. I don't want to know how they do it.

Man, our parents treated us more like boarding-school students than as their own children. Yet we were *their* children. Every time I got beaten by either of them, I asked, "For what?" It was either for doing this little thing or that little thing. I got beaten for going against their regulations, like leaning against the wall or bending my knees while I was walking, or for talking "too loud", or whistling, or for not lowering my eyes fast enough when one of my parents approached. It got to a point where every one of us was always afraid at the slightest sight of our parents because we didn't know what we were doing wrong. All we knew is that they would descend on us and start beating us. Caress their children? They wouldn't indulge in that shit-o. They called it indulgence. Hold us in their arms? Never. I remember that when I was very, very small, my father would sit me on his lap once in a while. I would feel so exalted! But my parents didn't go for that shit. Only when I was very small, my father would stroke my hair every morning but he would never hold me in his arms. For our parents, the rule was "Spare the rod and spoil the child". In Africa, colonial parents are never close to their children.

Fela's mother, Funmilayo ("Bere") Ransome-Kuti
(*née* Thomas)

3

Funmilayo

"Give Me Happiness"

My mother was a motherfucker, you know. She would flog
you like a man. You know how? She'd say: "Touch your
toes. Bend down." And it was *batabatabatabatabatabata-
batabata* . . .! She and my father wanted their son to be an
example. So any time there was punishment, I would get
the most. Man, my mother and father were so honest with
their discipline, their child had to be flogged. They were the
baddest parents I ever met in my life. It was systematic
flogging. There was no week I didn't take sometimes three,
sometimes six floggings. Any time my mother flogged me, it
was rough flogging-o: *chagachagachagachagachagacha* . . .!
If I tried getting away, she would say in a severe, com-
manding voice: "Come back here." And I'd have to come
back.
   I remember very well the first rough flogging she gave
me. I nearly died from it, man! My mother's mother,
Adejonwo, was at the house that day, sitting down in the
big room. I think she asked me to do something for her that
had to do with food. But you know how children are, don't
want to listen to old women, man. So since I thought she
was bothering me, I told her, "Mama, leave me alone!" My
mother overheard.
   "What? Whaaaat did you saaaaay?"
   Heeeeeeeyyyyyyyyy! Ohhhhhhhhh, she flogged me
rough-o! Man, I'll never forget that day. I was flogged to
the bone! Ohhhhhhhhhhhh!
   Strange! But something just kept attracting me to her. I
didn't know why she was kicking my ass. I don't think
anybody kicked my ass as much as my mother. But I dug
her. I liked to hear her talk, discuss. Something always
made me sit with her, to listen. I vaguely remember when
she started getting into politics. No, not vaguely. I

41

remember very well, because when she was running around doing politics she didn't have time to flog me. The more she got into politics the less time she had to beat me. So I, too, began liking politics.

It wasn't until around 1946 or '47 that I began understanding what my mother was fighting for. She was organizing a big protest demonstration with the women of Abeokuta. She was protesting on the streets with the women. And they went straight to see the District Officer of Abeokuta. He was a young white boy; one of those fresh British guys who tried getting arrogant with my mother. She had gone to see him to expose the demonstrators' grievances. The District Officer must have said something in a disdainful voice, like: "Go on back home." To which my mother exploded: "You bastard, rude little rat . . .!" Something like that. Ohhhhhhhh! What a scandal! It was something heavy at that time. And the news went around like fire, man. The *Daily News,* the national newspaper then, printed the story immediately. Imagine insulting the highest motherfucking representative of the British imperial crown in Abeokuta. Ohhhhhhhh, man! I was proud. People in Abeokuta talked about nothing else but that incident and "Bere". "Bere" was my mother's nickname. And I would just beam with pride.

The Nigerian Women's Union was a powerful organization. My mother founded it in the early '40s. As I got older, she started taking me around with her in the car to her campaign meetings. You know, she was the first woman to drive a car in Nigeria, man. Eventually I got to know what she was doing because she'd take me *everywhere* with her. I admired her. That was when I began getting close to her a little bit. I was close but not as close as I should have been.

My mother was quite heavy politically. And, ohhhhhhhh, I liked the way she took on those old politicians, all those dishonest rogues. She wouldn't have anything to do with them. None of them. Except Nnamdi Azikiwe ("Zik"), for whom she had a little sympathy. But she was against all the others, all those politicians like the Obafemi Awolowo ("Awo") type. She even finished with Zik later on because he began playing a double game with her. It happened when she went to London with Zik for a press conference. When she returned, she said that Zik was sabotaging her.

She said that Zik didn't want progress for her at all. Awolowo? To her, he was the biggest crook. She could tolerate Zik, but not Awolowo. At the time – in 1949 – I was one of those encouraging her to join NCNC, the National Council of Nigeria-Cameroons, Zik's party. Everybody loved Zik, because he was a nationalist. I wanted my mother to be in his party. I wanted her to *win* the elections. She was so popular, man! Oh, those politicians of that time destroyed the country, man. And look at what they're doing today! They're the same politicians: Awolowo, Azikiwe. . . .

But in 1949 Zik's party was a national party. The Yorubas voted for him. He won many times. He won over Awolowo. Even in Yorubaland he beat Awolowo. Awolowo's party, Action Group, wasn't a national party at all. I was hearing a lot about all that then. I'd always sit down with my mother when she was talking politics. I was interested in her progress. I didn't know why she was kicking my ass, but I dug my mother so much.

The more my mother got involved in the political movement, the worse things got between her and my father. The confrontation of my mother with the *Oba* (chief) of Abeokuta didn't help either to improve things between my parents. You see, the Oba Alake Sir Ladapo Ademola II was the Chief of Abeokuta. But my mother never called him a king, as he had titled himself. She called him a chief. Her reasons are historically right because Abeokuta never had a king. Odùduwà, the ancestor of all Yorubas, founded the sacred city of Ilè-Ifè. Odùduwà had only seven children and they were the only kings of Yorubaland. They founded seven kingdoms: Ondo, Oyo, Ife, Benin and three others I don't remember offhand. The Alake was not one of those seven kings. So my mother would never call him king. When she spoke to the press or to white people she would always say, "The Chief of Abeokuta, the Alake." You see, Alake is a title.

My mother was against the Alake because he was working for the white District Officer. He was a lackey of the colonial system. When the Alake declared he would collect taxes from the market women of Abeokuta, my mother decided to take their side. So she went to see the Alake on their behalf. She said to him: "How can you collect taxes from women who are selling small, small things in the

The Oba Alake Sir Ladapo Ademola II, Chief of Abeokuta

market?" The Alake would collect taxes from them for his own pockets. That was in '46, '47, '48. My mother said: "This must stop!" She mobilized all the women. Then they took to the streets and protested. That's how the whole thing started. She also got all the market women to boycott sales for as long as the British colonial administration did not recognize their rights as traders. From there, it progressed to demanding more rights. It expanded to become a Nigerian opposition. At first, it was called the Nigerian Women's Union, then it became the Federation of Nigerian Women's Union.

Ohhh, those were fantastic times-o! My mother succeeded in dethroning this pseudo-king, the Alake. How did she do it? It was ingenious. She got all the women together and told them: "Now, we are going to take over the Alake's house." Everybody hated the Alake. There was a huge courtyard outside his house. So my mother said, "Let's all go and take over the entire house." About 50,000 women went, with my mother at the head. They went and slept there in the yard of his house. The Alake was surrounded by 50,000 women. They were everywhere, in the front, behind the house, everywhere. The Alake couldn't get out of his own house. You know what that means? What would you do? You would flee too. And, man, that's exactly what the Alake did. He fled to Oshogbo. My mother had succeeded in chasing the Alake out of Abeokuta; she chased him into exile. And the Alake stayed in Oshogbo for three years. It wasn't until around 1950, '51, I think, that he came back to Abeokuta. And guess who brought him back? It was Chief Obafemi Awolowo who brought the Alake back in 1951 when he launched his political party, Action Group, and was attempting to get the British to put him at the head of the first Nigerian government.

Bringing the Alake back was such a demagogic move! When my mother heard the news, I remember seeing her come storming into the house. And a few minutes later, come back out, dressed as a . . . man. She had on shorts, like Bermudas, a man's shirt, a beret and sandals. I swear she got dressed like that because she realized she was going to fight men. It was her way of saying, "It takes a man to fight another man!" But the Alake came back anyway. . . .

My mother, she was something else! Tireless, man! After

45

the Alake, she shifted her fight· to getting the right of suffrage for Nigerian women. And she won that one too, because women did cast votes in the first elections in Nigeria during colonial times. An amazing woman, my mother! In the early 1950s she became the only Nigerian woman – and perhaps the first African woman ever – to travel to the USSR, China, Poland, Yugoslavia and East Berlin. In China, she met with Mao Tse-tung. I don't know who she met in Russia. You see, at that time she was one of the vice-presidents of the Women's International Democratic Federation (WIDF). Remember that was at a time when it was considered a crime to travel to the so-called "iron-curtain" countries. So, in 1955, upon returning from her trip to China, her passport was seized. Abubakar Tafawa Balewa was then Prime Minister. Nigeria was still a colony but under a régime of "internal self-government". Then, some time in the early '60s, she was awarded the Lenin Peace Prize. I don't remember well, but I think they gave it to her in Lagos.

But there is something I do remember very clearly. That's when my mother took me to meet Kwame Nkrumah. Ghana was already independent and Nkrumah was President. Nigeria wasn't independent yet – and still isn't. That was around early 1957.* She had met with Nkrumah many times in her life. But on that particular day she took me with her to see Nkrumah. You know, if my mother wants to see somebody like that and she takes me, it means she's going to see a friend. Nkrumah was her friend. At that time he would come now and then to Lagos in his yacht on holidays. I remember his yacht being anchored somewhere in Lagos harbour. He was wearing a white shirt and trousers, man. Nkrumah told my mother he didn't want to see anybody; that he hadn't come for any official visit; that he didn't want to see any minister, nobody at all. Not even Tafawa Balewa, the Prime Minister. He had come to meditate. But he had sent a message to my mother, saying that he wanted to see her. When she got there they started joking. My mother said teasingly:

"Ah, you come to Nigeria and you don't want to see your brothers here."

* On 28 February 1957 the British colony of the Gold Coast became independent under the name of Ghana, with Dr Kwame Nkrumah as President.

46

"I don't deal with corrupt people," he answered.

My mother looked at him and smiled.

Nkrumah went on: "They are slaves to the people in England. You know that."

He was smiling while saying it. Man, he was so cool. My mother thought a lot of him. But she never spoke much about him to me. He was her friend, a very good friend. Nkrumah! Man, I'll never forget his face.

4

Hello, Life!
Goodbye, Daudu

Nobody was more in a hurry than I was to become an adult. Adulthood meant freedom, man! Freedom at last to do whatever I felt like. And what I felt like doing most was having fun, enjoying myself. So the older I got, the happier I got. At least outside of my house. I was glad to finish primary school and be somewhat out of my father's reach. I began feeling like a different person in secondary school. A total extrovert. I was in the forefront of entertainment in school. I'd run around, always joking, laughing, making others laugh. I was easily the most popular boy in the school.

I'd given myself a nickname just for fun: "Simon Templar". But before that I'd called myself "El Paso Kid", a real colonial nickname. Then one day I changed it to "Simon Templar". You see, at the time I had read this novel – *The Saint* – whose main character was named Simon Templar. This guy was very, very clever. In fact, he impressed me as being so clever that one day I went into the classroom, straight to the blackboard and wrote: "Don't call me El Paso Kid any more. I'm now Simon Templar." Ohhhhh, can you imagine how stupid I was then, man? I was so full of complexes, you know. But all of that was great fun. After the horrors my father had put me through in primary school, I was entitled to some fun.

In school I remember we had a newspaper and there was a club formed around it. That was always the system of schools. So I decided to form a club too. Guess what I named it? The "Planless Society". I was sixteen then and was in Class Four. The rule of the club was simple: we had no plans. You could be called upon to disobey orders at any time. Disobedience was our "law". We'd take my mother's car, for example. We loved the night, man. We'd go to Lagos, nightclubbing. Oh, wow, I was finally getting a taste of life, the real life!

Oh, how I loved the feel of driving! I remember the day I taught myself to drive my parents' car. I was only twelve and a half years old then. There was only one car; my parents shared it. I wanted to drive so badly. I told my mother to teach me. She said she would when I got to be sixteen. But that was too far away for me. So I'd always watch them. I watched what they would do. I watched their legs. And I'd ask them questions, like, "What is this or that for?" Then one day, when I was alone with the driver, I begged him to let me drive the car. He said, "OK." Man, I couldn't even see. I was so small. Anyway, I released the clutch and the car bounced forward. Shit, I'd forgot my foot was on the accelerator, so the car was just going zzzzzzzzzzzz. The driver shouted, "Press the brake!" I pressed the brake and the car stopped in a big jerk, man. Oooooooooo. I was fucking scared. I was shaking man. I didn't get in that car again for two years.

Then when I was fourteen I got a bit braver. One night when everybody was sleeping I went to the garage. I kept thinking of the brake. "Brake. Brake. Don't forget the brake." I went out of the garage gently in first gear. This time I wasn't gonna make any mistake. I went into second gear, then I pressed the accelerator, gently. The car was going slowly under my control. I said, "Fine." But at that point my mother leaned out the window. She was surprised:

"FELA! Who told you to drive that car? Come upstairs here!"

I got out and went upstairs.

"Who told you how to drive the car?"

"Me, Mum," I answered.

"You NAUGHTY boy!" she said sternly.

And would you believe it? That was the end of it. So from then on it was nothing but good times.

Coming back though to our "Planless Society" and the fun we had. The club was our own way of commenting on the society we were living in. So a lot of students were attracted to it. Our club developed to the point where we started a newspaper: *The Planless Times*. We would pass around copies – to the teachers first. We were only a few members. I can give you their names: Shiji Sowetan, who is now an Attorney-General and Solicitor-General in Nigeria; Dapo Teju-Osho, who owns a big factory, a big company in

Nigeria now; my brother Beko, who's now a doctor; Bumi Sowetan, a business boy, running around town now; Akin Shogbamu who's now a doctor in Lagos; and Beekersteth, a boy with an English name; and there was me. It was marvellous, man. Ohhhh, we were doing our thing, *The Planless Times.*

At the end of the year, we heard that the Principal wanted to bring a new prefect. We heard about it underground. So we brought out a special issue which carried two protests in it. We printed 500 copies. That caused a riot in our school. When the police came to our school we fought, man. That was part of the things we did in school at that time.

It was during those days that I met the most important guy in my whole life: Jimo Kombi Braimah. But he's always been called J.K. for short. It was in 1954 that we first met. I was sixteen and he was nineteen. Was it on one of my trips to Lagos that we met? I don't remember. J.K. even thinks we met in 1955 instead. So he doesn't remember either. But, man, we hit it off right away. It was quite a natural attraction. Nothing forced. We just started doing things together. We used to meet in Lagos. Since those days, J.K. and I have become inseparable. And today – after thirty years of friendship – I can say that J.K. is the closest person to me, except my wives.

The funny thing about J.K. is that he was boarding at the school in Ijebu-Ode where my father had been the Principal some years before. Even funnier is that he had been assigned to the Kuti boarding house, named after my father. You see, Reverend I.O. Ransome-Kuti had become a sort of legendary figure. J.K. knew everything about him: his terrible beatings, his disciplinarianism, his fucking obsession with colonial education. . . . Everything. So, in a way, J.K. had also lived under the roof of the Ransome-Kuti family. Isn't it strange how the roads of people cross?

Once we had met, we just stuck together. We would hook up in Lagos and go around town together. J.K. was then a singer and he introduced me to the musical world of Lagos. Both of us were struggling through secondary school. (We graduated more or less the same year: 1956–7.) But we always found time to have a lot of fucking good fun!

Music is what really made J.K. and I so tight. He was already singing with a band – "The Cool Cats" – and was

50

popular in Lagos. Whenever I came to Lagos, man, we would have a holiday around that band – playing music, singing, dancing. Oh, wow! That was real life!

J.K. was a helluva woman-chaser then. Not me. At home, my parents didn't allow me to smoke. I wanted to smoke. I wanted to drink. They didn't allow me to drink alcohol. I wanted to go with women. But they used to make me fear women and all those things. . . . I was never free at home, man. So I got used to the training. I wasn't the cause of it. I was taught the cause-of-it-ism. So I was very colonial, a good Christian boy. I never used to smoke, drink, or run around with girls. I was always wearing a suit and tie and was very proper. I loved women, wanted to go with them, but I was afraid of women, you see. Everything made me afraid of women. Would you believe that?

Not J.K. J.K. wasn't a Christian, so he was just doing as he liked. He wasn't from a Christian home. He was a different man from me completely. He was all so free. The girls always liked J.K. He was a nice guy with a fucking nice voice. He used to be a guest artist to several local bands, like Victor Olaiya's. Actually, he was the steady singer for the Cool Cats. Since he had lived for a while in Ghana, J.K. became popular singing Ghanaian tunes. At that time, man, there was nothing more popular in Nigeria than Ghanaian highlife. Women everywhere would be shouting, "J.K.," "J.K.," "J.K." That's how I got my first break in singing. J.K. introduced me to Victor Olaiya and the Cool Cats and I began singing with them. J.K. got a *Kumba* band together – with people like Godrich Khan, who is now a doctor, Femi Williams, and some other boys – and we would go on the air. We were playing highlife and some jazz on the radio, man! Oh, those were such beautiful days!

Happiness. Why is it so shortlived? Why should suffering bear more weight than joy? My father's sickness was announced to me with the suddenness of any bad news. I saw him rapidly fading away. And then he died. Cancer of the prostate. That was in 1955 and I was seventeen. I remember looking at him lying there on the bed, motionless. Whatever went through my mind then I have forgotten. Everybody around me was crying. I did too. But I didn't really know what I was crying for. The motherfucker had beaten me so much, man, that his death was also a little bit of relief. But I missed him afterwards. I didn't want

51

him to die. I was both sad and *not* sad at the same time.

The death of my father made me think about his idiosyncracies. I started remembering many things about him. We had never had anything like a close relationship. But he was an honest man. Strict. With a colonial attitude towards training, education and discipline. But yet an honest man. I liked my father. I *didn't* want him to die. But as I went over the past of brutal beatings, I felt glad that he had died. And many times after, I would find myself being thankful that the man had died, because at least I would have peace from then on. But again, my father was my father, after all. . . . And I had lost him. Does any of that make sense?

Strangely enough, it was my father's death that opened doors to my parents' life together. Doors which till then had been shut to us children. Only then did we find out that for years – in fact, ever since I was a young child – our parents had been estranged from one another, to the point that they had even stopped sleeping together from the time I was seven, which would make it around 1945. They kept on living under the same roof but as total strangers to one another, and none of us even suspected it. I don't know what happened. There was a misunderstanding. I believe my father didn't support our mother's political activities. We only knew this on the day of his burial. You see, my mother was in her room that day. And there were all of these women from Abeokuta who had come to mourn my father's death with her. She was crying and sobbing. The women were consoling her. Then she spoke to them:

"For ten years I haven't moved near my husband. And you women, you caused it!"

I knew then that she blamed the rupture with our father on the women of Abeokuta for whose rights she had fought since the early '40s.

"You women, you caused it!" she cried aloud, over and over again.

Christian or not, my father was still a Yoruba man and I don't think he liked the idea of not seeing his woman in the house any more, once "Bere" had begun her fight.

I remember J.K. being at the memorial service held for my father in Ijebu-Ode. J.K. claims that that was the first time we ever met. But I always tell him that's bullshit, man. We had met the year before. I remember well because at the time we used to spend our holidays together, including

Christmas. We would talk a lot. About what we wanted to do in life. About girls. About our childhood. Just about every and anything, man. He was then having trouble finishing secondary school, because all J.K. wanted was to hang out in Lagos, sing, make music and chase girls. All his pals in school said he would never make the "Cert".* J.K. was such a fantastic guy! Nobody alive knew more about my life at that time than he did. . . .

* West African School Certificate: equivalent to High School diploma.

Jimo Kombi Braimah ("J.K.")
Photo: Chico

5

J.K. Braimah

My Man Fela

Of average height, brown-skinned with almond-shaped eyes and a generous, contagious smile which lights up his face, J.K. Braimah is good-natured and calm whatever the circumstances. And will listen as attentively – even for hours on end – as he can engagingly carry on a conversation. Born in Lagos, Nigeria, in 1935, to an animist and polygamous Yoruba family (his father having two wives), J.K. grew up in a purely African environment. While the only boy of the three children born to his mother, J.K. has two other sisters and three brothers born to his father's second wife. His father, a Lagosian, was an accountant; his "blood-mother" a merchant trader. For unspecified reasons, J.K.'s father decided very early to send J.K. to Accra, Ghana, for his primary school education. J.K. only returned to Nigeria for his secondary schooling in Ijebu-Ode. And it was around that time when he would meet Fela.

Q: When you met Fela what was he like?
A: Ohhhhhhh! Fela was something else when I first met him. Outwardly, he looked like a nice, clean boy. A perfect square. But inside he was a *ruffian*, man. And I knew it. Many of my friends, they always tell me: "That crazy boy! What are you doing with that boy? Why don't you leave him alone?" But this guy, I've finished prospecting him a long time ago. This guy, you can *feel* him the way he does things. You knew that this guy was not a *young* guy. I told many guys, "This boy, he's a ruffian. He doesn't even know how to talk to people. You just wait. We'll see what this guy can do." And it was true. Even my family didn't like Fela and didn't want me associating with him.

55

Q: So how did you both hook up in London?

A: Well, after finishing my secondary school in Ijebu-Ode in 1956, I began working as a clerk in the High Court of Lagos. I loved law. I wanted to be a lawyer, man. It was with that in mind that I made my parents send me to England in 1958, where one of my sisters was living. I was then twenty-three years old. Can you imagine that, man? Going to England? At that time, that was like going to Heaven for Nigerians! Hoo-hooooooooo! Fela had left to England about two months ahead of me. So we had agreed beforehand on the hook-up. He'd gone to study music. Actually, I wrote Fela to tell him I was coming, but he didn't know where I was going to be in England. I went to London. At the beginning I enrolled myself at one of the Inns of Court, Gray's Inn. I was going to read law. . . . And, of course, Fela came round to my house one day.

Q: You mean he just dropped by?

A: Yeh . . . just like that! I was sitting down in my house in . . . what was this place? It's a very popular place in Shepherds Bush, you know. But I've forgotten the name of that street. Anyway, my sister took me there. She had been in England for some time. So she took me down to this place to go and stay there. And then one night I was sitting down there, talking to this West Indian guy who was my roommate. And I hear somebody knocking. "Who is that?" And in comes Fela. I say to myself, "This boy is looking for me again? I'm in trouble!" [*Laughter.*] And from that night I took my few bags and everything and left with him. I went to his place. He was staying in Brisley Gardens, in White City. I didn't come back to my house again.

We started sharing the room together. I was paying half. He was paying half. He was going to Trinity College of Music and I was going to North-Western Polytechnic at that time.

Q: What were you studying?

A: I told you I wanted to do law at the beginning, but I couldn't get in. I didn't make it. You see, I'm not so bright. [*Laughter.*] When me and Fela started living together we used to go out in town a lot, you know. One day I told him: "Man, we can form a band. We

56

can form a band on our own, man. Why not?" Fela said, "Yeah, we can form a band. Let's go and do something." And we went into a shop. We started hiring – you know, hire-purchase – some of the instruments. I got drums. Fela got trumpet, I think. He had enough bread to buy it. Besides, that was his instrument then and not the saxophone like now.

Q: Who was giving him bread at that time?

A: His mama, man! But I didn't have bread to buy shit, man. If I had told the folks at home that I was going to buy drums, they'd say, "What???? That's not what we sent him there for!"

Q: So who was supporting you?

A: My family. He-he-he-hey! Even at the beginning they were doing their ass over when I started doing music, man. They were fucking mad. "We're not going to send you any more money," my parents wrote me. They stopped my allowance. Man, I couldn't understand how people could hate such a beautiful thing as music, and look down on it. I said, "Never mind. I love to play music. Finish." So me and Fela formed this group called the Koola Lobitos. We started out playing for Nigerian students who were studying in England. You know, all the dances in the halls and that sort of stuff.

Q: Why that name: *Koola Lobitos?*

A: I don't know why that name. Fela gave it that name. I wanted something different. Anyway, he had his way and we formed Koola Lobitos with some West Indian guys. I played guitar and Fela played trumpet. We used to play highlife, Fela's compositions, and some other numbers like "I am the O-by-a-wo-wh-y", and things like that. It caught on. So we were playing with this group till about '61, or '62.

Q: In London?

A: Yeah, in London. It came to be our thing that at the weekend we get money to spend in our pockets. We used to have gigs, in places where we'd play for students on Fridays, Saturdays. We were always having money with us, Fela and myself. Wole Buckner, who's now a high-ranking officer in the

Nigerian Navy, was there with us. He was playing piano with the group. But he wasn't deeply in it. You know what I mean? It was the two of us, Fela and myself, who actually started Koola Lobitos.

Q: How many were you?
A: We were about a nine-, ten-piece band.

Q: You used to play for mainly West Indian and African audiences?
A: Yeah, but we started going more and more into all the jazz clubs, like. . . . The Marquee, the JCC, Birdland and . . . what's the name of that club in Gower Street? A very, very popular jazz club? Anyway, we played there.

Q: What type of person was Fela then?
A: He was very quiet, although he was very speedy, you know. He was speeding all the time. He was a cool guy, nice to work with. And he loved to play, man!

Q: Did he drink a lot?
A: Fela? Drink? He used to drink cider at that time; that's all he'd drink. [Laughter.] He never got drunk off anything but cider, man. [Roaring laughter.] Whenever we went to parties he would start dancing. He would fill up on cider first. Then he would start challenging the others to dance. Girls, you know . . . Nigerian girls, they loved us because we were straight. We didn't fool with anybody. We weren't the kind of family type who wanted to get married and settle down. We were just doing our own thing. Chasing women? [Laughter.] Fela was very green at that time. Well, not green in the sense that he didn't know. . . . Well, you know what I mean? He was afraid to fuck, man. [Roaring laughter.]

Q: He didn't smoke?
A: Not even cigarettes. Let alone grass, even for fucking. He was afraid to fuck! We had to take his prick by hand, hold it and put it in the cunt for him. I swear! Well, for example, I tell Fela, "Fuck this woman. This girl will leave if you don't fuck her." Fela would answer, "Ohhhhh, she go get pregnant-o!" And I'd have to persuade him. Guys like Richard Buckner – that's Wole Buckner's senior brother – didn't know

how to go after women. So they would hang around us. When we'd get women they'd come around and take the girls away from us. All that was Fela's fault. But we didn't care because we were very popular.

Q: That's incredible.
A: Man, it's me, J.K. telling you! . . . We used to go around town. We were almost every night in the West End. Oh, man, when you would see me in London then. . . . For two years, you could never see me without tie or three-piece suit. I became like a gigolo. Gold rings everywhere. You know. . . . But, shit, Fela was a square, man! A nice guy, really beautiful guy. But as square as they come!

Q: Your sister must have been happy to know you were in good company, uh?
A: Shit, no! They were all against it. While I was in England my sisters, my parents kept up their shit: "What are you doing with this guy? Are you crazy? What are you doing with Fela?" I said, "Just leave me alone. I know he's my friend. He's my close friend."

Q: Then, your family's opposition had a contrary effect?
A: Definitely so! How could I drop Fela just because my family didn't dig him? I dug him, man. We used to sleep together, eat together, sleep on the same bed, you know, things like that. I could never abandon a feeling like that, a friend like that. You know what I mean? If it's a male friend, like a school friend, say, then we meet at school or we meet outside. That's a different thing. But we were living together, you know. Telling each other secrets and everything, you know. Right from the time when we were away from our country. So it brought that close love between us because we were not in Nigeria.

NEW YORK Tribune

☆ A European Edition Is Published Daily in Paris ☆

SUNDAY, JANUARY 4, 1959

Castro Is On Way To Havana, Rebels Move Into Capitol

Evacuation of Americans Sped; Army Chief of Staff Arrested

By United Press International

HAVANA, Jan. 3.—Fidel Castro's rebels today occupied the
national capit_____ strategic points in and around
Havana. The c_____ the arrival of the victorious
rebel chief a_____ ___ Urrutia Lleo.

The rebe_____ _hat Ca___

Castro Hit- U.S. Idea of Quota Cut

Threatens to Seiz__
Holdings in Cub__

Troops Fire on Rioters In Belgian Congo Capital

NEW YORK HERALD TRIBUNE

LEOPOLDVILLE, Belgian Con-|north to work in this capi-
_go, Jan. 5 (UPI).—Troops|area. They recently form
_opened fire on charging native|political party demand-
mobs in this Belgian Congo|Belgium. immediate
capital today in new rioting by|independen___
Abako Congolese agitating for|Several ___ _he
independence from Belgium.|were r__ _he
The governor general declared|Cairo __
a "state of alert."|br__
Eleven Congolese were re-
_ported killed in forty-eigh-
_hours of rioting, which was
_fined to the African qua-
the city. At least fif__
_persons, including at l__
_Europeans, were in__
_ashes.
Two Catholic missi__
_ police commissioner__
_ng the wounded.
_ratrooper reinforcem__
_being flown in.
_European quarter of the i__
_mained quiet. In the __
_quarter, residents were __
a government ban on __
_s of more than __

Troops Halt Congo Riot; Belgian Cabinet Called

JANUARY 6, 1959

LEOPOLDVILLE, Belgian|disperse mobs at several points
Congo, Jan. 6 (UPI).—Rein-|this morning.
_forced security forces today re-|Mobs had surged through the
_____order in Leopoldville|streets of the native quarter
__ days of anti-Belgian|shouting such slogans
____ which thirty-five|"Belgians, go home!"
__illed and more|Gov. Gen. Henri Bosma__
|said all of those killed a__
|more than 100 of those inju__
|in the rioting were native
|the rioting was touche__
|_lice broke up a __
|_ass meetin__
|of th__

6

A Long Way From Home

Imagine me, Fela, eighteen years old, School Certificate in pocket, working as an office employee in Lagos, in a government office, Commerce and Industries? My first job ever in life, man. But I couldn't stand that rigid shit. I resigned after six months. Soon after, I found another job in the same building. At that time they weren't needing any workers. They were only needing people to sort of fill in the offices. So I saw no point in sticking around. Music was all I wanted to work at. And now that my father wasn't there, it was easier to persuade my mother to let me go study music abroad.

August 1958. I was nineteen. And off to a new life when I left to England! Trinity College of Music meant real hard work. No bullshit, man. I studied there from 1958 to December 1962. The final exam was in two parts, practical and theory. For theory, you had two books: one in harmony and counterpoint and the other in history. I failed theory but passed the practical on my instrument, which was then the trumpet. At Trinity, if you failed one part but passed the other, you had three years to pass the one failed. And if you didn't pass it again within those three years, you had to pass both parts all over. In two and a half years I passed theory. It took me that much time because I was unable to concentrate on my written studies. You see, I couldn't *read*. It was a real effort for me to read anything. I wouldn't even read a newspaper at the time. Somehow the urge to read had been killed in me. And I came to feel the same way about films too.

You see, one day I went to watch this film, Hitchcock's *Psycho*. There was a billboard outside the cinema house which said: "No entry into cinema house 15 minutes before start of the show." So, if you're not there fifteen minutes before the show starts, you're not allowed to enter. That's how scary the film is. Then when you enter the cinema house fifteen minutes before the film starts, they start to fill your mind with some fucking music, man. And they put the cinema house dark. And that was the intention of the producer of the film. Everybody wonders what's going to happen. Then the film starts rolling. It started so coolly, like nothing was happening. You know how terrible this film was? The actress, Janet Leigh, a big star then, died very early in the film. They killed her very early in the film and the film had another hour and a half to go. The way she was killed I almost jumped out of my chair. That thing scared me! It started me thinking. Like when I read that book about that Simon Templar guy. He was so smart, man. Just a clever man who decides to go and catch crooks. Then, when he's ready he hands them over to the police or private detective . . . after he has got their bread. He spends the bread lavishly to make people happy. So, you see why I wanted to be Simon Templar, man.

These films, these books really made me think twice. When do you see someone like Simon Templar around? Then, you go in the film house to watch *Psycho* and these fucking films scare you. I said to myself: "I see. So, this is what people do now? Somebody goes into his room, locks himself up, and decides he's gonna scare the whole world." I said, "Shit! I ain't gonna watch no motherfucking scary film again. And I ain't gonna read no fucking novel or stories unless they are history or true books or education." That's why I stopped reading novels and seeing those films, man. The first book I ever read since those days, man, was in 1969 when I went to the States: *The Autobiography of Malcolm X*.

Grey. Wintry. Cold. Lonely. That was London, man. I was out of my natural environment. And I've always enjoyed being around a lot of people. But my four and a half years in Britain allowed me to really get in touch with jazz. At school I studied classical music. But outside of Trinity I *played* jazz.

So it was shortly after I arrived, when I had been feeling the most lonely, that my mother made arrangements for me to visit, of all places, East Berlin. At that time they had just put up the Berlin wall, man. And I don't want to travel nowhere. I didn't even have money to travel. But my mother wanted to arrange a holiday for me. Why . . . East Berlin? The "Iron Curtain" was getting big publicity in England then. It was newspaper headlines. It was said that if you went into communist countries you would never come out; that communist countries were dangerous for human beings. So I was scared to go, man. I didn't want to go. But how could I disobey my mother?

On departure day, at London airport, passengers were being called to board the different flights. When they called, "Pan Am, Pan Am," a whole lot of people got up When they called our flight, everyone in the airport looked to see who was going to stand up, because they knew that this flight was going to East Berlin, man. Only *three* of us got up in the whole airport! All eyes were on us. I was so scared. I knew I was going to die. Two hundred people had gotten up for the Pan Am flight. But only *three* for East Berlin! I swear, I was shaking. On top of that, the plane turned out to be the oldest plane on the airfield. I said to myself: "I'm gonna die today." When we finally arrived at our destination, you know what I saw? It wasn't like an airport at all. I saw sheds and these Gestapo-like dressed soldiers with boots. A man came up to me and said:

"Mr Fela Ransome-Kuti?"

"Yes."

He said: "Follow me." He was so military.

I said: "Follow you? Where?"

He took me to this big hotel in East Berlin. It was so big, so great. But I was so afraid, it looked to me like the biggest prison. You see what brainwashing does to human beings? Here was this big hotel. Actually, it was a beautiful place; but to me, it was like prison.

We went down a long corridor. "Here's your room," he said. It was about 9 o'clock at night. I locked the door. Went and sat on the bed. Then I thought I heard footsteps. I tiptoed to the door. Slowly opened it and looked in the corridor. No one. I went back and sat on the bed. Again I would go. Again I'd come back. Go. Come back. That's how I spent the whole night. In the morning, I heard them calling for me. I said to myself: "It's time for trouble-o." They said to me, "Follow us now. We're going to start the tour." I was thinking, "Tour to hell!" Then when I got downstairs I saw many Africans waiting to go on this tour too. Then I felt a bit comfortable. I at last started to cool down, man. Then we all went sightseeing. I had the most beautiful time of my life those ten days I spent there. All the racist thing I experienced as a student in England wasn't there. Happiness, man. Ten happy days. So I took a different view on that whole shit about communism. But, ten years after, on a second visit to Berlin for the Berlin Jazz Festival in 1978, I would see communism's real face. But during my first visit I could only see all of those good things. I was thrilled.

Politics! Man, I was so fucking ignorant about world politics then, I didn't know shit! And I really didn't give a fuck either! The first time I'd heard about race riots was when I got to London, man. The press was full of that racial shit. NOTTING HILL, AUGUST 1958. STICK-WIELDING POLICE CONTAIN NEGRO RIOTERS! No, man, I wasn't ready for that!

At that time, I wasn't even reading newspapers, man. Music. Music is all that interested me! And parties, of course, where I could play, dance, meet people and have fun. I'd just go from party to party. Then. . . . Fuck it! When I saw her, I said: "This is NEWS!" That girl, man, was so fucking beautiful! I said to myself: "Shit, I've got to make it with her." What attracted me to Remi? Her face. It was a beautiful face. What did I feel? I felt to . . . fuck.

Remi Taylor and Fela at the time of their marriage in
London, 1961

7

Remi

The One with the Beautiful Face

She's tall, slender and graceful, with the poised, self-assured dignity of a woman who has been through a hell of a lot. Remi is Fela's first wife, the mother of his first three children. Vivacious and eloquent in private, she keeps a distant and low-keyed profile in public.

Remilekun* Taylor was born on 12 July 1941, in Maidenhead (England), during the Second World War when, as she relates, "pregnant mothers were being shipped to the outskirts of London". Her father was Nigerian, her mother is a blend of Black American ("which also means African," she proudly affirms), Red Indian and British.

Growing up in England then was not easy, she recalls. "Now I can say it was stinking, but then I didn't know any different. You know, when I was growing up I always thought I was very ugly 'cause I judged myself against the white girls. I didn't know any Blacks except my sister and cousins." Not until she was sixteen did that negative self-image begin to lose its hold. "When I got to sixteen and left for school in Birmingham I saw a lot of Black girls. So I knew I wasn't as ugly as I thought. There were so many things I had to fight against then, like religion. After I left school I couldn't be bothered with it." And it was soon after leaving school that Fela walked into Remi's life.

Q: When did you meet Fela?
A: I met Fela when I was eighteen, in 1959.

Q: How did you meet him?

---

* Remilekun: "Wipe My Tears".

Nigerians Freed On Quiet Note

Rockefeller: U.S. for Nigerian Neutrali

By Richard C. Wald

LAGOS, Sept. 30—American ap-

'Massacre' of Lumumba and Two Aids Announced in Katang

By Villagers

Chief ...ands ...iry

PARIS, FRIDAY, APRIL 21, 1961

Kennedy: Cuba 'Must Not' Go to Red

Castro: 'Foe Suffered Crushing Defeat

President: Restraint Is Limited

Warns America On Passive Stand

Minis Term 'Exce

Agitator's Rise
Tool to Foes

Patrice Lumumba

A: At a party. I first met him in London at a party and I didn't like him. He was too rough. [*Laughter.*]

Q: What were you doing at the time you met him?
A: I was working and training to be a secretary.

Q: I see. And why do you say he was too rough?
A: The way he dressed, you know. No tie. Open shirt. Everything. Like a Teddy Boy, I called him.

Q: Like a ruffian?
A: Yes. [*Laughter.*] It's true. Then when I met him six months later he had a suit on and was playing with his band. So he appealed to me then and so OK.

Q: What appealed to you then?
A: [*Laughter.*] Sex appeal.

Q: Sex appeal! [*Laughter.*] And what happened afterwards?
A: We started going out together and then we got married. In London. In 1961.

Q: And when was the first child born?
A: The same year. It was Yeni, our oldest daughter. Next came our son, Femi, in June 1962. Then another daughter, Sola, on 24 November 1963. She was born in Lagos.

Q: So you were pregnant once a year?
A: More or less.

Q: Tell me something. How was Fela with you then? At that period? Those were the hard years in London then for him.
A: Those years may have been hard, but not as hard as the years to come. We got along well and Fela was attentive to me.

Q: Were you all living together?
A: No, he lived in his place. I lived in mine.

Q: That's how you always lived?
A: Yes, ever since we met.

Q: Why is that?
A: Well, in the beginning because he couldn't practise in my place. And then, I just liked it like that.

Q: So there was never any misunderstanding because of that?

A: No. Although he did say when we came home we'd start to live together, which we did when we came back to Nigeria.

Q: When he returned to Nigeria, you came back with him also?

A: Yes. He came by boat and I came by plane two weeks later, so he arrived the day before me. In '63.

Q: Then what happened? How was life then?

A: It was OK at first. He started his band, I think, the following year or the same year. I can't remember. It was OK at first and then I got sick. He went to America and I got worse. When he came back I decided to live in my own place, like before.

Q: Why?

A: Why not?

Mob Uses Guns,
Molotov Cocktails

WEDNESDAY, JULY 1, 1962

Algeria Becomes Independe

Ben Khedda Hailed in Algi

Congo Terrorists Reported
To Have Slain 'at Least 100'

From Cable Dispatches

LEOPOLDVILLE, Jan. 28. —
ilu Province representatives said
ay that Communist-led terrorists
e murdered about 100 adminis-
rs, missionaries and other of-
there and that the situation
f control.

incial government dele-
here to request the
take emergency
estern Congo
les from

PARIS, TUESDAY, OCTOBER 2, 1962

Mississippi Students
Battle Marshals;
2 Killed as
Meredith Attends Cl

De G
Stat
Pu

Jea

Russia Says Blockade of Cuba Could Start Wa

Kennedy Orders Navy to Stop Ships As of To

Warsaw
Put or

PARIS, WEDNESDAY, OCTOBER 24, 1962

iet Ships May Be
e Within Hours

Mulele
'Presumed'
Dead in Congo

By the Associated Press

LEOPOLDVILLE, Aug. 19.—The
ment today announced the
ed death of Peking-traine
Pierre Mulele
here
Mulele, a fo
mini

Civil-Rights Day in Washington

210,000 Take Part in 'March'

Crowd Gay and Well

In Accra, as Citizen of Ghana

Dr. William E. B. Du Bois, 96, Dies; Long U.S. Negro Leader

From Cable Dispatches

ACCRA, Aug. 28.—Dr. William E.B. Du Bois, 96, a pioneer Negro leader in the United States, died here last night.

Dr. Du Bois, who had lived in Ghana since 1960, was working as editor of an encyclopedia of Africana at the time of his death. He was naturalized as a Ghanaian citizen early this year.

He was an organizer of the first Niagara Movement, one of the first American integration organizations.

The Niagara Movement grew directly into the National Association for the Advancement of Colored People, and Dr. Du Bois was on the NAACP staff until 1948, when he was forced out because of his political activities.

the first "All-Africa Congress," which met in Manchester, England, in 1919.

And 39 years later he told an "All-Africa Peoples' Conference" meeting here, that "today Africa has no choice between private capitalism and socialism."

"The whole world, including the capitalist countries, are moving toward socialism inevitably, inexorably," he said in a message read to the congress by his wife.

When Dr. Du Bois won his Lenin Peace Prize he told reporters that he intended to use the prize money "to eat with" and his wife could use his writings.

"Now it is a worry to carry around," said

Bomb in Birmingham Church Kills 4 Negro Girls

Children Attended Sunday School

Dozens of Negroes Injured

U.S.-Soviet A Bar to

KENNEDY ASSASSINATED

Is Shot Down in Car by a Hidden Sniper As He Rides Through Downtown Dallas

8

From Highlife Jazz to Afro-Beat
Getting My Shit Together

From England I went back home in 1963 and worked for
Nigeria Broadcasting as a producer. It was a terrible job. A
stupid job. Unprogressive work. But I got into records and
heard African music, the music I love. I had my band called
Koola Lobitos. The NBC gig didn't last. My appointment
with them was terminated. I had to resign. Why? Uncount-
able reasons, man, like: "You're always coming late to
work." (Yeah, at eleven o'clock instead of eight.) Or:
"You're not recording new bands for new programmes."
(Yeah, true sometimes.) Or: "You insist on playing *your*
music rather than what is programmed!" (Yeah, I wanted
to play jazz, man.) My boss wanted jazz too, but straight
jazz. I wanted to play highlife jazz, as I called my music at
the beginning.

In '66 I was playing highlife jazz with my Koola Lobitos
band. Eventually I dropped that name too. 'Cause my
mother had told me: "Start playing music your people
understand, not jazz." So those were years of experimen-
tation, man. Even with . . . *grass.*

How did I get into grass? You may not believe me, man.
But it was a girl who started me "smoking" in Nigeria. Her
name is Eunice. I'd always see her eyes red and a friend
said she "smoked" a bit. So one day I asked her: "Do you
smoke?" She said: "Tell me, man; tell me, make him some
try some too." So I tried it. I'd tried it before in London,
but you didn't get it in London so much. I tried it once or
twice in London. I liked it when I "smoked" it in London.
But my brother professor told me a long time ago that if I
"smoked" I would go crazy, so that is why I run away from
it. But when this girl gave me the smoke and I had sex with
it. . . . Ohhhhhhhhh, it was fantastic! I'd never had sex with
it before. That was '66.

When did I start calling my music *Afro-beat?* Let me tell

you. I was playing highlife jazz when Geraldo Pino came to town in '66 or a bit earlier with soul. That's what upset everything, man. He came to town with James Brown's music, singing, "Hey, hey, I feel all right, ta, ta, ta, ta. . . ." And with such equipment you've never seen, man. This man was tearing Lagos to pieces. Woooooooh, man! He had all Nigeria in his pocket. Made me fall right on my ass, man. Ahhhhhh, this Sierra Leonian guy was too much. Geraldo Pino from Sierra Leone. I'll never forget him. I never heard this kind of music before-o, I'm telling you. Only when I went to Ghana shortly after that did I hear music like that again, soul music. Shit! If you could have seen him, man. And his equipment . . . something else!

When that guy Pino came to Lagos in '66, he came in a big way: in a convertible Pontiac; you know, one of those big American cars, man. Flashy, new equipment. Lots of bread. He was doing his thing, man. He had everything I didn't have. He did a three-day show in Lagos. Then he went up country to the North for a month, then came back to Lagos again for five days. After that, he was to go back to Ghana. What worried me was that he was going to come back again to Nigeria. I'd seen the impact this motherfucker had in Lagos. He had everyone in his pocket! That was my mind, you know. I wanted to split town, leave, disappear. Go far away. To America. Find my own way, in any case. Make it myself. 'Cause I saw I couldn't make it with this man around, even in Nigeria. In '67 he came back to Nigeria for a tour, then split back to Ghana. Ouuuuf!

After that motherfucking Pino tore up the scene, there wasn't shit I could do in Lagos. So I went to Ghana in '67 with Zill Oniya, a trumpeter from Nigeria, to look for work, because at that time I didn't have funds in Nigeria. I was even giving up the music-o! I swear, man! I was so fucking discouraged. Then Zill came to me and said, "Let's try and find work in Ghana." At that time that's where the action and the bread was. So we went to Ghana. And one day in Accra we entered this club, Ringway Hotel. The place was packed, man! Geraldo Pino was playing there. Ohhhhh, come and hear this music-o! See this guy's equipment! I'd never seen such equipment before. In Lagos, I was using this old equipment . . . museum antiques, man. I had only one microphone for the whole band. One microphone! This motherfucking Pino had six!

The whole place was jumping. The music carried me away completely. To me, it was really swinging music. I say, "Look the drummer, how he play drums!" Ohhhhh, I say, "Whaaaaat? This is heavy-o!" I was saying to myself, "I need equipment like this, man!" Oooooooo, I was enjoying the music! Can you understand my situation at that club that night? Needing to find a job myself, but enjoying the music so much that I even forgot I myself was a fucking musician. I was there digging the music, thinking about all that. Finally, I did get my own job at a club in Ghana. I stayed there for a year. That was in '67. After seeing this Pino, I knew I had to get my shit together. And quick!

I went back to Nigeria, but soon after returned to Ghana in '68. One day I was with a friend sitting down in a club in Accra, listening to soul music. Everybody was playing soul, man, trying to copy Pino. I said to myself: "This James Brown music. . . . This is what's gonna happen in Nigeria soon-o." I saw it so clearly. That's why I said to myself, "I have to be very original and clear myself from shit." I was still hustling. Hustling to make bread. "I must clear myself from this mess. I must identify myself with Africa. Then I will have an identity." That's what I was thinking to myself. Raymond Aziz, a Nigerian-Ghanaian who was sitting next to me, looked at me kind of pensively.

"You OK, man?" he asked.

I said: "Raymond, you see that my music. I must give it a name-o, a real African name that is catchy. I've been looking for names to give it. And I've been thinking of calling it *Afro-beat.*"

He said: "Yehhhhhh! That's a good name."

I said: "Thank you."

So when I got back to Lagos, I called the press, gave them money, and told them I was changing to Afro-beat. I had to "dash" the press, bribe them, have a press conference. All that shit. Then I started a club: Afro-Spot. It gave me some of the prestige I needed. Even if Geraldo Pino came – I was thinking – I had Afro-Spot. But then he arrived and started to take Lagos! Ohhh, waoooooooooh!

All the while, terrible things were happening in Nigeria. Atrocious things, man. The Biafran war had started in '66 and was now fully underway. I was in Lagos, playing music. I didn't like the Biafran war though. I thought the Nigerian government was wrong. I thought the Biafrans were right.

JUNE 3, 1967

War in the News

Lagos Orders Blockade of Seceded East

General Mobilization Begins in Nigeria

LAGOS, Nigeria, May 31

Ojukwu Leads Ibo Tribe Out of Nigerian Federation

By Lloyd Garrison
The New York Times

LAGOS, Nigeria, May 30

Nigerian Easterners Declare Independence

British, U.S. Interests Hit By 'Oil War'

JUNE 13, 1967

Stokely Carmichael

Arrest of Carmichael Triggers Alabama Riot

PRATTVILLE, Ala., June 13—Black power leader Stokely Carmichael, whose arrest last night

Arabs Say U.S., U.K. Planes Aid Israelis

Egypt Breaks Relations With U.S.
Israel Captures Gaza

Arabs Burn U.S., British Consulates

23 Deaths in Newark Race Riots

JULY 15

JULY 24, 1967 — Established 1887

Racial Violence Breaks Out In Seven Cities Across the U.S.

The Yoruba are not Ibo. I thought the Ibos were right. I said to myself, "This whole thing is a cheap, big hustle to put the Ibos in a bad light in the world." And, in fact, what was happening was the beginning of corruption in Nigeria. That's evident now.

The Biafrans were fucking right to secede, man. If it was secession, it was good secession. Because secession is what could have brought Africa together at that time. From secession we could come together again. But by not seceding, we're put together *by force*. Uhuhhhhhh! That's what's happening in Nigeria today. The Ibos don't understand why they're in Nigeria. The Yorubas don't know what's happening. And the Hausas, they want to dominate everybody. The whole thing is fucking confusion. I don't even know myself why we're in Nigeria; how we all got to be together in this country, in the first place. No politician has ever gone into that. If Ojukwu* had seceded, we would have started our own history. We would have known why we seceded and what happened. How did we get together in the first place? Uh? That's the real question. Why don't any of the politicians ever ask that question? Eh? Anyway, at that time, when the war was going on, I wasn't politically minded at all. I made my comments as a citizen. I was just another musician, playing with Koola Lobitos and singing love songs, songs about rain, about people. . . . What did I know? That's when I split to America.

The idea to split to America came suddenly. One day I was in this club when this guy came and told me he wanted to take me to America. He said he would give me tickets and everything. So we started to plan America. We went and got our passports, then went to get visas. We had already told the press we were leaving that same Friday. So when I went to the American Embassy for visa, they said, "Where are your tickets?" So I went and asked this guy for the tickets. He started to scratch his head and talk shit, saying that they were with his brother, and that we'd reimburse him when we got back from America. The motherfucker didn't even have bread to buy the tickets. So I went with him to see his brother. Of course, he had no tickets either. Anyway, this guy told his brother we would

---

* General Odemegwu Ojukwu, Commander-in-Chief of the secessionist Biafran army and President of the shortlived Republic of Biafra.

77

refund the money to him when we got back, that we would work, do African music, make shows, and send him back the money. You know, he was trying to convince him. Finally, his brother said, "OK," and he went to the bank to borrow the money. So he didn't have money either.

Anyway, I went to America and when I did come back, I only had $10 in my pocket. I was completely broke, man. I didn't even dare go to see the man at all. I was saying to myself, "I can't see you-o. 'Cause your brother fucked me up in America." You see, man, this guy had advanced us £2,400 sterling for the tickets of the whole band. We'd left on three-month excursion tickets. Imagine that, three months! And, man, we stayed there *ten* months instead. When I got really popular in Lagos though I paid this man back from what I got off the records released. That's how I paid my debts.

All the while I'd kept in touch with J.K. who'd been living in London, Paris, then in London again. I used to wonder, "How is that motherfucker doing?" We'd keep in touch, but irregularly, off and on. I was convinced that together we could pull off whatever motherfucking shit we wanted. "If I make it in America," I was thinking to myself, "then we could get together and really do our thing!" Finish.

Martin Luther King Slaying Brings Rising Tide of Violence; Riots Hit 41 Cities

APRIL 6... 1968

150,000 at Dr. King Rites

9

Lost and Found
in the Jungle of Skyscrapers

New York! New York! Buildings going up, up, up, high like that! Pata-pata-pata-pata! Skyscrapers! Oooooooooh! Today I'd say: "Go up that high? To *scrape* what? Jo, make 'em scrape dirty streets fo' Harlem an' Mushin-o!* Make 'em scrape 'way poverty from this, the land we're standing on-o! . . ." But at that time, man, I was taken back. I said to myself: "Fuck! Look those motherfucking tall buildings! Africans ain't shit! Just savages, man! When did Black man ever build things great like that-o?" Oh, I was so impressed by America! So blind, man! No, my life in England hadn't prepared me for America-o. That place was so big, man! Shiiiiiit! And we really had a chance to *see* America 'cause we didn't have bread to fly to Los Angeles. So my whole group, seven musicians, myself and one girl dancer, set out to L.A. by road. Woooooowh! Who would believe me back home? "Great" Britain? *Little* Britain beside America!

Nigeria was now three months behind us. And we weren't *in* the America we'd dreamt of. No, man. We were *in* trouble! No gigs! No bread! No shit! Nothing! And our visas finish-o! I said, "Now we're illegal immigrant motherfuckers!" No visa, no work permit. . . . Stalemate! Terrible times, man. I had already made the rounds of all the big recording companies: not one would even audition us 'cause we were . . . Africans! That "racial shit" again, man! That's when I met Duke Lumumba, a Ghanaian boy residing in America, who was in the recording business. I thought, "Well, maybe we'll now get a break soon!"

The Biafran war was still on. One day Duke came up with an idea: to release a pro-government record just so we could get some bread, man. I wanted to hustle the Nigerian

---

* Mushin: A sprawling "ghetto" of nearly half a million people on the outskirts of Lagos city.

Fela and Sandra, 1970

government to back my band. So I wrote a song: "Keep Nigeria One". Now, wait a minute-o. You see, it wasn't my idea. It was Duke Lumumba's idea. It was he who was putting the money down. You see, Duke had this old woman he would take money from. He went to the old woman and she gave him $2,500. So he got this studio to do this recording and said to me, "Fela, I have to make just one record that the Nigerian government will like, just in case the government will want to back the band." So we made this tune. It was just bullshit: "Nigeria, we must not fight ourselves we must be like brothers. . . ." I feel so bad about that record now; I was on Biafra's side. But it wasn't my idea. Anyway, nothing came of it.

It was right after the record was released that I met Sandra. Saaaandraaa! Shit! Yeh, man! Let me tell you *how* I met her.

August 1969. Los Angeles. There was this African band in town, so they came to invite us to play at this club – Ambassador Hotel – in Los Angeles. I was on the stand playing when I saw this lady standing in the crowd, man. She stood out to me. She had come to this NAACP show there. The NAACP? A big political organization for Black civil rights in America. But at that time I wasn't political at all-o. The NAACP wanted me to play, so my business manager said, and got me the gig, you know. So that's how I got to play there, not because I was political. I wasn't political. I just wanted to play, to make bread, to make myself a great artist. So that night I went on the stage to play and I saw this woman standing in the crowd there. Her eyes! Different from all the eyes there! She was very beautiful that day. She was the most beautiful woman there. I said to Allen, my drummer then: "Who is that woman?" He didn't know. I said, "Look at that woman!" Then I saw her looking at me. I said to myself, "Good! Let's go now." I left my band then and went to speak to her. I said, "When I finish here, I've got a recording to do and I want you to come with me." She said, "Yeah, yeah, I'll come." Then I went back on the stage, happy, man. After the show she took me straight – bam – to the recording studio. Then we decided to drive around after that in Los Angeles. Where to go? Who to visit to have some smoke?

We wanted to find some friends where we could smoke

some grass, get high. That's why we went to this Nigerian boy's house. I don't remember his name. Anyway, he brought out a tray of grass. Ohhhhhhh, it was too much! You know, I can't fuck without grass, man. If you fuck with grass once you won't want to fuck without grass any more. It would be a useless exercise, I tell you, I swear. It's fantastic! That's why I started smoking grass-o. The first time was in London with J.K. That day I felt to fuck, I felt nice, you know. By the time I went to Lagos, my older brother Koye had convinced me that smoke was bad. Anyway, this Nigerian boy, he knew what was happening and left Sandra and me there in the living-room. There were these plush carpets, man. And we did our thing, man. It was a beautiful, beautiful night, that night-o! When we woke up in the morning, Sandra drove me straight to my house. (When an African man say "his house" he mean where he's living, man.) So she took me to my house and said she'd phone me later. She went home, phoned me, then came and picked me up. . . . That's how it all started.

The second night I went to her house. I was feeling good. . . . The third night, she took away my clothes bit by bit because she said they be dirty. First my shirt, then another. Then she went to bring another suit for me to wear and took the one I had to wash it. When this other one got dirty, she took it too. Then she brought a whole bag of clothes for me to wear. . . . That's how all my clothes gradually left my house to her house. She was the saviour of that my trip-o! Ohhhhh! Ohhhhh! Sandra Smith . . .!

Then one day I was in her house sleeping. We weren't talking about politics then, just business. I don't remember what happened exactly. I must have said something 'cause she said, "Fela, don't say *that*! Africans taught the white man. Look, the Africans have history!" I said, "They don't have shit, man. No history, man. We are slaves." She got up and brought me a book. She said I should read it. Then she said, "I was in jail for three months, Fela." I asked her why. She got up, brought a newspaper cutting, showed it to me. She said, "Look, one day, I went to a Black Panther protest rally in Los Angeles and during the protest. . . ." You see, she was so mad, man. She had gone up to this policeman and kicked this policeman's ass, man. Whaaaaam! She escaped that day. But when they played back what happened on the television, they recognized her.

That's how they found her. They went to her house to arrest her. She spent three months, man, in jail. I got jealous. "How can a woman do that and a man can't do it, a man like me?" Then she started giving me the political reasons why she'd done it.

Sandra gave me the education I wanted to know. She was the one who opened my eyes. I swear, man! She's the one who spoke to me about . . . Africa! For the first time I heard things I'd never heard before about Africa! Sandra was my adviser. She talked to me about politics, history. She taught me what she knew and what she knew was enough for me to start on. Yeah, Sandra taught me a lot, man. She blew my mind really. She's beautiful. Too much. Nothing about my life is complete without her. Sandra was the woman . . . I swear.

I was heavy into the book she'd given me to read. It was the first book I'd read since I'd stopped reading all that nonsense from when I was in London. The only book I'd read then was a music history book for my college examination. But this book, I couldn't put it down: *The Autobiography of Malcolm X*. It was the first book since the long spell of not reading. This man was talking about the history of Africa, talking about the white man. . . . Ohhhhhh! I never read a book like that before in my life. After Simon Templar – that fictitious man I'd wanted to imitate – here was a *true* story, about a MAN! Can you imagine how it took me? Ohhhhh! I said, "This is a MAN!" I wanted to be like Malcolm X! Fuck it! Shit! I wanted to *be* Malcolm X, you know. I was so unhappy that this man was killed. Everything about Africa started coming back to me.

Then one day I sat down at the piano in Sandra's house. I said to Sandra: "Do you know what? I've just been fooling around. I haven't been playing AFRICAN music. So now I want to write African music . . . for the first time. I want to try." Then I started to write and write. In my mind I put a bass here . . . a piano there. . . . Then I started humming, then singing. I said to myself, "How do Africans sing songs? They sing with chants. Now let me chant into this song: *la-la-la-laaa*. . . ." Looking for the right beat I remembered this very old guy I'd met in London – Ambrose Campbell. He used to play African music with a special beat. I used that beat to write my tune, man. Later on, I said to Sandra: "Sandra, I must rehearse this tune."

Sandra said: "Use the back yard, man, my father's back yard." So I called my boys and said: "We're having rehearsal tomorrow. We must make some new tunes, man, If we got to make bread in this country, let's work for it." I convinced these boys, so they all came to rehearse, man. And we did this tune.

By then, you see, we'd secured a gig at the "Citadel de Haiti", a club at 6666 Sunset Boulevard. No joke, man: 6666 S-u-n-s-e-t B-o-u-l-e-v-a-r-d! The place was painted in black with the name in red. At first, we were playing there Fridays, Saturdays and Sundays. Then later on we played Wednesdays and Thursdays too. Five days a week. The club was owned by Bernie Hamilton, a Black guy. He has a series on television now; he's getting back small-small now. Bernie Hamilton! Always on a trip, man. Besides he was the fucking barman of his own club. He dug my band. Let me tell you how I got into that place.

We'd been roaming around L.A., doing nothing. No place to stay. Going from place to place. Then this guy named Juno came up to me and said: "Fela, there's this 'Haiti' club. The guy who owns it wants you badly to come there and play. He told me he wants to hear you, audition you. You see, he ain't got bread, but he ain't got licence either, so he can employ you, see?" I said, "Shit, that sounds good!" You see, the reason why I couldn't get work in America was because I didn't have a visa to work. The clubs wanted me to work but immigration wouldn't give me a visa to play 'cause I'd gone on a . . . cultural visa. So Juno said: "Bernie hasn't got a licence, so he can employ you 'cause you're not in the union. He can employ you and pay you anything he wants to pay and you can accept, man, 'cause you're not in the union." I said, "Yeah." So I went to see Bernie Hamilton, who told us to come back the next day. When we went back, he said we should start the next week.

Man, the Citadel de Haiti was the emptiest club on the whole Sunset Boulevard. When I got there I saw this ugly thing painted in black, a warehouse, with a big yard. It was the afternoon. I said to myself, looking at that big yard, "This is where all the cars must park." So when we went there in the night to audition we were expecting the whole place to be filled with cars. What do I see when we get there? One car, man. Only Bernie Hamilton's car. And his car was the oldest thing in town! You imagine how I felt, man? Then we went inside the club. They'd put red cloth on all the tables. Inside it was a nice place, you know. There were two people sitting down, friends of his. He said, "Set up. Set up. Let's hear it." I said to myself: "Shit, I'll take this job. 'Cause even if his club is empty if I can play my music I'll pull a crowd in here." So we auditioned and he told us to start next day. Then we talked deal. He said he would pay me $300 a week for the whole band (seven guys, one woman and myself). Then he said he'd give us a place to stay. I was so happy.

When Bernie said he had a place for us, I thought to myself: "What place isn't good in America? When someone says a place isn't good in America, it's still better than Ikoyi, in Lagos." That's what I was thinking. So I said, "Let's go." Now when we got to that house, man! Heeeeey! It was so bad, I can't describe it. I was still staying with Sandra at that time, but my boys, they were suffering. That bothered me. So I'd made up my mind to get a room in this house with them. Solidarity, you know. Besides, I'd have two places. If I wanted to sleep with another woman, apart from Sandra, I could go to my house and stop going to hotels. That was my plan. It was a good one. But when I saw the house – oh, shit! – I said: "I am going to stay in Sandra's house-o! I can't stay here-o." My boys, though, they suffered-o. That house was too much! There was a carpet in the back of the house but none nowhere else. It was a small comfort to keep them happy 'cause that house was a complete suffer. That's how I saw it. It was around September, October, getting cold. We were all wearing coats, man. That's how I got to play in this club, OK?

Coming back to what I was saying about the tune I wrote. I didn't put any words to it, you know. At that time I only sang short songs. Things like, "Why did you take our wife from us? Now we've come to take our wife back." Finish. Another one went: "You rich woman, you will go home and you will bring back what you saw." I was just singing nonsense. Nothing. But on this day, I didn't want to sing any song. I knew I wasn't going to sing any song in that tune I wrote. I was going to chant.

Sandra asked me, "Fela, what are you gonna call this thing, man? Why not call it 'My Lady's Frustration'?"

It has a meaning today-o. It had a meaning on that day too. But I told her I couldn't call it that 'cause I hate to name my tunes after women. So I challenged her:

"Why should I call it 'My Lady's Frustration'?"

You know what she answered? She said:

"Fela, I'm your woman, man. And you've been in America for five months and you haven't made it and we're frustrated, man. I'm frustrated. I'm a lady frustrated, man! Yeh, that title does have a meaning!"

And she was right.

Oh, this woman, she has helped me in America-o. She has fed me for five months. There are telephone bills I've run up; they've even cut one telephone line of their house. . . . I've almost made her family bankrupt. . . . I've spoiled their cars. . . . This was what was going on in my head, you know. So I said to myself, if I'm gonna sing about any one woman, I would sing about this one. At least to clear my conscience. That's how low I was at that time, man. I hated to give women any fucking credit, man. Everybody was singing about women. How could I sing about a woman in my tune? I didn't want to start singing about women.

So on this day, I went to play this new number. By this time, I'd been playing there for about two months and we had a steady crowd then. About sixty, seventy people on weekdays. Weekends two hundred. That was good for an American club. So Bernie was getting happy. That's why he had us play five days a week and raised the pay to $500. So on that day, I took the microphone and said I was going to play "My Lady's Frustration". I didn't know how the crowd would take the sound, you know. I just started. Bernie was behind the bar and he almost jumped over it. . . . "Fela, where did you get this fucking tune from? Whaaaaaat!" The whole club started jumping and everybody started dancing. I knew then I'd found the thing, man. To me, it was the first *African* tune I'd written till then.

Ten months in America. Ten terrible months. I can now say it could fill a book. America had been both bitter and sweet. As me and my band headed back to Lagos, I remembered a joke told to me only a few days before getting on the plane. I kept laughing to myself, thinking about it. . . . It was about this man in Los Angeles who had thrown a party in his house. LSD liquid, acid, was passed around. They all took small-small. Then this guy went to the toilet. Suddenly, he runs out with a towel around him. "Goddamn, there's a fucking gorilla in the bathroom!" Everyone was so high, man. "A gorilla?" they asked. "In Los Angeles?" The man himself was so fucking confused, he said: "I tell you I saw a fucking gorilla in the bathroom. Shit! I know what I saw. Fuck L.A.!" So they all decided to go and see the gorilla in the bathroom for themselves. They're all so scared, but they go and push open the door ever so s-l-o-w-l-y. Then put in head bit by bit to see the gorilla, "There ain't no fucking gorilla in here, man. Shiiit!" Now the guy who said he'd seen a gorilla came and went inside. There was a mirror on the wall. When the guy looked up, he screamed: "The gorilla! The gorilla!" They all said, "That's you, motherfucker!" I laughed and laughed over that one.

Who was I? It was in America I saw I was making a mistake. I didn't know myself. I realized that neither me nor my music was going in the right direction. I came back home with the intent to change the whole system. I didn't know I was going to have . . . such horrors! I didn't know they were gonna give me such opposition because of my new Africanism. How could I have known? As soon as I got back home I started to preach. I had decided to change my music. And my music did start changing according to how I experienced the life and culture of my people.

Sandra

10

Sandra

Woman, Lover, Friend

Her "dreadlocks", like her varied African headwraps, offset
an oval face and large, almond-shaped eyes. Brown-satin in
hue, of average height and slight build. With numerous bead
necklaces and gris-gris to complement an attire of African
cloth or Indian cotton, Sandra, with a style all her own,
hardly goes unnoticed. A frank, open look and a dynamic,
self-assured gait. Sandra, with her lively, rhythmic voice and
animated gestures, loves to talk . . . which she does mov-
ingly, passionately.

Born Sandra Smith in Los Angeles, California, to Posey
and Sulillian Smith, she now goes by the name of Sandra
Isidore. Her parents come from Arkansas in the south of the
USA, as do her grandparents and great-grandparents. On
her maternal side, little is known. But on her father's side,
she has traced her genealogy to her great-grandfather, Ned,
who was born into slavery; as well as to her great-grand-
mother, Mary, who as a child was sold in Jamaica to slave
planters in Arkansas. Going back even further, Sandra
traces her origins to the Ashanti people of Ghana.

Holding a degree in computer science, Sandra did both
her secondary and university studies in Los Angeles (including courses in anthropology "to discover the true history of
Blacks"). Of devout, Protestant parents, Sandra began
singing quite young in the church choir. "My mother wanted
me to be a pianist and she paid for me to have private
lessons. But I wanted to be a dancer. So I wouldn't do the
practice although I do know the theories." In any case,
music made its imprint, for "throughout my life," says
Sandra, "every man I ever met or became involved with was
musically inclined or had a musical background."

Q: So when you met Fela you were just meeting another musician?

A: No, it wasn't just another musician. There was something in particular about Fela. . . .

Q: Were you a member of the Black Panther Party when you met Fela?

A: Yeah. Black power was very, very strong at that time. I wasn't a leader in the organization. Then I wanted to participate, I was a member. It was Black. It was something that was making a connection to my roots. I was very rebellious because I thought I had been taught wrongly about being Black. I went through the whole stigma of being ashamed of my colour, of wondering why I had been born with black skin. . . . I grew up in white America with no knowledge of myself, no self-pride.

Q: But what triggered off your own Blackism?

A: You see, my parents were religious, so I heard about Martin Luther King from them. From that it was Elijah Muhammad, Malcolm X, Rap Brown, Stokely Carmichael, Ron Karenga, Huey Newton . . . all these voices, different speakers coming from different places at different times. You'd never know where the message was coming from. It might be Martin Luther King one day, Elijah Muhammad another. . . . There were all these Black leaders talking and you had to pick it up.

Q: Weren't you thrown in jail at one point?

A: I was thrown in jail a couple of times behind political activities.

Q: Connected with the Black Panther Party?

A: Not necessarily. It was the movement that was happening at that time. There was a lot of rioting, things that were just happening in the streets. I would see things. One incident was when police officers were unjustly harassing a brother and I happened to be there and I came with rhetoric, questioning them as to "Why?" Coming to his defence, they arrested us both. Another time. . . .

Q: How long were you in jail?

Three hundred policemen
pre-dawn raids on the
ters and two houses, se
Panther offices, in th
area of Los Angeles
riots in 1965.
The two hou
ost casualti
women a
who su
quar
oth

Machine Guns Used

Pitched Battle Fought in L.A.

As Police Besiege Panthers

-ANGELES, Dec
Black, Pan
sandbag
a bir

FRIDAY, DECEMBER 5, 1969

-ce and two appar
es were
bu

Probe Asked On Death of Two Panthers

By William Greider

WASHINGTON, Dec. 10 (WP)
—Nine congressmen called on
President Nixon yesterday to ex-
tend the life of the National Commission on Violence so that it can
investigate the unanswered questions surrounding the Chicago
police slaying of two Black Panther leaders.

The 13-member commission, appointed last year to study violence
in the nation after the assassination of Sen. Robert F. Kennedy,
is scheduled to go out of business at midnight tonight. Its final
report is scheduled for relea
and.

The White House
he request, but
commission sai
nlikely that
ue to fun
mission
enhowe
an

Chicago Blacks Quiet, Bitter At Funeral of Slain Leade

By William Chapman

CHICAGO, Dec. 10 (WP)—
Chicago's blacks—from middle-
class matrons to uniformed street
gang members paid their
respects last night to Fred Hamp-
ton, the slain Black
leader.

They paraded for h
in a pack
in sub
ch in
murf

MARCH 17, 1969

Associated Press

BATTLE DEATH—Black Panther chiefslain Fred
pton, who was killed yesterday during a gun battle
Chicago police, as he addressed a rally in October.
him is anti-war leader Dr. Benjamin Spock.

inois Panther Chief Killed

h Gun Battle With P

CHICAGO, Dec. 4 (UP
pton, th

New Soviet-China

Clash on Borde

After Civil War
dants
trial als
as State Penitentiary
e compound, most of
built just after the
Inside the walls there
or dormitory, which has
on the cells, some of the
shops, which make soap,
nd license plates for the
and the three main cell

Blacks Keep L.A. Peace
LOS ANGELES, Dec. 10 (AP)
A peace-keeping force of some
Negroes yesterday patrolled a
square-mile are
small
Panthe

anged on tiers within the
blocks are the rows of 5-foot

Mr. Hilliard, 27, was seized here
Secret Service agents. He was
before U.S

-orium rally an anti-
Nov. 15.

stor, the Rev
set the tone when
asking that there
that we meet hate
but he added,
more of us will have to die
fore we get justice?"

A: They arrested me and then my parents came and put up bail. Then they let me go like that.

Q: And the second time?

A: The same thing. They came and arrested me but this time they locked me up for five days. After that I vowed I would never go to jail again. Even if they had found me guilty of other charges, my parents were prepared to pay my passage out of the country.

Q: When you met Fela you were therefore very, very aware of your Blackness, of Africa, and looking very intensely for your own historical and cultural roots. But when Fela met you he wasn't someone who was that aware of his own Africanness. Fela told me it was you who "Africanized" him. How did you do that?

A: By me being so Black at that time. I was rebellious, then, willing to fight, willing to die. We had a saying: "By any means necessary." I thought if we Blacks in America had to die for what we believed in, even if it meant your mother and father had to go, then let them go. That's how rebellious I was, so much so that my parents couldn't understand me. I just rebelled against them because I felt that everything they had taught me was wrong. Now I know they did their best because they didn't know any better.

Q: After that did Fela move to your place?

A: No, I moved into his place and then he moved into mine.

Q: He told me you gave him a book to read: *The Auto-biography of Malcolm X*. . . .

A: That's right. I had just completed that book and I gave it to him to read. I also showed him pictures of me physically fighting the system.

Q: What did you say to Fela that made such an impact?

A: There were so many things I shared with Fela: novels, poetry, politics, history, music. Poems by Nikki Giovanni, The Last Poets (you know, "Niggers Are Afraid of Revolution"), Angela Davis, Martin Luther King, Stokeley Carmichael, Jesse Jackson, Nina Simone's "Four Women", Miles Davis. . . . It was something that happened over a period of time. It was constant talking every night, every day, over a period of six months. Politics. Love. Love and politics. Just the two of us. At that time I was so strong. I believed so strongly in the Black movement. . . . I told Fela about things that had happened to me, like my being jailed and why. I talked about my ancestral background. I was trying to let him know that we too are African. We might be a watered-down version but African all the same. We are trying to go back to the African way.

Q: How did he react when you were telling him this?
A: At the time, Fela was just listening. He just listened to me. He never said anything. I was telling him my side of the story 'cause I was convinced that he was already there. I assumed Fela was already there.

Q: So you didn't know that Fela wasn't there? That it was you who was "Africanizing" him? When did you find out?
A: I didn't know at that time. I found out in 1976 when I returned to Africa to do the "Upside Down" album. I realized then that everything in 1970 was upside down. But on my first trip to Africa I went on with my rhetoric 'cause I was so into what I was talking about and so happy to be on the continent that I was like a sponge. I was just ready to absorb all of the Black I could get and bring it back to America to spread. And if you could have seen the Black I took back and how it manifested there in my friends. . . . There are American women you would swear are African because they are blacker than a lot of the African women, which is surprising. On my first trip to Africa I wasn't critical of Nigeria or Ghana. I was open. I was only there to absorb and take the blackness that was there. There was so much culture, so much for me to see, it was like I was a blind woman. I couldn't see the forest for the trees. It was so much. So I couldn't be bothered with where Fela was or with Fela's trip. I was into Fela. I assumed that Fela was already there. Fela never said anything. He just went along with whatever I had to say. He would agree, so I couldn't have known at the time that Fela wasn't there.

Q: How was Fela when you first met him? Shy? Boisterous? . . .

A: Aggressive! He's always been aggressive. And that's what I liked about him. Immediately he started telling me what I was going to do. I never had a man just come up and say, "You're going to do this." Because he was so aggressive towards me, my reaction was: "Who is he? Let me check him out. Let me see what he's saying."

Q: What did he tell you to do?

A: Well, when we first met there was this strong, vivid eye contact. . . . You see, in '69 I was dancing with this African dance troupe called "Swaba". I was an American Black trying to do an African thing. A Guinean named Mamadou had founded this dance troupe. One of my friends, Juno, who played conga drums with the troupe, was the one who'd talked to me about Fela before and who took me to the Ambassador Hotel and introduced me to Fela. So when Fela came off the stage that night, Juno came and told me that Fela wanted to see me and I went to the bar where he was. I was immediately subdued by Fela. I felt that by Fela being an African from Africa, he would more or less laugh at me trying to do an African thing, as if I couldn't do it good enough. But I didn't know at that time that I was surprising Fela and teaching him at the same time.

Q: But what was it he told you to do?

A: Fela asked me my name and I told him. Then he asked me if I had a car and I said, "Yes". He said, "Good." He just said, "Good," like that. Then, "You're going with me." It just blew my mind 'cause I'd never had anybody be so aggressive with me. I didn't say, "NO." You don't say, "No," if it's something new, a new culture. You don't turn away from it. If you want to learn about it, you walk into it. So I went into it with both feet and I got deep into it before I knew what was happening. So I fell in love with Fela. I fell in love with the man. I fell in love with the music. Then I fell in love with the band. I was already in love with the country.

Q: Fela told me that it was because of you that he played African music for the first time. And that the name of one of his compositions, "My Lady's Frustration", was for you.

A: Yeah. Because I was so frustrated. Just dealing with him. Plus, his band went through a lot of hardships in America. I, too, was so aggressive then. I was a fighter. Now I'm very passive. But, then, if you didn't want to hear it my way, I was ready to fight. Physically. Whatever. By any means. And I used to physically attack Fela. I used to attack him all the time.

Q: And what would he do?

A: Not much of anything 'cause I always did it in the right places, where there were plenty of people around. I slapped him one time on stage in front of an audience. Let me tell you what happened. My father and I had come to the show late. It was a known fact that I was Fela's lady. And because I was Fela's lady, it was like, "Everybody get back." That's just the way American women are – the possessive, domineering type. So we were at the club and all the girlfriends, wives, whatever, of the guys in the band were sitting at this one table, along with my father and two other ladies I didn't know but to whom I was very cordial. Also at the table was the girlfriend of Felix, the bass player. Fela's band was then called Nigeria 70. When they first came the name was Koola Lobitos, but this Jewish promoter got hooked up in it and the name was changed. Fela doesn't know, but I still got some old contracts of copyrights and tunes he did in America as a joke and which he signed. I still have them. My mother kept them. . . . Well, we were at the table and my father was there. I was so proud in front of those ladies. I had taken out a photo of Fela and me together to show everyone. Then Fela came and said that I should go home and that he would be home later. So I said, "Fine." I'm so happy 'cause I know Fela's coming as soon as the gig is over, so I leave. We get in the car. My father's driving. There's about three or four of us women and my father's taking us home. We get halfway down the freeway, almost to the house, when I remember I left my picture in the nightclub. Then one of the women in the car says it's not worth

98

going back to get since the other woman probably tore it up. Turning to her, I asked, "What you mean, tore it up?" "Didn't you know," she said, "that that woman is there waiting for Fela?" I said, "Whaaaat? You mean the one I was being so nice to?" I told my father, "Stop the car! Turn it around!" Just like that, my Daddy turns the car around, right in the middle of the Hollywood Freeway, and we go back to the club. You see, my father likes trouble. He enjoys seeing two women fight. When we got there, it's intermission. I go storming into the nightclub and walk right up to the stage. Fela was just getting ready to come on to play the second set. "Fela," I said, "I want to talk to you!" Irritated, he answered, "Not now! Don't you see I'm busy? Go sit down!" "Fela," I insisted, "I want to talk to you." Again he answered, "I said not now!" "Fela, I want to talk to you. N-O-W!!!!" "NOT NOW!" he said. And I just went whaaaaaaam . . . in front of the whole audience.

Q: How did Fela react?
A: The members of the band had grabbed him. They all grabbed him. Isaac, his saxophone player, said: "Good! It serves you right."

Q: Was that the only time you'd hit him?
A: No. We had fought before. He's the one who stopped me from having them temper tantrums.

Q: How many times did he slap or hit you?
A: Never.

Q: You mean every time you'd slap him he would never retaliate?
A: No. He might grab me or maybe hit me on my ass. Then by the time I realized what I'd done, I'd be scared.

Q: Who were some of the people Fela met then?
A: There was Stu Gilliam, a very big comedian in America today, and his wife who had an African name, Akeeda, a very fine woman. Then, Esther Phillips, the singer. . . .

Q: Fela knew Esther Phillips?
A: Oh, yeah! All the Black people that Fela knew in

America then, they're big, big people today. Like, Bernie Hamilton, Chico Hamilton's brother; he's the star of the weekly TV series, "Starsky and Hutch", and one of the few actors who works on a regular basis. He was the owner of the "Citadel de Haiti" club where Fela was playing, but it's been torn down since. These are big-time people. John Brown used to come to the club to hear Fela; he, too, is a big star now on the TV programme "Good Times". Fela knew all those people. Jim Brown, Melvin van Peebles, you name it, he knows them all. They were all on the set at that time in '69. Like Fela has told me since, '69 was a turning year. Everyone who made the hook-up formed a nucleus back then and Fela was in America at that time.

Q: Was Fela depressed at that time?
A: Yeah. It was very hard for him. The way his band was living, the trips they had to go through. It was depressing. I think that's probably why I loved Fela even more because I knew how hard it was and I wanted so much to give to them because they were African and I didn't want them to see a bad time in America.

Q: What was making things so hard for them?
A: They were foreigners, number one. You know, America has a way of putting obstacles in your way: no visas, no union. You see, you have to be a member of the union to get a gig, but before you can be a member of a union you got to get a gig. But you can't get a gig unless you're a member of the union. So it's a closed shop.

Q: Did you ever see Fela break down at that time?
A: No. I knew he was depressed. He'd be sort of quiet, staying in bed. . . .

Q: That's not being depressed if he stays in *bed* with you.
A: If I'm there, yeah, so I didn't mind him being depressed. [*Laughter.*]

Q: When you first went to Nigeria in 1970, you had problems in getting a visa. Do you remember who you were dealing with in immigration?

A: Yalla. I could never forget his name. He's a bastard. He was the Nigerian ambassador in Washington D.C. I went to that asshole puppet to get my visa and I thought by me being Black and because I wanted to know about Africa, wanted to go, that they would open their arms to receive me. But he was one of them pseudo-Blacks that was there. . . .

Q: What happened?

A: You see, I had mailed my passport to Washington and it was taking so long and I was wondering why they hadn't mailed it back, why I hadn't received the visa. Finally, I got on a plane and went to Washington in person to collect my passport and have them give me a visa. Ever since I can remember I've wanted to know the truth about Africa. So I go to this Yalla, thinking I'll get the visa. And he tells me I can't go. He wouldn't give me a visa. I told him: "Well, hey, I'm gonna go anyway. I've come this far and I'm not turning around!"

Q: But Fela was waiting for you. He knew you were coming. . . .

A: That's right. Fela sent me this telegram. Fortunately thanks to that telegram, that's what got me through.

Q: What did it say?

A: It just said: "Come. Your visa is waiting for you at the airport." So I went to Spain in transit and while there I met Art Allade, who hosts a TV programme in Nigeria. I told him my situation and he told me not to worry. So when they questioned me in Spain about my visa, I told them that it was waiting for me at Lagos airport and showed them the telegram. That's how they let me board the plane in Spain to go to Lagos.

Q: What happened at Ikeja airport in Lagos?

A: They took my passport, but Fela's people came and took me on through.

Q: Who took your passport, the immigration?

A: It was the army then. They kept my passport. But my attitude then was: "Hey, you can have the passport 'cause I don't want to come back." At that time I didn't care. Anything they wanted from me, with the

101

exception of my life, they could have gotten because I wasn't interested in any of those things. I didn't want to come back to America.

Q: How long did you stay in Nigeria that first time?

A: I spent six months in Nigeria. I came in 1970 and left in '71. When I came to Africa in 1970 I came with the idea of not going back to America. I had escaped Babylon and I was now at home in the Motherland.

Q: When you came to Nigeria, did you expect to be Fela's wife?

A: I don't know if you could say "expected to be Fela's wife". I loved Fela. I still have a great love for Fela. Although the love I have for Fela today is platonic. It has grown beyond. So the love I have for him, nobody can ever take it away. Because we went through a growing period. He showed me something and, I guess, in turn I showed him something. So that bond is there and it can't be broken.

Q: In Africa, you found yourself having to deal for the first time with a polygamous situation. How did you feel about that?

A: I dealt with it when I dealt with Fela in America. It was, like, Fela had a lot of girlfriends but still he was basically mine. That's the way women have this thing: He's *mine*. That possessive thing. I've grown beyond that now. The African women have taught me how to grow. I'm not trying to pat myself on the back, but I was already walking on high ground when I met Fela. And every encounter I've had has taken me ten steps ahead of the average woman. So even now, very few women can come from where I'm coming from. The American women I associate with now, they accept polygamy.

Q: So you came with the expectation of being his woman. How did you find Fela when you came to Nigeria?

A: The same. He treated me well. Although like any other woman, not understanding African women, not understanding African culture, I had my jealousies. They were jealous of me and I was jealous of them, so we were jealous of each other. It was just natural. Everybody was jealous. But since everybody felt it was

102

because of me, I caught more hell than anybody.

Q: What did Fela do?

A: What could he do? In the situation I gave Fela hell. My thing was, like, if I can't have my way, then I will find another way to deal with you. So I had my little temper tantrums and I'd have my own way of dealing with Fela. You see, there was a lot of hatred too among the women living at Fela's because they didn't want me there. Call it *obeah, juju,* or *voodoo.* They were using everything on me. Everything! The forces were against me. You see, even before I left America I used to have nightmares. Each time I would see myself in Africa, always running. It's like *déjà vu.* My dreams were black. I was always in dark places. I was always in fear in my dreams before going to Lagos. And what my dreams were trying to tell me is what I encountered. For me in Africa, it was a period of total unrest. Even to the point that I believed someone was definitely working *obeah* on me. I assumed who it was but I won't mention any names. I knew who it was at that time and she was definitely sending her evil force.

Q: You never told Fela about it?

A: I didn't tell Fela anything about it. At that time, Fela didn't believe in none of that. Fela didn't believe in spirits. But you see, my parents had taught me about it in America.

Q: When did Fela start believing in it?

A: When I came back in '76 I found Fela a believer then, which surprised me.

Q: But you already believed in 1970?

A: As a small child, my parents used to talk about the spirits. They'd talk about how people would do evil deeds to another person. Then I would hear older people talking about it. So I was aware of it. In Africa, when this started happening to me, I said, "They are trying to work this on me." And I called my mother in America and told her to do whatever she could. But I never told anyone in Africa the whole time I was there.

Q: What did your mother do?

103

A: I don't know what she did. But I told my mother what was happening and she must have told my father. I think my mother and this Black woman from Louisiana were in connection. It's known that in Louisiana they deal and delve in witchcraft; it's called *voodoo*. . . . I never told anyone in Africa whether I believed in it or not. They never knew. I only confided in my own mother. I had something that was on my side, a belief that my own family had given me and that even to this day is strong. I believe in it and no one can do shit.

Q: During your stay in Nigeria, Fela said they even had to hide you so the immigration authorities wouldn't deport you.

A: That's right. They ran me all over Lagos. I'm telling you, I had so many obstacles against me, but I was still there regardless because it was meant for me to be there.

Q: In which village did they hide you?

A: In Fela's mother's village in Abeokuta. I call the compound where they lived a village because it was self-contained, like Fisk University. Everything they needed was there – chickens, goats, the school, the house. . . .

Q: How long did you stay?

A: Some days.

Q: Did you like it?

A: Yeah. While I was there, Fela's mother turned me on to books. She turned me on to *Chariots of the Gods*. That's another thing I got to tell Fela too, 'cause it was his mama who started me on this religious thing. That's where that started. . . .

Q: What other books did Fela's mother give you to read?

A: She gave me this communist book to read. I believe it was called *Lenin*. While I was there I just read different books and got different knowledge. Fela's mother and I didn't do much talking. She'd just give me different books to read. That's all I did was sleep, eat and read.

Q: You never talked?

A: Nothing heavy and detailed. I talked to her about her going to China because that really fascinated me. She was the first Black woman to have gone there. I was fascinated with the fact that she had gone to a communist country because at that time Americans couldn't travel there. . . . Everything she told me about communist China was good. She liked it. She liked what communism was doing; it was benefiting the people.

Q: She met Mao Tse-tung?

A: Yes. I don't remember the year. But Fela's mother went. She told me about different things, the struggles in Nigeria and how she came about to make change for women, how she overthrew the Alake. It was just women talking, the older one telling the younger one 'cause she was schooling me. I don't know what made her start struggling. The only thing I can attribute it to is that she was aggressive, an aggressive fighter. When you would meet her or if you had known her, she seemed to be very mild-mannered. But she was very strong too when she had a point to get across. If I can put it in American slang, Fela's mama didn't take no shit!

Q: What did she think about Fela? Did she talk to you about him?

A: Well, you know, not really. At that time, Fela was more or less the underdog of the family. They couldn't understand Fela. Then later his mother was right with him; it was like he was the favourite son. She never talked to me at that time to downgrade him. It was Fela who told me and I could tell by the way the family acted towards him that they weren't too happy. Fela had disappointed them. He was the black sheep of the family.

Q: Did you get that feeling from his mother at that time?

A: Not in 1976. In 1970 I felt she was a little disappointed in Fela. They were all disappointed in Fela. They expected more. They had expected Fela to go to Europe and become a doctor like the rest of them. Then Fela goes and comes back a musician. And you know the African attitude about musicians.

Q: So his mother also shared that point of view?

A: She didn't verbally say it, but you could see it in her reactions.

Q: Why did she protect him?

A: I don't know. In any case, it was Fela's mother who intervened and took me to the officials. Because his mother went with me, they gave me a visa for two weeks. Then I left to Ghana and then came back. After that everything was downhill as far as I was concerned. Anyway, as I said to myself, I had already been in Africa. I had talked my political rhetoric. I had gone back home. But emotionally I was distraught. I didn't want to go back to America but I knew I had to go back because of the Nigerian government. They wouldn't renew my visa. They didn't want me there and I couldn't understand why. I didn't want to go back to America. I wanted to be an African woman. I wanted to live in Africa. But at the time, the Nigerian government was saying: "This is impossible, you American *Negro* woman!" They were calling me a "Negro". I was hurt emotionally.

Q: So you left Nigeria in 1971 after being there six months. Then you returned in 1976 to cut the album *Upside Down*. Who chose the title for that album?

A: Fela. He wrote the lyrics and I sang. I stayed about two and a half months. I wanted to stay on but I had so many commitments then in the States.

Q: What were you doing in the States then?

A: I still had family there. My mother was there and. . . . You see, when I came back to the States in '71 I went through a hell of an adjustment. It was difficult for me. I found it very difficult to readjust in America. People couldn't relate to me because not that many Blacks had travelled outside and they were still brainwashed. My return to America hurt me so bad. I had gotten so heavy into the African culture that I was African. So on returning, I went through a heavy mental trip, very close to a breakdown. It was like a cultural shock. Nobody knows the trip that Sandra went through, the adjustment. My mother, my father had a chance to see 'cause I lived with them. Me being their child, they lived with me and helped me through that period of

106

readjustment of coming back to America. I hated America. I did not want to be there.

Q: To that extent?
A: There was nothing there for me. I could not relate. Plus I had such a strong love for Fela. It was like a love that could not be fulfilled because he was over there and I was over here. The only thing that would really make me feel good was music. I loved music. Anything that was African, that I could relate to I clinched to. I was supposed to record with the group Osibisa, so I went to England and made some hookups there. It was like I had no direction, no one to lead me or gear me in any way. I tried writing some songs. I don't know what happened to those songs. There just wasn't the energy I needed. The energy wasn't there. All those years I had been away from Fela I still loved him. Then it was a physical, emotional love. . . .

Q: Describe your love for Fela today
A: I consider there are two main men in my life: my parental father and Fela. I've been spiritually informed that Fela is my brother. I don't think there's anything Fela could ask me to do that I would refuse him. It's that kind of love.

The new Fela
Photo: Chico

11

The Birth of Kalakuta Republic

Imagine me, Fela, in America! That's one motherfucking country! *I no dey tok fo' dat one yet-o. Cos na one big fuckin' story wey de full one book-o!** Fuckin' racist! . . . Hatred! . . . Violent! . . . A bitch! Ohhhhhh, man, you ain't seen shit till you hit America. I thought motherfuckin' England was bad! America na worse than bad-o! America *na-wa-o!*** People in Africa don't know how much their American Black brothers are suffering *wey dey fo'* that place-o. I swear, they no know! But Black Americans were beautiful to me, man. When I came back home, I said to myself: "All African countries should open their doors to Africans from everywhere, especially those in the Americas." That's what I wanted to do if I'd been in power. But I wasn't.

So the idea of creating a place open to every African escaping persecution began taking shape in this my mind. Was that my first pan-Africanist idea? Maybe. At any rate, that's how the idea of setting up a communal compound – one like Africans had been living in for thousands of years – came about. A place open to everybody. A real compound, you know. I'd think to myself: "Ah-ah! What is this city shit-o? One man, one wife, one house isolated from everybody else in the neighbourhood? Is an African not even to know his neighbours?" Man, even the Bible says, "Know thy neighbour!" So why all this individualism shit? This "mine". That "yours". That "theirs". What's that shit? Is it African?

My communal compound came about naturally, right there in Surulere. Later on, in '74, it was given the name "Kalakuta". Then I added . . . Republic! Why Kalakuta? You see, when I was first put in jail, the name of my prison

---

* Pidgin: "I haven't yet talked about that one (America) for that's a helluva story, enough to fill an entire book."
** "America is like hell-o!"

cell was "Kalakuta". And "Republic"? Well, 'cause I wanted to identify the ways· of myself or someone who didn't agree with that your Federal Republic of Nigeria created by Britishman. I was in non-agreement, man. General Yakubu Gowon was then in power. That foolish man! 'Cause Biafra war had just finished, you see.* Federal soldiers were walking round with fuckin' guns and sticks; pushing people around and acting so big-o! They'd been the "victors", you see! You get me now? So I said, "OK. Good."

I changed the name of my club from Afro-Spot to Shrine. That was in '71, I think. I'd just released my first hit, a record called "Jeun Ko'ku", which means "Chop and Die" (Eat and Die). It was my first African record, you know. I'd also changed the name of my group from Koola Lobitos to Africa 70. To my knowledge, Koola Lobitos meant nothing. It was a foolish name, a stupid name, you see. How could other people think straight? *Africa 70* had a meaning. It was looking to the future, to the coming decade. Then we opened the Shrine. Why *Shrine*? 'Cause I wanted some place meaningful, of progressive, mindful background with roots. I didn't believe playing any more in nightclubs.

Right from the start, the Shrine was successful; it was getting on. Since I'd just released "Jeun Ko'ku", things were going well. It was a big hit then in Nigeria. But that's when all my troubles began! At the Shrine. I was only singing my own songs: "Jeun Ko'ku", "Buy Africa", "Why Black Man Dey Suffer", "Lady". . . . But police came to try stop me from sing, man. First they tried to intimidate club owner. But me, I dey have contract-o! Then, they physically tried to bar my entry into the club. You see thaaaat? I said, "Ah-ah! These foolish people!" I went to court and won. Court said I was entitled to play in the club 'cause I had contract.

Was that in '70, '71 or '72? In any case, my mind was still heavy with the US thing-o: Black Panthers . . . Malcolm X . . . racism . . . the horrors . . . Sandra. . . . At the time, and even today, man, I think about that woman! A wonderful woman, man! She's definitely one of the most important

* The surrender of Biafra was announced on 12 January 1970 by Major-General Phillip Effiong, Chief of General Staff of the Biafran Armed Forces, ending a two-and-a-half-year war that left *one million* people dead.

women that ever crossed my life! Because of what she'd done for me in America, I'd promised to bring her to Nigeria for a visit. Sandra's visit to Nigeria was one of the heavy experiences of my life. It was my first fight with government officials.

I didn't know it was so difficult for people to come to a country. I'd simply said to Sandra, "Come to Nigeria and have a show with me." I wrote her that in a letter in 1970, when I'd started to make small-small money. At the time the club was still called Afro-Spot. So I sent her a ticket. She phoned me and told me she had to have a visa to come. "Ah-ah! What is this visa for come to Nigeria?" She said she would go get visa in Washington, at the Nigerian Embassy there, 'cause she was living in Los Angeles. I told her, "Me, I will go get visa for you here in Lagos." So I went to the office to get a visa for her. Then I phoned her and told her, "Take a plane and come." She went to Washington anyway 'cause she still wanted to get the visa. The Embassy told her she cannot get it yet. She insisted to see the Ambassador.

"Why won't you give me a visa?"

He started giving her a lot of shit. . . . She cut him off, man, and cursed his ass out. What didn't she say? Ooooooooo! You don't know Sandra, man! Batabatabata-batabatabata! "Idiot. . . . Bastard. . . . Son of a bitch. . . . Motherfucker. . . ."

Man, Sandra is something else!!! The ambassador got pale! Imagine that? An African Nigerian get pale, man! Ohhhh, Sandra, she's a motherfucker. She'd kicked a policeman's ass in America, so what wouldn't she do to an ambassador? You know what she told him?

"You nigger! Shit! You with your slave mentality! You should be in chains permanently!"

She told me all that later.

"I cursed his ass out!" she said.

So I told her over the phone:

"Good. Just come directly to the airport. I'm coming to get you."

Sandra arrived. I met her at airport and brought her in.

Sandra started playing with me in the band. She was fantastic. Everybody loved Sandra. Newspapers wrote about her. All over Lagos people started talking about "Sandra . . . Sandra . . . Sandra. . . ." When I was teaching

111

her to sing, I saw that she had a very unique voice. I swear that that woman's voice is the wildest woman's voice you've ever heard. I never heard any voice like it. I wanted for people to hear her. So I recorded her on an album, *Upside Down*. That was in '76, on her second trip to Nigeria. She came back specially to record it. Everybody liked her. And, ohhhh, the way she dressed! She was so. . . . She wore see-through top, halfway short skirts. . . . She was fuckin' popular, man. Now when the Nigerian ambassador to Washington arrived in Lagos and saw this Sandra in the newspaper, it cursed him out. "So this motherfuckin' woman is here!" He quickly contacted the officials. He set up a plan for her, to throw her out.

You see, her three months' visa was up. And they wanted to get her out. They began to chase Sandra about the country, those immigration officers. They were really chasing her physically, looking for her everywhere. We went to hide her out in our village, in Abeokuta. My mother took her, I swear. She liked Sandra. And she hid her in village for one week. Sandra only left Nigeria when she was ready. They were looking for her to deport her, but they didn't find her. When she was ready to go we let them see her and we said, "She's going." So she left. I can't remember how many months she stayed, but it was a long time-o, a long time.

I was confident now. I knew I would succeed. Success was in reach, man. And I thought: "J.K., J.K. Now is the fuckin' moment!" That same year – '71 – we got the chance to hook up again. 'Cause, you see, I wanted to record in a proper studio. I insisted that a proper studio be set up in Nigeria, otherwise I wouldn't record. Or else they'd have to take us to London to record again. So they changed the studio from two tracks to eight tracks.

In the meantime, I went to London anyway. I was already successful in Nigeria, but they wouldn't release my records overseas. Why? I didn't know that EMI was against me 'cause they were saying I was too "political". So I said: "Fuck these bastards!" I left EMI and became independent. I started releasing records on my own, with my own musicians. It got to be heavy-o. I was making eight albums a year in Nigeria.

I was getting very powerful. Very listened to. Very liked. But, for the authorities, very . . . daaaaannnnngerous!

Fela and J.K.: The inseparables

12

J.K. Braimah

The Reunion

Q: So you and Fela finally hooked up again. How was Fela then?

A: He had changed completely, man. By the time he came back from America he smoked, he drank, he fucked. He was more lively. He was a new man. A completely different man! Yeh, he even tried conning me. I'd say, "Look at him. He wants to con me!" [*Laughter.*] I asked myself, "But how did Fela get to be like this?" I was wondering what had happened. It was the American thing, you know. He saw the light over there and everything came out in him. Fantastically good things came out.

Q: But give me the whole story!

A: Well, as I told you before, I was doing fine-fine in England. I was into a lot of bread, man. I was making plenty-plenty by '70. I was comfortable. I bought big car. I was drinking a lot. '70, '71, '72 were all right, man. Actually, this was how I left. Fela came to London with his group in June '71 on a recording tour. So when he came, he said: "Why don't you come home and we join together? We'll team up together. I have Africa 70. We could do something together." He said I could be his PR man. I said, "OK, I'll think about it." You know, I would have liked to come home. So I came home in '71 just on holidays. I saw the band, what was happening. It was all right, promising. So I went back to London, sold my house, and then. . . . Shit! There was this trouble, a whole mess that led to court. Ginger Baker was one of those involved. Anyway, they freezed my money. They freezed about £60,000 of my money in England. Up until today I haven't got it back, man. Up till today!

115

Original album cover of *Shakara*
Design: Africa 70 Organization
Photo: Africa 70 Agency

They even charged me. They wanted to charge me with some other guys for conspiracy.

Q: Conspiracy with Indian hemp?

A: Yes. Fela had sent this American guy with the drum. This was a long time ago. Fela was not the one who did it, you know. Anyway, the drum was full of shit. When they caught the guy – who I won't name – at the airport, he just started talking. He said Fela gave it to him and all that bullshit. You see, Fela was supposed to play with Ginger Baker and Ginger Baker was supposed to come and live in my house, you know. And things like that. So the police came over to my place and raided me. They didn't find a thing. But I'm so clever to the extent that the police can't see anything. Yet they still said they would charge me with conspiring. 'Cause they said I was supposedly the one giving them the stuff. . . . They started with their inquiries and everything. They charged me to the Old Bailey, one of their biggest courts. Afterwards, I thought, "Why did they charge me to the Old Bailey?" That was in '72. I said to myself, "Well, we'll see!" Then I came to France. I sold my car there and moved on to Italy. From Italy I went to Accra (Ghana). Africa, at last!

Q: Once in Africa, you were OK! [*Laugh.*]

A: Damned right! [*Laughter.*] So I got to Accra. Fela came to meet me in Accra and then we crossed over to Nigeria by land. I came home and said: "I'm home. Nobody can do me anything here. That's for sure!" Then I started settling down, man. We started with Africa 70. Our first number then was "Shakara", which was a smash. I was the one who gave the name *Shakara* to that record. And that was my first album with Fela. I had joined the Africa 70 organization.

Q: As PR man or as Fela's manager?

A: As everything, man. Yeah, 'cause at that time he started rising up like that [*motions to the sky*]. After "Shakara", all our numbers were making it. '73, '74 we toured the Cameroons, all over the place. . . . We were making big hits, man. But we also began to get *hit*! And fuckin' hard, too!

Defiant Fela
Photo: Chico

13

*Alagbon Close**

"Expensive Shit",
"Kalakuta Show", "Confusion"

"Name?"

"Fela!"

The police officer looked up at me. "Just Fela?"

"Yeah, jus' Fela!"

I knew very well that motherfucker knew my name.

"Address?"

"My house. . . ."

"Where?"

"Right here in Surulere, man, yeah!"

That was the first time in my life I was taken to jail, man. That first time, it's a funny feeling. Not the other times. Just that first one. You know how people are brought up thinking that jail is just for criminals, man. For people who've "gone against society. . . ." You know what I mean? That "law and order" shit. But after they put me in that cell with the people they call "criminals", I started thinking: "Who the fuck is Society? Who jails Society when it does horrors to people? Why Society does nothing to help beggars; to provide jobs and keep people from having to steal just to *chop*? Why don't Society fight against corruption, punish the powerful . . .?" I concluded to myself: "Fuck society, man. It's unjust!" I knew I would be in jail for another *ten* years 'cause the shit they had on me carried *ten* motherfucking years, man. But still I said, "Fuck society, man. . . . Fuck! Fuck! Fuck iiiiiiiiiit!!"

Whenever I look back on my past, there are things that

---

* *Alagbon Close* – an album title hit of Fela's in 1975, along with the others mentioned above – is the central police station of the Nigerian CID, located in the residential area of Ikoyi, Lagos.

119

make me feel so bad, man! 1974! That's the year when all the horrors started. The arrests . . . the clubbings . . . the imprisonments . . . everything! Sometimes it all comes back to me and I ask myself: "Why all this shit? Why do all these horrors happen to me? . . . All the shit I've been through in this motherfuckin' world ever since I was born. . . . What kind of world is this? A world where you get your ass kicked if you do good . . . but given a medal if you kill some guy in the name of patriotism! What shit is that?"

My first clash with "law and order" people was on 30 April 1974. I can't forget that, man! Oh, what bastards! There I was in my house in Surulere. At that time, you know, there wasn't any barbed-wire fence around my place. I had nothing to fear. I wasn't even thinking they could have something against me. I was just preaching revolution for Africa, you know. I didn't know they were planning against me, man. So my house was open. I didn't have a fence or a gate. So when those motherfuckers came to bust me for grass, they had no trouble getting in, at all. . . . How did the shit start? I'll tell you.

That day I was in my house giving interview to someone. Talking 'bout the scandals and corruption of the Gowon régime. About how people were being whipped in the streets by soldiers, man. Yeah, soldiers hitting your *nyash* with whips, man! Now, where else in the world does that happen? In South Africa? Not even. So while I was heavy into this interview-o, fifty motherfucking policemen just walked in. F-i-f-t-y, I'm telling you, man!

At that time, man, you got up to ten fucking years for just smoking grass. But I never use to hide the shit. And these bastards, man, found grass everywhere. Under the carpets, in toilet, in kitchen . . . every fucking place. All my people smoke. Everybody has his own shit. We all went to prison, man: Alagbon Close. About sixty of us were packed in the same cell like animals, man! It was the first time I ever see prison in my life-o! I use to think prisoners were criminals until that day. Inside there I found guys who were also looking for a better life.

The day I was busted I was getting ready to leave for Cameroons on my first big tour outside of Nigeria. On that day, the fucking police didn't touch me-o. No, not that time. They didn't beat up anybody. There were already many girls living at my house. They were all taken to

Welfare. Me, they put in prison. That was on Monday. . . .
Then, they took me to court on Thursday or Friday. The
police told the court that they opposed bail 'cause they
hadn't finished investigations. So the magistrate gave them
another three days. I went back to jail. That was Friday and
I stayed the weekend plus Monday.

Tuesday, they took me back to court. I got my bail. I'd
spent eight days in jail, man. Now, when they raided my
house that time, they'd taken my passport-o. The bastards!
In fact, I'm sure they busted me just to keep me from going
to Cameroons on that big tour I was to make. So I got out
of jail on Tuesday. And Wednesday I went looking for my
passport. Me and my lawyer went to see Sunday Adewusi.*
I told him I had to travel on Friday to Cameroons.

He said: "OK. Come tomorrow morning at 9 a.m. for the
passport."

So that Wednesday I went home to sleep, expecting to go
see him next morning for the passport.

While I had been in jail those eight days, all my girls had
been taken into custody by Welfare. Can you imagine that,
man? Police had took everybody from the house. The
women spent about two months at Welfare. They had to
escape by themselves. They jumped over the fence of
Welfare. They escaped; all of them escaped, except maybe
five or so. Those, my girls! That's why I had to marry them,
man. They were a bunch of wild motherfuckers, man!

When I went home, the house was almost completely
empty. I got fucking high and went fast asleep. At 4 a.m. –
it's now Thursday morning – guess who shows up? Police!
Fuck it! I swear, I didn't know police would come again.
And there they were to raid me again. I hear: *tam . . . tam
. . . tam. . . .* I had a spy-glass on my door, but I didn't even
bother to use it. I just opened the door and . . . *Baaaam!*
What do I see? Five detectives! Now, I'd smoked some
joints earlier. What was left was in the ashtray on a small
table near my bed. They'd just finished raiding me, man, so
I wasn't ready to have them catch me again. I said:

"Police? What do you want?"

They said they'd come to search me again.

"Again? You just finished. I left on bail yesterday.
What's happening?"

* Chief of the Criminal Investigations Department (CID) of Nigeria at the
time.

121

They said they'd come to raid me again. I said:

"Fine. I have a woman inside there. She's naked. You cannot come in here until she is dressed."

"OK," they said.

I banged the door in their face. I quickly went to my ashtray, man. I put all the grass in my mouth, plenty, man. About a handful . . . in my mouth . . . just like that . . . mmmmmmmmmm. You follow me? I stood at the door and suddenly opened it. Boinggggg! I did like I was feeling sick, holding my mouth like I wanted to vomit and I ran to my toilet. I just rushed through them. They didn't know what I was doing. I was too fast for them. My toilet was just there. I opened the sink. Spit everything into it. Ran the water. Pushing everything down the drain in a rush. Then I went back into my room, closed the door again. Just to make sure, I searched every corner and cleared my room. My room was safe. Then I opened the door. "Come in."

They came in. They started to search here, there . . . under . . . everywhere. They didn't find shit. Then they dropped one joint that they brought themselves, just *one* joint. Enough to send me in for ten years, man. It was wrapped in a paper like how we wrap joints for sale in Lagos. So they brought it out from under somewhere.

"We found this," they said.

"You found this?"

He unrolled it and opened it to show me, saying, "I found this."

"I can't see it." They brought it close to my face and showed it to me. I again said, "I can't see it."

And they brought it right up to my face like that.

They said: "Look!"

I looked at it. I was thinking fast, man. Then suddenly, in a split second – really fast! – I went for the paper, grabbed it, put it in my mouth and jumped on my bed, man. I'd swallowed it! I took the whisky bottle by my bed, put it to my mouth and washed the shit down. Then I started to lecture them. "Motherfuckers, what's the matter with you? Look-o, I'm trying to save this country, man. You want to put me in jail. What have I done? Whaaat have I done? 'Cause I smoke? Fuckin'. . . ."

They were looking at me while I was eating it. There was left about one tiny grain inside the paper. And they took that one tiny grain, looked at me and said: "Let's go!"

And they took me. This time they were so sure they'd got me! 'Cause that first raid wasn't a clean one. They'd done everything roughly. This time they made sure they had a neat one. A police officer was even waiting for me in the office, at Alagbon Close, the big police station.

"Fela is coming. This time we've got him," he said.

When we got there, this man was sitting on his chair. I stood there, with four detectives standing next to me. So, the man, looking big, stood up in the front. He asked them:

"So you got him?"

"Yes, sah. But when we showed it to him, he grabbed it and ate it."

The man was so shocked. He looked at me as if I was the biggest criminal he ever saw. Motherfucker wants to put me in jail, man, and I'm trying to get myself out of jail and he thinks I'm a criminal for that, man! What he has planned-o. . . . He's the criminal now! He looks at me, so annoyed.

"Lock him up!"

They locked me up, man, a second time. Motherfuckers! Second time in one same week! I didn't know what was gonna happen. Have I told you the part about the hospital? I didn't? It's fantastic! I must tell you, fuck!

Look, they put me in the cell. I was there for hours, waiting. I could see the officers through the cell door, running up and down, planning. Motherfuckers were planning on me, man. I was jus' looking at them and thinking: "What are they up to? They can't charge me with that shit there, man, 'cause they ain't got nothing to test, nothing to show. So what do they intend to do?" I was waiting when they came and opened the door.

"Come out."

"Where?"

"Just follow us."

They make me get into a Peugeot and zooooooooooooom. Where they're taking me, I don't know. Straight! They took me to a military . . . hospital. I was thinking, "Now, what do they want to do?"

Once inside, they take me to see Dr Peters, head of the military doctors at that hospital. He's my cousin, you know.

"Oh, Fela, how are you?" he asked.

"Ah. . . ."

"What's happened?" he asked, like as if he didn't know.

"I don't know what they brought me here for," I said.

"Follow me."

So, you see, he knew. They had already told him, see, why they'd brought me to him. He took me to an operating theatre. I'm standing there, still not knowing what was up. Then a nurse came. She was carrying two new shoes, the type you wear in operating theatres. She put them on the ground and said: "Wear these!"

"Shoes? Are you blind? Don't you see shoes for my foot?"

Then, blaaaaaaam! It occurred to me. I said to myself, "So that's it?" I look at nurse, I look at doctor, I look at police.

"So, you people want to wash my stomach! Fine! Go ahead! Wash my stomach. Fine. You will do it 'cause you can do it, can't you? 'Cause you will take me in there by *force,* right? You're ready to take me in there by force? OK-o! Make you take me by force-o! It's my *nyash* you want to put somethin' inside? Well, you'll never get any-thing in my *nyash*! Let me tell you somethin': before you do anything to me, all that theatre, I will break it down. So take me inside. Let me see you take me inside, you mother-fuckin' police! Bastards! Take me inside! Ba-s-t-a-rds!"

Oh, man, I was so fuckin' mad! When the doctor heard I was gonna break his theatre, he told police: "If you can't get your prisoner under control, I can't do it."

"You doctor," I said. "I know one thing. You cannot do anything to my body unless by my express permission. So you get that into your head. I know that law!"

That one just messed him up. Po-po-po-po-po-po! He went away. He left me there with the police. And I say to police: "What do you want to do now?"

"Follow us," they say.

I follow them. We reach outside. Guess who was outside waiting for me? The boss of Nigerian Interpol, man: Mr Atta! He was there waiting for the results of my shit thing! When he saw me and the police coming out, he asked them: "Have you done it?"

"Fela no agree for them to do it, Sah," they answered.

He looked at me like I was a criminal. You know what he said? "Get in *my* car!"

Not in the car I came in, you know. He'd brought another car. He must have thought I was a stupid man. He put me at the back seat. It was a Peugeot Station Wagon, three seat lines – front seat, middle seat and back seat. He put me in the back seat and he sat in the middle seat. His driver took off! Then he turns round to me, still looking at me like I'm a criminal.

"I'm going to talk to you in my office."

"You get office?" I asked sarcastically. "You foolish stupid bastard! Low-down sonofabitch. . . ."

Oh, I abused him like a dog. I was cussing, calling him dirty names, "dog", "bastard", "goat", things like that!

As soon as we arrived at Alagbon, Atta ordered:

"Lock him up!"

When I was finally taken to court, they charged me with possession of Indian hemp. However, they said in court that I had *eaten* the Indian hemp; that it was still in my stomach, and so they wanted me kept in jail to collect samples. You understand, man? When I hear that in court again, I say: "Collect my shit? These police never give up."

So the magistrate asked: "How many days do you need to collect that 'thing', the samples?"

"Three days."

So they took me back and locked me up for three more days. When my mother found out, she started to send me vegetables. I was just eating vegetables. You know, to quench the vegetables inside there. I refused to shit. That first day I didn't shit-o. Then, in the middle of the night, the prisoners woke me up. They said:

"Fela, all the police are asleep now. Why don't you come and shit in the pail 'cause they won't see you shitting. Then they go throw it away tomorrow with everybody's shit."

I said, "That's a good idea, man."

So I crept out of my bed . . . not bed, man. There was no bed. Just a position on the cell floor where I was sleeping. And I got to where the pail was. You see, the cell was a room with different positions. A small room, roughly the size of an average sitting-room. There were eight of us in there at that time. Everybody had a position. The pail of shit, too, had its own position in the corner of the same room. So I went to the pail position and I did my shit there. In the morning the police threw it away thinking it was the shit of the other prisoners. Then, police come and say:

"Fela, you don't want to shit yet?"

"Shit? No, I don't want to shit, man!"

Second day, my mother send vegetables again. The

Original album cover of *Expensive Shit*
Design: Remi Olowookere
Photo: Peter Obe Photo Agency

second night, the prisoners again say: "Fela, the. . . ." The "president" of the cell at that time was a guy named Rockwell. He was in jail for forgery of notes. He had been in the cell for eight months. No investigation. Nothing. They just kept him there. So he said:

"Fela, these people are bastards. That one shit not enough-o. So you go shit another one tonight, to make sure your stomach is clear."

I said, "Thank you."

So that night, again, when everybody's asleep, I do the same thing. Then, in morning, they throw it away. Now, when police came, they again asked me:

"Fela, you want shit-o?"

"Me, I don't want to shit yet-o. Shit? Shit no come!"

The morning I was due in court, I woke up at 6.30 a.m. and call out: "Hey, police, I want to shit."

Ooooooooooh, see the commotion in the police station, man! "Fela wants to shit!" Helter-skelter! Everybody looking for chamber pot – policeman, orderly, constable, everyone! They all want Fela's shit! They took me to the backyard, put the chamber pot under my *nyash*. I shit. When I look at my shit, man, it was clean like a baby's shit. Clean! That's how I got myself out of that shit that time, man. The motherfuckers couldn't charge me for any fucking thing. No evidence!*

In spite of that I still had two cases in court. The first didn't last long: four and a half months. One day, the magistrate just said: "Look, I'm tired of this case. Everybody go home." Finish! That's how the first case ended. It had seven counts: three counts of abduction. But the case connected with the second raid went on for *five* years in court before it was thrown out, too! You know what police did to me in court for the first case though? Adewusi tried to jail me for abduction that time. Man, he put three counts of abduction on my *nyash*. They brought a man and a woman to court to swear that they were the mother and father of a girl they said was kidnapped by me. Imagine that! Fela kidnapping woman! You see, what these "law and order" people can do? The girl's name is Ibekwedi. She was one of the twenty-seven girls I married in '78, but she has left me since, though I still see her once in a while. . . .

---

* This and another similar experience which Fela had that same year, 1974, inspired his hit "Expensive Shit". (See Discography.)

Fela protects himself

Photo: Peter Obe Photo Agency: from album cover of *Alagbon Close*

14

From Adewusi to Obasanjo

I was free. Back on the streets, back to playing at my Shrine. Oooooooooooh, the place was fuckin' packed every night! The shit with the police had made me more popular than ever. But every single day for the four and a half months that my first case lasted, I had to appear in court. I'd thought, "Everything is finish-o." But, man, you don't know Adewusi! Guess what he did, that man? They had set the date for judgment on 27 November 1974. And on 23 November police showed up at my house. They said they were looking for a girl. Again, a girl! The police were many, man. That time, they almost . . . killed me! They beat the hell outta me, man! My head is still scarred. You can see it. That was the first violent attack I experienced. It was terrible, man. It was so fuckin' terrible that I don't want to talk about it any longer. . . . They said they were looking for Folake Oladende. She's no longer with me either.

You see, to protect myself and my people from police and keep these fucking police from just walking into my bedroom like that, I'd decided to put up a three-and-a-half-metre-high barbed-wire fence around the entire Kalakuta Republic compound. I also kept guards at the gate. But one day the police came anyway with axes to cut down the fence. That was November '74. They threw tear-gas and beat the shit outta us. They'd come – so they said – to look for one girl they say I "abducted". Fela abducting woman? Oh, man, these people! They tried using her against me but the girl didn't co-operate. She refused. The bastards! Ooooooooooh, I was beaten by police! So much. . . . How can a human being stand so much beating with clubs and not die? I was cut, bleeding profusely. Couldn't even stand up, or walk. This time I was taken to hospital, not jail. I was there for three days. Police wouldn't allow visitors to see me. Later, I was taken to court. Again I got bail and went home. It was bad, man. It was horrible! Another cycle of horrors had begun in my life.

When I went for judgment on 27 November, I was all in bandages and had to lean for support on my friends. The case was thrown out of court. But Adewusi still wouldn't give up. The next year again, in February '75, he did it to me again. You know where? In Ilorin. Adewusi's hometown. Arrangements had been made for me to go and play at the university there. It was a trap; I'm convinced of that today. When I got there, the police were ready for me, man. Road police, just to raid me again. Raids. Raids. Raids. This shit went on for about two or three weeks at Ilorin. But I fucked the whole police up in Ilorin.

I got out of the Ilorin one. It was a real mess for Adewusi and his stupid police. By now everybody was convinced Adewusi and his police were after me for nothing. After that one they laid off until '76. But in '75, there had been so many raids. You know what I mean? I've only talked about the three main ones. You can't count how many times they beat my people – in my house, on the streets. . . . So I had to go out and face them, man. They did many things, you know. Like arresting my people anyhow, anyway, for anything!

Then around the middle of '75, I think, M.D. Yusufu rose up in rank. He became the IG. Inspector-General of police. It was he who cooled everybody down. When he said, "Fela is not a criminal," that took the heat off. You know, a *coup d'état* had overthrown General Yakubu Gowon. It was the military who overthrew him on 29 July 1975. And the new Head of State, General Murtala Mohammed, appointed M.D. Yusufu Inspector-General of the police. Right then and there, Yusufu said I wasn't a criminal, just an artist. That I had my ideas and that the police should stop worrying me. That's exactly what happened. Because as IG, he controlled the whole police and secret services. So police didn't worry me again until Obasanjo came to power.* Then that man started his own shit against me, man. Not right away, though. He used *soldiers* against me, not police, 'cause M.D. Yusufu con-

---

* Born in Abeokuta, Ogun State, on 5 March 1937, Olusegun Obasanjo joined the Nigerian Army in 1958, after completing secondary studies at Baptist Boys' High School in Abeokuta. During the Biafran war he was Commander of the third Marine Commando Division. He became Head of State in February 1976 after the assassination of General Murtala Mohammed in an abortive *coup*.

trolled the police. Obasanjo began his shit in '76, shortly after taking power. He was so cruel, man! He'd have my people beat up all the time he'd worry them, provoke, attack. All sort of harassments, man. Until one day when he sent *one thousand* soldiers to Kalakuta Republic . . . to kill me, man.

Supposedly Obasanjo's family knew mine. At least, that's what I've been told. But I can't remember meeting him when I was a child. One of my friends told me I had. He even showed me a picture of Obasanjo visiting my school. He said we'd met at that time. He even told me that Obasanjo would often come to our school to play with us. But I don't remember him, man. I swear. He's only a year older than me, so we're about the same age. We were born in the same town. We went to school at about the same time, he to Baptist Boys' High School and me to Abeokuta Grammar School. Both schools always had things together, like sports and things like that.

But I don't remember him from that time.

Olusegun Obasanjo! No, he didn't start all his horrors against me right away. I was even invited to participate in the Second World Black Festival of Arts and Culture (FESTAC). That thing was real confusion! Corruption left and right! People running in all directions with no orientation! FESTAC was just one big hustle, so a whole lot of little military men and useless politicians could fill their pockets. They *chop* plenty-plenty naira.

It was around then that Sandra came back to Nigeria to record an album with me: *Upside Down.* She only stayed about two and a half months. That was in '76. The album was heavy, man! Her voice is unique! The lyrics, the beat, the rhythm, the music, man! Ohhhhh, *Upside Down* was a fucking good album! It dealt with all the confusion and corruption of the Gowon-Obasanjo period. All the shit, man! The chaos! The foolishness of those Africans who look down on the names of their ancestors and take European names. Me, myself, I'd just changed my own name. . . .

You see, at the end of '75, I got rid of "Ransome". I replaced it by . . . Anikulapo. My mother, too, she understood, man, and dropped "Ransome". What does *Anikulapo* really mean? It means "Having Control Over Death". Literally, it means having death inside your quiver.

Original album cover of *Upside Down* with Sandra

Design: Remi Olowookere

Photo: Tunde Kuboye

And *Fela*? Of course, you know: "He Who Emanates Greatness". *Kuti*? It means "Death cannot be caused by human entity". My full name means: "He who emanates greatness, who has control over death and who cannot be killed by man".

What's the importance of a name? A lot, man. Malcolm X knew that. That's why he chose "X". Slavery had taken away his African name. So he preferred an "X" rather than the slave-master's name. But so many people, man, are just brainwashed! They'd come and ask him: "Why X?" That reminds me of that French journalist who just the other day, there in Paris, asked me: "Why did you change your name from Ransome to Anikulapo?" I looked at him surprised. 'Cause he'd asked just the opposite of what he should have asked. That i-d-i-o-t! He should've asked why my name had been Ransome in the first place. Me, do I look like Englishman? But what was I talking about? Oh, yes . . . about Yusufu.

Really, M.D. Yusufu was a heavy guy. Let me first of all tell you a story one boy told me about him, when M.D. Yusufu was just an intelligence officer. This boy had done something and had to run away to hide in Abidjan, Dakar, somewhere like that. Anyway, Yusufu was the one who was supposed to be looking for this guy. He finally found him sitting in a nightclub in Abidjan or Dakar. Yusufu just faced him and said:

"I've got you! . . . But I'm not going to take you back. I'm going to leave you. That thing you did, you will never do it again, will you?"

Imagine that guy's surprise, man.

"No, Sir, I won't do it again. I promise. . . ."

And Yusufu left him there.

That's M.D. Yusufu. A very humane person. He's someone who really loves Nigeria. A real man! When I met him he was very revolutionary inclined. Yusufu really kept that government from messing up entirely, man. He kept it from doing too many atrocities. That's what M.D. Yusufu did. That man doesn't like blood-o! All revolutionaries in Africa have met him, know him. He was the liaison guy between the liberation movements and the successive Nigerian governments. He was beautiful to the revolutionaries in Africa. He's not corrupt. When he left government in '79 he didn't own shit. He didn't even own a house in Lagos, for instance. Every other government man was owning ten big houses in Lagos and he owned none. He's a great guy. That's what I want to say about him. All Nigerians love and respect that man.

Yusufu himself came many times to Shrine. He understood what I was saying in my songs about African emancipation, the struggle against corruption, abuse of power, dictatorship, poverty. . . . And he protected me against those other bastards. One day, end '75, I think, I said to myself: "What could I give M.D. Yusufu just to show small-small appreciation?" So I said: "I go *make* 'am something."

I made him a nice box of multi-colour spotlights. I *made* it, man. I conceived it and made it with my own hands. It was only for my very close friends that I ever did that: J.K., Kanmi Oshobu – who was then my lawyer – and a few other friends. When I'd finished Yusufu's, I took all my girls and boys, packed them in my bus, and went off to Ikoyi, where M.D.'s residence was then. You remember, he lived near military hospital. When we pulled up at the gate, guards with sub-machine guns came up to us.

"Yes?"

"I come see IG. Tell 'am Fela is here!"

"Wait a moment, Sir."

Police never call me Sir-o! Then, after a moment, they said:

"You can pass."

My gift was nice, man. It was a white box with four coloured bulbs fitted inside: green, yellow, blue and red. My favourite colours. And you could combine them together. For example, you could mix the red and green lights, the yellow and blue. . . . It was a wild spotlight box, man. Invented by Fela for someone he dug very much. Those lights were my creation. Just like my music. I felt so happy giving it to him. As happy as when I play. Oh, I could see he was moved. And me, too, I was moved. 'Cause I. . . . Well, I dug him a lot, M.D. Yusufu!

15

The Sack of Kalakuta

"Sorrow, Tears and Blood",
"Unknown Soldier", "Stalemate"

FESTAC! One big hustle, man! A rip-off! They tried getting me into it. They started out being nice to me and that sort of shit, man. First, I was invited to attend a Nigerian National Participation Committee meeting which was being held at Bagauda Lake Hotel in Kano. That was in '76. It was Major-General I.B.M. Haruna who'd called the meeting. Anyway, he started demagoguing, man, saying he was "open" to fresh ideas and that kind of thing. So I presented a nine-point programme to make the festival meaningful. The first point of my programme called for the *participation of the people.* Then I denounced the under-handed dealings going on; the way in which the cultures of Nigerian peoples were being treated trivially; and so forth. But Major-General Haruna rejected these proposals. It was then that I resigned.

I didn't know that my resigning would cause so much shit. You see, the stage was being set for a very serious confrontation. But I didn't know it. I had asked myself: "How is it possible that General Haruna, a *military* man, could be the chairman of a committee which dealt with *cultural* matters?" Haruna felt offended. The next thing he did was to use the mass media to lambast me, saying Fela had refused to participate in the festival "because he wanted the government to purchase new equipment for him". Now, you hear that shit, man? I wanted the govern-ment to buy equipment for my own motherfuckin' use?

You see, what was worrying Obasanjo was that by then I'd purchased a printing press. I'd started publishing a small-small newspaper, *YAP.* The name stood for *Young African Pioneers,* a youth organization I had launched. The

135

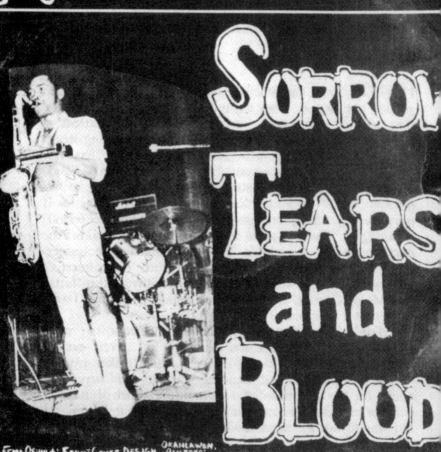

Fela playing at Shrine after Kalakuta attack: original album
cover of *Sorrow, Tears and Blood*
Design: Okanlawan Banjoko
Photo: Femi Osunla

military had imposed a ban on political parties since it took over in '66. So we were printing our own anti-government propaganda, man. Denouncing those corrupt, unprogressive politicians and military men to the people.

So FESTAC came for one month, January to February '77. I didn't go to that thing-o! I stayed at Shrine and made my counter-FESTAC there! All the big musicians and artists FESTAC brought in wanted to see me, man. For one whole month, man, every night, Shrine was packed with Blacks from all over the world. And since they wanted to know what was happening in Nigeria I told them. I used the stage at Shrine to denounce all of the shit and corruption of that government which had invited them. That one they never forgave-o! But Obasanjo held off till FESTAC finished and everybody had left town. He knew he could not rely on M.D. Yusufu's police. So this time it was *soldiers* of regular army, man, that he used. I'm telling you.

Because of the FESTAC thing, the government had brought out an operation called "Operation Ease the Traffic". It was a campaign against "go-slow" – traffic jams – in Lagos. To carry it out, Obasanjo had put soldiers in the streets with *horsewhips*. They had orders to deliver on-the-spot beatings. With no legal trials for offenders. None! Man, those street soldiers were so brutal that the people began to complain. Of course, you know me, I couldn't turn a deaf ear to that, so I denounced that shit to the press and at the Shrine. . . . And then I set out to defend and protect the interests of those victimized, by denouncing the government for having taken those measures. I attacked Colonel Tarfa openly, 'cause as officer of the Nigerian Army he was also chairman of the "Ease the Traffic Campaign". My public condemnations of the government's actions and all the military and social oppression – at a time when something like 60,000 people had come together in Nigeria for this huge black Festival – brought a violent reaction.

The shit really started on 12 February 1977 when a group of armed soldiers fought with youth in the area around Kalakuta Republic. The soldiers were beaten up by the boys, but they vowed to come back. They did a week later, on 18 February 1977. But this time, there were about a thousand soldiers, armed to the teeth.

Let me tell you how the thing went-o!

I'd sent one of my boys out to fetch something. He came

back saying that when he was coming back he had a row with some soldiers over a one-way street. The boy had answered them back, so they beat him up. The other boys tried to retaliate, since the incident happened only three hundred yards away from the house. Man, they'd almost beaten my boy to death. So we carried him into the house and were gonna put him into our car to take him to hospital. But then the army men showed up. There were eight of them. They wanted the boy they'd beaten up. I told them:

"You want who? He's wounded. You can't have him."

The boy is so badly wounded, you know. But even if he weren't injured I wouldn't give him to anybody, to any police or soldier.

"You can come with bazookas, rifles and bombs if you want. . . ."

The soldiers had no right to arrest anyone. So they went back in the streets and lined up there. I realized they were going to try and force the gate open. They started to cut the fence.

Since the last police raid on Kalakuta, when they'd already cut my barbed-wire fence to come in, I'd taken my precautions. I'd bought a big 65 Kwt generator, put it on a Ford truck, so as to electrify the entire fence around Kalakuta. I had a system in the house which allowed me to switch the electricity on whenever needed. You see the type of shit I was forced to do then? Just to protect myself and my people, not from robbers, but from the authorities! I'd never electrified the fence till that day. When I saw the soldiers trying to cut it, I switched on the electricity. The soldiers jumped and moved back.

I went upstairs to the balcony and I saw Kalakuta completely surrounded!!! I saw a high officer going around in his car. There was a flag on it. Then I felt so happy. I said, "Oh, good. When this big officer will see this commotion, he will stop this thing from happening." But that's precisely when everything started. 'Cause that officer was there to . . . lead the shit-o!!!

From then on, everything happened very quickly. The military put fire to the generator, like they did to the bus and my cars. They used petrol to start the fires. Then, they came in, busted the gate open, broke the door down . . . went everywhere in the house . . . beating . . . flogging . . .

138

Home of Dissident Musician
Attacked by Nigeria Troops

By John Darnton

LAGOS, Feb. 20 (NYT) —
everal hundred soldiers attack-
d the home of Nigeria's est-
nown musician and most
ent dissident Friday, se
blaze and sparking off
our disturbance in the
g slum section of Las

The riot, in which th
eat passersby with
ere themselves p
ones and bottles, w
a series of clas
vilians and the
nder Nigeria's
ent.

Ten days earl
s violent dist
ar the commu
re-protected
an, Fela An
Mr. Anikul
ar-old off
igeria's mo

a gadfly
nment,
tacks in
e stage
m ram
as th
at m
tho
The
the country
e government of
tions in such things a
g Lagos traffic jams by whip-
ng motorists.

The cause of Friday's disturb-
ce was not immediately known.
dents who were fleeing the
diers with their arms raised

in the air said that it began
when the soldiers attacked the
two-story yellow house called the
"Kalekute Republic" in retalia-
the beating of a soldier
oys."

that the
le and
mmune.
ed, and
Hospital

to three
the night-
way. There
orts on the
r the where-
nikulepo-Kuti,
ested six times
rently pressing
wsuit stemming
the compound in
his

military govern-
ular with many
ntaneous fights be-
ns and soldiers are
on. Thirteen months
was a 20-hour melee
on the outskirts of
which 4 were killed,
an 50 injured and 100
urned to the ground.

military is sometimes un-
ned and not under the
ve control of the officer
corps which is small for a 250,000-
man force. Because of a lack of
barracks, soldiers are often quar-
tered in civilian areas, contribut-
ing to tensions.

Protest Singer Said Beaten by Nigerian Police

LAGOS, Feb. 22
Anikulapo-Kuti
sician who
fie
(UPI).—Fela
erian mu-
ttack the
e in this
ondition
th in-
military
the
this

art-
and set fire
The 45-year-
other, pushed from
and his brother were
also hospitalized, members of the
colony said.

Mr. Anikulapo-Kuti is under
an armed military guard barring
entrance to all but hospital
personnel.

May 11, 1982

₦10m fraud claim for police investigation

THE police have
been directed to in-
vestigate an alleged
₦10 million fraud
during the FESTAC
77.

The House of Re-
presentatives yester-
day adopted the report
of the Committee on
Public Petitions which
recommended that an
allegation that an
Special FESTAC Task
Force embezzled over
₦10 million be referred
to the police for inve-
stigation.

The committee also
recommended that the
police be directed to
investigate another

allegation that ₦4
million was paid to a
London firm
Francis Associate
for equipment not
supplied in respect of
the festival.

The investigation
would also cover the
allegation of sale of
fake cinema tickets at
the National Arts
Theatre.

kicking ass with their boots . . . hitting with rifle butts. . . . The first one they brought out was Najite, one of the girls. Oooooooooh! They beat her! When I saw that, I said to myself: "The way they beat her, today they will *kill* me!" They beat her, tore her clothes off, naked her. . . . Then they began flogging her, to make her run to the barracks. . . . Oooooooooh! It was too much, man. They were flogging away, beating everybody, cutting, using bayonets, broken bottles . . . raping the women! It was terrible! Oooooooooh!! Terrible!!!

At that moment I was still up on the balcony. I'd been calling out 'cause I wanted all Nigerians around to see it wasn't me who'd started the trouble. I wanted to speak to the Nigerians with a microphone. It was then they switched off the electricity altogether. The soldiers were everywhere! All in the yard, inside the house, in all the rooms on the ground floor. They beat up the girls, raped some of them and did horrors to them, man. They beat up my boys. Then they stormed upstairs. They beat my brother, Dr Beko, who was trying to protect my mother. They fractured his leg, his arm. They beat him so bad he had to be taken to hospital. My brother was in a wheelchair for several weeks after. Then, they grabbed my mother. And you know what they did to this seventy-seven-year-old woman, man? They threw her out the window of the first floor. And me? Oh, man, I could *hear* my own bones being broken by the blows! Then, the whole Kalakuta Republic – at 14-A Agege Motor Road, Surulere – went up in flames. The soldiers had set fire to the house.

First, the hospital. Then prison. I stayed in jail for twenty-seven fuckin' days with wounds all over my body and several bone fractures. I was told by my lawyer that *all* of my people who were in the house were either in hospitals or in jail. My mother was in hospital with a leg fracture, contusions and bruises. I was taken to court and charged. Imagine that! I – not the army – was taken to court. So I sued the Chief of Staff of the Nigerian Army along with army officers from Abalti barracks for twenty-five million naira for special damages. After a one-year delay, the court ruled that I was not entitled to compensation. An official inquiry was made on the attack and burning of my house. In that inquiry I was called a "hooligan". No apologies to my mother whose leg they broke.

140

The government probe by a two-man administrative panel established that there was a burning of the residence of 14-A Agege Motor Road, but ended saying that the house was burnt by "unknown soldiers". So that's why the next two albums I released after the sack of Kalakuta were named *Sorrow, Tears and Blood* and *Unknown Soldier*. They were dedicated to the memory of those who were beaten, raped, tortured or injured during that attack.

16

Shuffering and Shmiling

"ITT", *"Authority Stealing"**

Whaaaaaaaaam! Here I was, in one blow, out in the streets with all my people: about *eighty* of us! My case in court? It was thrown out, man. They didn't even hear it. They withdrew all of the bullshit charges against me. Eventually the courts also threw out my multi-million naira compensation claim. Oh, the corruption of those courts! Those people are such bastards, man. Where to seek justice?

Jobless. Homeless. Still in a cast, my body all bandaged. So I told everybody, "OK, motherfuckers, we must all get back to work!" We had to try to get the Shrine moving again 'cause we didn't have shit. All of my equipment, my belongings, they'd all gone up in flames with the house. Not a fuckin' thing was left. Me, my girls, and the rest of my people slept in my brother Beko's garage for a while. We still kept our dignity, though, man. We started the Shrine back. I began playing again, with one arm and a leg in a cast. That's when I composed "Sorrow, Tears and Blood". We were penniless, man. Then I thought to myself: "Don't I have money coming to me from Decca or EMI?" We're now in June-July. . . .

Now, what was this whole thing with Decca? It's a long story, man. You see, Decca is a motherfucker, man. Wow! Decca signed with me when I was popular. When they burned my house, Chief Abiola of ITT took over Decca and drove out Mr Booth, the white man who was managing Decca. The white man wanted me, so they drove him away to London. Then Decca started giving me horrors. First I

---

* The album title, *ITT: International Thief Thief*, is a play on words. The tune "ITT" is a violent indictment of the multinational company International Telegraph and Telecommunications, represented in Nigeria by Chief Abiola, owner of the record company Decca. "Shuffering and Shmiling", the title of this
* chapter, is another of Fela's hits, composed right after the sacking and burning down of Kalakuta by soldiers of the Nigerian army.

must tell you that, before my house was burnt down, Mr Booth had told me I was popular and that Decca wanted to sign me. But that he was afraid 'cause people were saying I was a hooligan and things like that. They were telling him that I wouldn't deliver. So he was afraid. When he talked to me though he said he liked me and that he wasn't afraid of me. But really underneath he was afraid. So in the contract he put a clause that whoever – Decca, me, or anyone – fucked the contract up, they would have to pay 250,000 naira. That was what he put in the contract. You see what I mean?

Penniless as I was, I decided to go to Decca. That first day I took along all my women and our mattresses to the Director's office. I didn't take over Decca office right away. Remember, I didn't have a house 'cause they'd burnt my house down, right, so I don't have a place to stay. So we went prepared. Now Abiola had just put this guy there as Director of Decca. His name is Mr Ogeus, a Dutchman, from Holland. So I meet this Mr Ogeus to tell him to give me my 250,000 naira for breach of contract, man!

"Mr Ogeus," I said, "if you don't pay me I will stay here with you until you do. We don't have a place to stay, so I brought my mattresses. I'm not going to court. Just give me my money."

Ogeus went to the police. You see that! I come peacefully and he goes to get the police! The police came. They asked him:

"You want to force them out?"

"No," he said. "But I think I should discuss things with Fela."

"OK," I said. "I agree, we should discuss it."

So we agreed to meet at the police office the following morning. I said, "I agree." So I left with my wives and mattresses. We met at the police station the next day and we discussed. The police agreed that their lawyer investigate the contract, and that they would give their opinion after the investigation. You understand? The police kept the contract for two weeks and the lawyer gave his opinion: breach of contract. So the police promised to bring Abiola to the police station to discuss it. The first time, he didn't come. Second time, he came. That was the first day I ever met Abiola. I didn't even know the man existed. So he comes to the police station and swears on his mother's life that he never did anything to me wrongly and that he promises to settle the matter. So we left. One week . . . two weeks . . . one month . . . nothing! OK. Good. So me and my women, we took our mattresses and went to Decca again, for a second time.

"Now, where is my money?" I asked Ogeus.

"OK, if that is what you want, I'm leaving the office for you," he answered.

Now, he had a very big sitting-room and thick carpets everywhere, so we laid our mattresses down. Ogeus, the white man, left the office and went to the police station. When he got to the police though, they wouldn't move 'cause they'd already been to investigate the matter. So I was there in Decca office with my women for seven weeks. It was the Inspector-General of Police himself who got me out. You know how Yusufu got me out?

Here I am one night, sleeping at Decca, when police come. Not to arrest me-o! But to take me to see the Inspector General. Yusufu had sent for me in the middle of the night to'go to his house, man. When I got there, he said:

"Fela, you have to leave now."

"Why?" I asked. "Sir, they have to pay me-o. Or else you send your police to batter me if you like."

"Fela, you *know* I can't do that."

"Fine. Then, they'll have to pay."

That's when he said to me: "Fela, you know they've taken *me* to court now." I understood then what was happening.

You see, while I was living at Decca office, those mother-fuckers had taken me to court. The lawyers, they lie. And the magistrate issues a bench order on me for . . . "illegal occupation". Of course, the court didn't hear my side of the case at all. But the police who knew my side of the story and everything about the matter refused to execute the bench warrant. In court, they said that every time they would go to the premises of Decca to get me out, they couldn't find me! Ha-ha-ha-ha-ha-ha! So Decca sued the police in court for not executing the bench warrant.

That's why M.D. Yusufu said to me: "If I go to court, they'll embarrass me."

"Yes," I said. "I know that." After a moment of silence, I said:

144

"OK. Fine. Give me one more week. Let me enjoy one more week, Sir, 'cause you know I don't have house any more. At Decca they have big sitting-room and offices with carpet everywhere." Yusufu shook his head, with a bit of a smile in his eyes.

"OK, stay there one more week."

That's how I finally left Decca, you know. But people don't know that Fela done his underground work legally and everything. They think I'm a hooligan who just went into Decca and sat down. But, man, I was the winner, you see. Let me tell you the reason why I always get victorious over people. People think I'm mad, but I don't do things rashly. People think I do things rashly because at the point when I'm gonna do action, those who do not know what's been happening will think I am being rash. At the time of my action I will really go full out and die there if I have to. What people don't know though is that when I go into action I have already done many underground things before. That's why I won out with Decca.

Even my own lawyer, Tunji Braithwaite, started messing me up over this Decca matter. He wanted me to go to court with EMI instead. I told him I didn't want to go to court with EMI 'cause I knew that EMI could settle. It was Decca I was after. They were the ones who were messing with me, the motherfuckers. That brought a clash between me and Braithwaite. So I closed him off completely. I said to myself: "I don't want no lawyer again. What for? Fuck!"

If M.D. Yusufu hadn't asked me to leave Decca, man, I would have stayed in that place till Abiola changed colour. We'd gone there in June or July and we left in August. We'd stayed there seven weeks anyhow. And in comfort, man. Just after that I left into exile, man. In October. Yeaaaah, into exile, you know. In Ghana. We all went together. But then Ghana depor. . . . No! Ghana didn't deport me. It was the fucking corrupt military government there that did it. Why? Well, that's another long story. Want to hear it? I'll make it short. . . .

Original album cover of *Zombie*
Design: Gharlokwu Lemi

17

Why I Was Deported from Ghana

"Zombie", "Mr Follow Follow", "Fear Not for Man", "V.I.P."

Here I was again, back in Ghana. Right off, I started playing at the Apollo Theatre. My latest album, *Zombie*, had gone over big in Ghana-o. Ghanaian students were singing it just to mock their own military government 'cause the words describe soldiers as zombies. Military! Ghana, home of Pan-Afrikanism, was under their boots then, man, just like in Nigeria. Ghana was the home of Kwame Nkrumah. So I started preaching Nkrumahism and soon ran into trouble with the military régime at that time, led by General Ignatius Acheampong.*

My first trouble came with an incident that occurred right in front of the hotel where I was putting up. You see, there was a Lebanese shop-owner just across the way from the hotel. This Lebanese had objected to Ghanaian women selling fruits in front of his shop. One day, he personally came out of his shop to pour cold water on the women to make them go away. One of my boys came to my room to tell me. I said, "Whaaaaaaaat?" I went out into the street and challenged that motherfucker. I told him that this was Africa and that he had no right to attack defenceless African women. I left, after warning him not to repeat such action again, man. Shit! The following day that bastard did the same thing. He drove the women away, even hitting some, and told them never to return again. If they did, he threatened to call the police. Man, when I heard that I took to the street again and confronted that Lebanese. I didn't

---

* General Ignatius Acheampong governed Ghana as a dictator from 1972 to 1978. He was executed in 1979 by the Armed Forces Revolutionary Council (AFRC), led by Flight Lt. Jerry Rawlings.

Durotimi Ikujenyo ("Duro")
Egypt 80 pianist and historical
researcher
Photo: André Bernabé

Mabinuori Kayode Idowu ("I.D.
Writer and Egypt 80 administra
Photo: André Bernabé

Lekan Animashaun
Egypt 80 Band leader and baritone saxaphonist,
with Fela since 1965
Photo: Raymond Sardaby

hit him, but I was gonna give him horrors, man. There was a scuffle and the Ghanaian police was called. They came and took me, then locked me up in a cell. At Police Head-quarters there was a big confrontation between me and a Ghana Inspector of Police who justified the action of the Arab man.

"This trader has the right to clear the front of his store. Those women are squatters."

That's what that fuckin' policeman said. Shiiiiit! Later I was taken down to the Accra Central Police Station and charged in a Federal Court for action "liable to bring about a breach of the peace". But I was released on bail and allowed to continue playing.

At the time, you see, students were seriously agitating against their corrupt government. It was the same struggle as in Nigeria. So I began meeting with the student leaders. They would even come to see me at hotel, man. The things they told me, man! Acheampong was a real motherfucker! The students told me that the police were beating . . . whipping left and right . . . and raping women at Winneba University. . . . So I called a meeting with leaders of four universities: Legon, Winneba, Kumasi, Cape Coast. Twelve of them came to my hotel. Man, I gave them a lecture for three hours. I told them why they should stop studying that nonsense there called law, 'cause colonial education was no good for them. "If you keep it up, your education is going to be useless." I advised these boys to do what they wanted to do. After that they made a public declaration. So every-body knew I'd met with them. Because of this and because I had a case in court over the shit with this Lebanese man, and also because of my album *Zombie,* the Ghanaian authorities deported me in '78. But I was so popular with the people! And, of course, with the students, man!

I dug those students, man. They were courageous. So I spoke to them openly. I told them Africa could not be non-aligned because Africa was the *centre* of the world. Not its south. Nor its north. Nor its east. Nor its west. But the centre! I told them things were so wrong. So very wrong! Imagine that, the fate of the entire world completely dependent on the whims of two fuckin' old men! Four billion people in the hands of two little motherfuckers over sixty who give themselves pompous titles, like "General", "Admiral", "President". . . . My motherfuckin' life, man,

149

and yours, and everybody's in the hands of a bunch of motherfuckers whose only problem is that they can't . . . *fuck*! As ridiculous as that, man.

Who are these "world leaders"? Destroyers, man. Not builders. Not creators. But destroyers. You see, I can't accept that *my* fate be in the hands of such fucked-up people. Does that seem normal to you? Do you accept the idea that your fate, your last hour on this earth, might depend on some motherfucker sitting up in the White House in Washington or up in the Kremlin in Moscow? Should the fate of the whole world depend on whether or not one of those bastards' pricks couldn't get hard one night? Is that normal? Not to me, man!

You see what I'm getting at? A handful of unnatural, unbalanced people are ruling this world. That's why when I hear that the non-aligned bloc is trying to be a third solution, I can only shake my head. 'Cause those people who call themselves non-aligned are un-balanced. Do you know what something which is non-aligned means? It means something which ain't *straight*, man. Something crooked, unbalanced, an out-of-line people, you know!

I also told them that Africans have to start by feeling that we belong to any part of the continent. We should not limit our area of belonging to that small enclave cut out for us at the Berlin Conference of 1884–5. Africa has to open her doors to every Black man in the world. Until Africa sees it that way, she won't have made it yet, man. White people, wherever they are, have a sense of belonging. They have even gone as far as electing a European Parliament to take care of their interests. White people are doing it for themselves. But instead of Africans doing it for ourselves, we go about copying foreign values, cultural concepts which permanently endear us to the whole world at large as certified slaves.

Industrialization? We don't need it unless it's industrialization the African way. That's what I told them. Technology, industrialization, the machine, they've all brought about a progressive loss of respect for life, for nature, for the environment we live in, man. And Africans worship nature and life. Technology's killing the spiritual things. Now, how can that be called modernization? No, man. That's regression. The white man is leading us astray. The right way is the one of our ancestors: traditional technology, or *naturalology*. That's the only viable way. Yeah, that's what I believe. You know what viable means? It means *life,* man. Life!

Why are Africans becoming technologists? I told the students: "I've rarely met any African doing the thing he really *wanted* to do." Most Africans do things 'cause that is what will bring them status, or make them important or give them bread. You see, man, some people think power is money. When you are rich; when you have many cars; when you have beautiful houses; when you have many women to show off. . . . But that's not power. Power is *knowledge.* Somebody who has knowledge cannot misuse power. Knowledge is not technology. Knowledge is power in the cosmic sense; it's rhythm, you know. Once you start to have rhythm you start having knowledge.

I said to those students that technology, industrialization will cause the downfall of white nations. That's what I think. I see the day when America will come to a standstill. I see a day when American people in America cannot stay there any more. Their environment will be too polluted. I think the Americans themselves see that day coming. The government sees it but not the people as yet. That's why America wants to keep Australia and Africa by all means. 'Cause the future of this world is based on nature, not the machine. Science will be completely wiped out. It'll be wiped out by those who live and swear by it today. Natural forces will wipe out science. Science means complications. Look at pollution!

Science is making the world get more and more expensive. When science brings out a new gadget it costs more than the others. People have to earn more to buy it. So science is making the world more difficult, more complex. It makes people run more. What we need is to rest more, talk more, walk more, fuck more and enjoy things in life more. There's a limit to what Europeans call technological and industrial development. When that limit is achieved society just crumbles. That's why I see the day Europe, America and Russia will come to a standstill.

At one point the students started asking me about Russia, communism and the liberation struggles in Southern Africa. I told them what I felt then, but now I could add two other experiences I had that same year, '78. You see, in '78, exactly ten years after my first visit to East Berlin, I went back to Berlin to play. It was for the West Berlin Jazz Festival. They paid me $100,000 for one concert. But, you see, I had to pay for the tickets for all my group and for hotel accommodation. So it was a lot less than $100,000 'cause, remember, there were seventy of us. The Berlin organizers should really have taken care of our accommodations and plane tickets. So what they paid me wasn't a real fee. You know what I mean? But since I had to buy the plane tickets myself I took the cheapest flight: Interflug, the East German Airlines. So it was in East Berlin that we landed. But we had to go to West Berlin to play for the Festival.

We did the concert. Then after that we went touring a bit of West Berlin before crossing back to East Berlin to leave back to Nigeria. Meanwhile, practically all our money was spent. We had about $4,000 or so left. So we go back to East Berlin. When we get there, they said I should come and pay for visas. I said:

"We paid for visas when we were coming into East Berlin. Now to cross to go back home again you're asking us to pay for visas again."

"That's the law," they said.

"Fair enough."

They stared at me.

I said: "Let me tell you my story. I came through here. You saw me. I went for that your Festival there. I'm Fela. I'm a socialist in concept. I believe in your ideology here. And I like it. Hear my story-o. I see that you are socialists. When people are in difficulty you help. So, you see, I spent all my bread in West Berlin, with the capitalist people. So you have to help me to pay $55 each again for so many people. This here is small bread I have."

I showed them the bread. The officer scratched his head, went away. He came back.

"You have to pay."

"You people are the same. You're looking for money. Just money. Now I know you."

That's how I know the communists, man. Me, I don't need no more experience, man. That one was enough for me to see their real face.

Today if I was talking again to those Ghanaian students, I would tell them about another experience I also had while coming back from East Berlin in '78. This one was with the leader of the South West Africa People's Organization (SWAPO), Sam Nujoma. We were all there at the East Berlin airport waiting to board the plane taking us home. This was just before we checked in. We started discussing with Nujoma and members of his entourage. One of my associates asked Sam Nujoma how long he envisaged the struggle would go on in Namibia. You know what he answered?

"Certainly, the struggle for the liberation of Africa will continue for a long time to come. Our children will have to continue where we stop. But *a lutta continua, a victoria e certa.*"

Minutes later, we all proceeded to board our plane and you know what happened? Well, Sam Nujoma and his group went towards the front of the plane, to the *first-class* passengers' section! And us? All seventy of us went into economy class. . . . What do you think of that? I'll tell you what I think. Sam Nujoma could have saved the extra money he was spending on first-class tickets to buy a gun for the freedom fighters who don't have the opportunity to take a plane, let alone travel in first class. Their homes, their permanent homes are their trenches. It's them, man, who are fighting for the total liberation of Africa.

A lutta continua. . . . *A lutta continua.* . . . *A lutta continua.* . . . Those words kept turning over and over in my mind during the flight. At first I didn't understand because it was Portuguese language. One of the boys finally translated it as "the struggle *continues!*" I said to myself: "How can a responsible leader ever want the struggle to *continue?*" Who can want a war to continue? War is massacring . . . and killing. How can anybody want that to go on indefinitely? Those were the things I kept turning round in my head on the flight back from Berlin to Nigeria. That's when I said to myself: "No! It must not continue. The struggle *must STOP!*" Since then, that's been my slogan.

Back in Lagos. What do I see at the airport? Mr Sam Nujoma and his group, escorted by Nigerian officials, leaving in a long line of Mercedes-Benz. I asked myself: "And how about the poor, ragged, barefoot, hungry guerrilla who *is fighting* on the front, exposing his life every day to the deadly bullets of the enemy? Suppose he showed up right now at this airport and walked up to those same

Original album cover of *V.I.P. – Vagabonds in Power*
Design: Fela
Photo: Tunde Kuboye

top officials who welcomed Nujoma? Would they receive him as they received Nujoma?" That day I understood the whole shit.* *A lutta continua* was the slogan of the . . . *leaders.* Those who will be eating the pie, not those who are getting killed to get the pie. I understood why it's Generals – leaders – who write their memoirs. And not the poor motherfucker who gets killed in their name!

The leaders of the African freedom struggle will always want the struggle to continue. For them, it means travelling around on first-class tickets and being given VIP treatment wherever they go. So when people talk to me about South Africa, I say:

"Our Heads of State, how do they dare talk about South Africa? South Africa? What? What about South Africa?"

We all agree that South Africa is a fascist, anti-Black, white supremacist régime. We all know that. But analyse the question well. Ask youself this: are the so-called independent states of Africa any better than the apartheid régime in South Africa? What do you think? Good. I'll tell you what I think. Me, I think that our Heads of State are in fact worse than those of South Africa! At least, the South African leaders are direct. The whites hate the Blacks and want to exterminate them. Finish. But our Heads of State, who are Black, tell us they want to protect us. It's these neo-colonial and reactionary African states that carry out genocide against their own Black people indiscriminately. Emperor Bokassa, isn't he Black? General Olusegun Obasanjo, isn't he Black? And all the reactionary African puppets, aren't they Blacks? So how can they go around condemning apartheid South Africa when they're doing exactly the same thing against their own innocent citizens in the countries where they hold power? Oh, man, Africa is not together at all! Africa *na wa-o!*

---

* Experiences such as the one related above are the source of Fela's '78 hit "V.I.P." – again a play on words, for instead of "Very Important Person", it stands for *Vagabonds in Power.*

18

My Second Marriage

Before this Ghana thing happened, you know, I'd made a short trip back to Nigeria to commemorate the first anniversary of the sacking of Kalakuta Republic. It was while we were there in Nigeria that I married the twenty-seven girls of my group Africa 70. After that, of course, I returned to Ghana. You know the rest. That Acheampong motherfucker, who's dead now, got his ass kicked good by Jerry Rawlings! But before that happened while I'd been in Nigeria, Acheampong had gotten in touch with the Nigerian government. So when I came back to Ghana I was deported shortly after.

Anyway, end January, I was with my group travelling by road back to Nigeria. I'd be looking at the fucking beautiful country and thinking how beautiful Africa is, man. My girls were tired. Most of them slept through that trip. Now and then I'd look at them sleeping. And I'd think: "These girls have suffered plenty-plenty for me-o! For years. Some for eight years! Fearless women, these my girls. Good women, man!" And I said to myself: "Fela, these na good women-o! Shiiiiit!"

On 20 February '78 I married all twenty-seven in a traditional ceremony. The marriage had been originally planned for the 18th of February, the anniversary of the sacking of Kalakuta. But my lawyer messed that up. You know what happened? He must have planned it with Steve. When I think about it, the two of them were working on it together. Steve Udah. You don't know him, man? A Black guy with plenty hair, a Bendel man, who used to be with me. Anyway, it was this Steve who came up to me and suggested: "Fela, why don't you marry all your women?" He suggested it, or at least that's what he thought then. Actually, I'd been thinking of it all along myself. All this time, man, I'd been fucking these girls. When I was in Ghana I'd reached a point where I was just fucking them. Nobody else from the outside any more. Just them! So I married them. I wanted to.

Now, coming back to that night when this Steve guy came to my house and said:

"Fela, why don't you marry these your girls?"

"Steve, I've been thinking about it, man."

That's how he got the idea that he's put it in my head. But, you see, he had a small mind. I had a big mind. I wanted to do it 'cause I wanted to do the right thing. He thought I wanted to do it for publicity. So the night before I was going to marry, Steve must have gone to the lawyer's to plan some dubious shit among themselves, man. But I don't know this at the time. You understand?

Tunji Braithwaite was still my lawyer then. Kanmi Oshobu? He'd already gone, man. He split when they burnt my house. So when I was in detention, my brother Koye had got Braithwaite for me. Kanmi had just disappeared! We couldn't find him, even to come and take up my case. He was too scared. So we had to find an alternative. That's how Braithwaite got involved, you know. Tunji Braithwaite! The day before the marriage, at 5 o'clock, we went to his office. We were to come next morning, 18 February at 10 o'clock. He said he had an apartment office upstairs which he would clean up for us and that the ceremony would take place there. It was planned. Everybody agreed.

The next morning we arrive. What do I see? Press, man. Nothing but press! I've never seen so much press people like that in my life! Now, I've been playing everywhere in the world but till today I've never seen so many press people! Understand? Place was full of cameras, reporters. There was no room to move. Then Tunji Braithwaite suddenly stands up in front of all those people.

"This marriage *cannot take place*. It is against public morals. And me, as Fela's lawyer, I am going to advise him that it's against the law of this country and that he may be prosecuted for bigamy."

Man, did you hear that? Can you imagine? Ohhhhhh!!! I don't know how I kept my body steady, man! I don't know how I kept my demeanour up! It was like I'd been hit by lightning! I don't know how I just stood cool. I was paralysed. I couldn't talk. I couldn't think. The place was in total confusion. All my women were there, standing behind me, dressed and made up, ready. They didn't know what to

157

think either. Flashbulbs were going off. Then the press asked:

"Fela, what are you going to do now?"

The press had asked the exact question I couldn't answer!

Ajanaku, the *Ifà** priest who was supposed to do the ceremony, was a fucking stupid man. He was supposed to be the leader of *Ifà* priests in Lagos. He was always following government people about. I thought he was respectable. But money has spoiled his mind. He doesn't know shit, man. He's just a fake. What does he know about *Ifà*? Nothing, man. Don't worry, man, one of these days I'm gonna deal with him! Idiot! When Braithwaite told him, "If you do this marriage, police will arrest you," he ran away.

I looked at the press people and said:

"You press, let me tell you something. I don't care what this man says. As far as I am concerned, *today* I consider myself married with my women. You understand that?"

Then I got up and went home. Oh, woooooooow! My head was turning around. I was thinking about everything that had just happened. I was broken, man. Yeah, broken! Then here comes this Steve again. He saw that I was completely broken, you know, unable to think. He also saw that if he didn't find a new suggestion, man, the whole group might collapse. How could Braithwaite have done this to me? That date was so important to me, man. To all of the girls. To all of my people, man. Shit! So I was sitting in my house, really down, man. And Steve says:

"Look, Fela, the best thing to do is to set another date for the marriage. We won't do it in his office. We'll do it somewhere else."

"Yeah. . . ," was all I could say.

He continued: "Let's do it in the hotel and call the press again."

"Good idea."

So we again announced that I'm gonna marry. This time on Monday, 20 February. The press announced it, and on Monday morning, *Punch* headlined: "FELA TO MARRY TODAY, LAW OR NO LAW". Press came again, man. Police or no police, I married. Braithwaite was disgraced, man. It made him look ridiculous. This time I'd gotten

---

* The Yoruba divination cult dedicated to the *orisha* of the same name. The Ifà Oracle is a divination done with sixteen palm-nuts.

158

another *Ifà* priest. We have plenty in Nigeria. Thousands, man.

At that time, I was full into my case against the government. And since Braithwaite was handling it, we were still in liaison with him. After the problems he raised over the Decca affair and now what had just happened, I didn't think I would ever go into his office again, or see him again. Because what he'd done made no sense, man. But on the morning I was married, my brother Beko was in Braithwaite's house. Now I've already told Beko I was marrying on Monday, understand? But Braithwaite didn't know anything. So while Beko was in the sitting-room talking with Braithwaite, the television people came to interview him about his cancellation of the marriage two days before.

"Mr Braithwaite, why did you cancel the marriage?" The television people wanted to make the *cancellation* into a big thing now. Not the marriage itself.

"How do think Fela will feel?"

Braithwaite was getting ready to make a small speech:

"Well, as you know, Fela is my friend, but. . . ."

Beko cut him off.

"Hey, you press and television people, lawyer, stop all this what you're doing! Fela is marrying *right now*!!!"

But Braithwaite had already talked. . . . So TV people just quickly took their cameras.

"Where? Where?"

"At Parisona Hotel, Ikorodu Road."

They left in a hurry.

We had finished the marriage when they got there. We were all having drinks. I saw one press man who wanted to ask me a question.

"Fela? . . ."

"We're married, man. We're all happy and everything." They took many photos of the marriage.

That night, we're watching news on the TV, network news, man. And who do we see? Braithwaite. They'd just put it on him! "Fela's lawyer is a liar." The news started like this:

— *TV announcer:* "Today we were at the house of Fela's lawyer, Mr Braithwaite. He made the following statement."

159

- *Mr Braithwaite* (who appears on the screen):
  "Unfortunately, Fela cannot marry since it is an illegal act against public order. It's unfortunate because, as you know, Fela is my friend, but. . . ."
- *TV announcer:* "But as Mr Braithwaite was saying this, Fela was calmly marrying his twenty-seven women. . . ."
  (Scenes of the marriage festivities flash on the screen.)

That disgraced Braithwaite, man! He was trying to use me for politics, man, and he ended up being disgraced. Tunji Braithwaite! Let me tell you who that man is. After the burning of my house, he was the one handling the case. I was suing for twenty-five *million* naira, man! The government wanted to settle. They went to see him in his house. But he didn't tell me that they wanted to settle. No. Just the opposite, man. He told me he wanted to go to court. So the case went to court. All of that was only to make his name popular, man. Nobody knew Braithwaite in Lagos before. Nobody heard his name anywhere. But when he started my case, he was on the front page, big: "Braithwaite in court with Fela." You want me to show you the press coverage of my case, man? If you stack the papers in a pile, they'd be so fucking high. I swear! They were carrying news on me for a year and a half, every day. So Braithwaite too was in the news. That's how everybody came to know him. See?

Braithwaite wanted people to think I was a hooligan, that I was just doing the marriage for publicity. As if I was any musician going round the street, looking for prestige, man. That's why he did that shit, man. After that I'd said, "I am not gonna see this man again. Let me show him a big mind." But then I thought it over, and said to myself, "Why not?" So one day me and my wives went to visit him at his home.

"FELA! How are you?"

"Fine, man. Cool."

Then he started saying he felt sorry about what had happened and stupid things like that. So we left, man. Later on I went back again to his place, but to discuss politics now. Throughout the case we had never discussed politics. It was time we did.

"Now, politics. You know I'm running for the presidency."

"Fela, look, let's work together in this thing 'cause I want to be president too."

So we discussed and decided to work together. I was ready to let him run for presidency in my place. Really, I don't want to be president, you know. Once the ideas I am fighting for are there, I don't need to be president. Right? Then, on another day, I went to see him to discuss the situation of poor people and what should be done. I gave him my ideas, not just on bettering the lot of people but changing it. But before I tell you what he said, let me ask you this. Have you ever seen his house in Ikoyi, man? It's a big, mighty house! Exactly like a ship, you know. He's very proud. He calls it a *mansion.*

"Fela, how do you like my mansion?"

His next statement was this exactly:

"You think I'm going to allow my children to go to school at *Mushin** with those *Mushin* boys? . . . So you want *Mushin* people to take over my house here?"

I looked him in the eyes.

"So, what do you want? . . . No use me arguing with you over this one."

When I went back outside, I started to think about it. I said to myself: "OK, I know this one now!"

Coming back to my wives. OK. What attracted me to each of them? *Sex!* I thought they were sexy and fuckable. That's what attracts me to a woman first. Some came to my house on their own. Others, I had come. Why? 'Cause I wanted to fuck them. That was all. I wanted a house where I could be fucking and I had it. It *grew* into something else after though. Something special. But it started just with *sex.* The desire to fuck. Man, the one most important thing in the human being is that life-giving and pleasurable sensation: sexual orgasm. And that's what's being condemned the most. Yeah. Somebody was asking me, trying to put down my ideas, if I thought sex was politics.

"No, I don't," I said. *"Sex is life."*

That's what I believe. Me, I fuck as often and as long as I can-o! Now, it's not even a matter of choice. When I married *twenty-seven* women I knew what I was doing-o!

* A sprawling "ghetto" on the outskirts of Lagos.

161

Did I sleep with all of them on the night of the marriage? No. Man, I said I married *twenty-seven*, not seven! I only slept with one. The one next in turn. I followed my normal procedure. You see, before I married them I'd told them:

"Look, when I marry you, I'm gonna do the same thing I was doing before with you. It's gonna be the same house, the same thing, but just that we're married."

Do I find living with them difficult? Naaaaah. I love it. It's not difficult at all. It's difficult if you don't think of them or deal with them as *women*. Now, if you put them in the same frame as men, then it would be difficult. But I don't do that, man.

Of the original twenty-seven I married – besides, of course, my first wife Remi – only fifteen are still with me. The others? Man, they've left. Life was too hard, you know. Where are they now? Well, I still hear from them, and see them. They come to house to visit me. They come to Shrine. How do I feel about their having left? I don't mind. I don't feel animosity against them. At all! I don't feel *nothing,* man. Ask *them* what they feel? I don't feel nothing 'bout them, man.

Do I beat my wives? Not *beat*; not that. Never! Not that brutal thing, man. Until I was seventeen I got beaten. Mercilessly! Me, I've never beaten my children-o. I swear! But sometimes it's necessary to give my wives some *paf-paf-paf-paf-paf-paf*. . . . I slap 'em. Yeah. You see, when you talk 'bout women, you're talking 'bout something else, man. A woman has to respect her husband. If she don't, I feel sorry for you. They need you to show authority, man. See what I mean? Then they'll say to themselves: "Ah-aaaaaaaah! This na good husband-o! He don't care fo' no bullshit!" See what I mean? But I never kick their asses, man. Never!

That's about everything on how and why I married those girls, man. I stopped calling them "my girls". After the marriage, they became my *queens*. Yeah, man. I'm very attached to them. They've been through it. But they've chosen to be with me and they stay with me. Why? *Me, I no dey speak fo' dem-o!* For that one, you have to ask them yourself, man! You have my permission.

19

My Queens

The only thing that the fifteen queens have in common is that they are all African. Diversity would best describe them, for theirs is an array of physical types: ranging from tiny to tall, slender to round; and a rainbow of skin tones, facial shapes and features. Their personalities are just as diverse: from timid to outgoing, from pensive to gay. Several ethnic groups are represented and not all are from Nigeria. Social origins differ as well. Some are of rural background, some are urbanites. Of modest or affluent families, all but one are from polygamous backgrounds.

What is it about Fela that has drawn women from such varied backgrounds and of such different temperaments and personalities to him? A recurring theme is that many of the queens, as young girls – often naïve, adventurous in spirit and suffocated by their family homes – went to Fela's as the place where they could fulfil their adolescent dreams. His door, they knew, was always open, for Fela was known never to turn anyone away from his house. To live at Fela's meant being free, as opposed to being held in strict check by their families. Smoking, drinking, fame, travelling, earning money, being with the man of their dreams. . . . Essentially, they found security in one man who was to become their husband, father, big brother, adviser and employer. But at what price?

Life with Fela is tough. At the time of the collective marriage in February 1978, there were many more women living at Kalakuta than the twenty-seven who married Fela. Of these, only fifteen remain, including Fela's first wife, Remi. Many have suffered raping, beating, imprisonment, family ostracism; and have been labelled "prostitutes" and "drug addicts" because of being with him. Unable to take the pressure, some have fled. Others have been forcibly taken by their parents. But what of those who remain? How do they continue amidst the daily hardships and, at times, horrors?

At first glance, none of the faces of the queens betray the troubles they have seen. Each is stunningly beautiful in 'her own way. Draped in the brilliantly coloured and varied styles of West African traditional attire – from the multi-coloured patterned *adire* and wax cloth to the luminous threaded handwoven strips of *ashoke;* with their matching and elegantly wrapped headties; and their braided, beaded hairstyles that are works of art in themselves – the queens are intent on preserving and embellishing even more the millennium-old beauty of African fashion.

In keeping with traditional practice, almost all the queens resplendently display their "wealth". Necks, wrists and often ankles are adorned with a myriad of necklaces and bracelets, made of an unending assortment of coral, ancient beads and cowrie shells – whose value, once equivalent to currency, was worn by women as such – along with ivory. These and the matching earrings are all made by the queens according to each individual taste.

As a crowning touch to a regalia befitting their title, an elaborate facial make-up is meticulously arranged in harmony with each individual face, temperament and personality. As they say, "Africans are the first people to wear make-up." Bold purple, blue or green eye-colours are lavishly applied; highly rouged cheeks, black gloss lips and green nail-varnish. They complete this already remarkable effect with designs of a white powder, called spiritual powder. Without this natural substance found in river beds, they say that the spirits are unable to communicate with them. The queens are eager to rediscover the original significance of these various designs in white powder which project a striking resemblance to sculptured masks.

The queens' first objective is to keep their husband satisfied. Failure to do so may mean their being refused the sharing of his bed when their turn comes.

Organization of the daily household chores, such as seeing to Fela's clothes, preparing the daily meals, etc., is apparently established by the senior wives who hold an authority over the younger ones though much less rigidly than is the traditional custom. As one of the queens related, her senior position vis-à-vis a more junior wife would traditionally mean that: "I could ask her to do anything I wanted. If I wanted my clothes washed, she would have to do it. But we have been so colonized she don't like to do it again."

Marriage has undoubtedly brought an even greater sense of security to the lives of the queens. Earlier bickering and rivalry has since slackened. There is a new willingness to co-operate. But despite efforts to avoid quarrelling, it is practically impossible not to. As one queen said, "We can fight any time and we can settle any time." Serious disputes (*yab*), or the rarer physical fights, are brought before Fela. Depending on the gravity of the offence, the queens can either be fined a sum of money or punished by slapping, enforced stringent household work, or sexual deprivation (for as long as one month). Are the queens slapped? Most of them, yes! (Although Fela does *not* beat or slap his own children.) However, outstanding work or behaviour is rewarded: gifts, additional "sexual time" with Fela.

Contrary to Yoruba traditional practice, whereby the first wife establishes the sexual calendar of the younger wives with the husband, in the Anikulapo-Kuti household it is Fela himself who has arranged the calendar. There would seem to be no set criteria, unless it is seniority and good behaviour, as some of the queens have said. According to certain of them, sexual frequency can vary from twice a week to every nine days. And in Fela's own words, two queens per day. One of the wives revealed that: "After he finish with one, he go jump on another straightaway!" Whatever the "technique", all the queens confess to being satisfied. None ever – at least openly – complained about sharing Fela sexually. And this may be due to the fact that all but one queen either come from polygamous families themselves or grew up in a polygamous environment. According to one queen, "Jealousy is not an African word." And, in any case, she added, "The African man has as many wives as he wants." This would echo Fela's own forewarning to the one queen who comes from a mono-gamous family. She was told she "could take it or leave it". And she took it.

Fela himself is aware of the dangers of favouritism in a polygamous marriage. "Man, even if I had favourites among my wives, I wouldn't tell you which ones they were." In any case, no one queen in particular is any closer to Fela than another. The sort of "special proximity" which prevails between a monogamous couple is thus absent. It may very well be that this lack of "proximity" acts as an

165

additional incentive for the queens to co-operate among themselves. In this way, the popularity of one queen would depend on how well she gets along with the others rather than on her particular relationship to Fela. The same would apply to those who bear the "unpopular" tag and tend to be the most withdrawn, haughty and less communicative – their "unpopularity" being in relation to the other wives rather than to Fela himself.

Every queen is expected to *work*. And whatever job they hold – whether as a singer, dancer, disc-jockey, cashier, or other – it is expected to be well done. Salaries vary according to job and seniority, but average thirty-five naira per week. Recording sessions and concert tours are remunerated by a special allowance. A separate budget is used for the running of the household and the person handling the money for such needs is never the same from month to month. At times it may be any one of the queens and at others, close friends and/or one of the musicians. It's a question of whomever Fela chooses.

To maintain the smooth running of a household which includes the fifteen queens, one queen's mother, five children, Fela, and a host of friends and passers-by is no easy task. Kalakuta itself is no palace. Or maybe *it is* after all. In any case, it's a focal point at the very centre of one of the poorest districts, Ikeja. Fela shuns exclusive areas, sharing all the discomforts with the ordinary people. Water and power shortages, cramped conditions and many other inconveniences that are the lot of the common man are accepted. Mattresses are placed wherever there is space. Privileges of life at Kalakuta are not of a material kind although some queens do aspire to fame and riches. Other queens, however, are into studying subjects as varied as astrology, traditional medicine, politics, African history, philosophy and traditional ways. Most of the queens would be content with just being good housewives and bearing children for Fela.

An unhesitating belief in Fela's ideology makes most queens loyal to the point of being reluctant to criticize their husband. They stay by him come what may in his struggle for PanAfrikanism. Even if it means spending two months behind walls in Welfare, being thrown behind barbed wire, locked in prison cells, or being brutalized and beaten by police and soldiers. These are the women who have stood by Fela through thick and thin. Everything. These are his queens!

The following individual presentations* of the queens are merely based on order of seniority:

Remi	*1961*
Naa Lamiley	*1971*
Aduni	*1971*
Kevwe	*1972*
Funmilayo	*1972*
Alake	*1973*
Adejonwo	*1974*
Najite	*1974*
Adeola	*1974*
Kikelomo	*1974*
Ihase	*1975*
Omowunmi	*1975*
Omolara	*1976*
Fehintola	*1976*
Sewaa	*1977*

* The queens' parlance differs depending on whether they attended Western schools or not. Some only speak their mother tongue plus *pidgin*. But for all of them, speaking *pidgin* is a way of stressing their Africanity. None of them see it as a "bastardized" creole.

Remi
Photo: André Bernabé

REMI

"Wipe My Tears"

After twenty years of marriage, Remi, Fela's first wife, occupies a special place in the Anikulapo-Kuti household. As senior wife and mother of Fela's first four children, she does not consider herself on the same plane as the other wives. Neither do the latter, nor Fela for that matter.

Resentful of any "uppity" manifestations by the younger and more flamboyant queens, she cultivates an olympian detachment borne out by her stately demeanour. Good-natured but serious. Both introverted and extroverted, Remi is always pensive.

Although living in her own place until recently, she now resides in Kalakuta with her mother and children, but in her own room.

Q: Until 1970 Fela and you lived as a monogamous couple.

A: When he came back from America I took the decision to live in my *own* place like before. And then he started the Kalakuta Residence.

Q: How did you feel when he started this communal living with other people?

A: To me, Fela's always lived like that. In England, in his place, you would find everybody living there. When we came back, we would always have people staying with us.

Q: So that was never a big thing to you that Fela had other women?

A: If we get into girlfriends, he always had them. He made me understand before I married him that he

169

would always have them. I could take it or leave it.

Q: Has this posed any problem for you? Are you just accommodating to the situation, or would you have liked it to be different?

A: I don't think I'm accommodating because he really didn't bother me. The only thing that bothered me was if any woman should come and try to act big over me. I wouldn't take that. It really didn't bother me because he had, you know, girlfriends outside. He never brought any woman to my house. And he wouldn't have done it anyway; whereas his friends, they took their women in whether the wife was in or not. He always respected me.

Q: Well, you said Fela has always respected you. So what type of relationship has prevailed between him and you? How would you designate, how would you qualify this relationship?

A: I don't know. I can't answer that really.

Q: What prevails mostly? Friendship? Understanding?

A: Respect. Everything.

Q: Would you say that you're satisfied with your life with Fela?

A: I wouldn't say I've always been or am. No woman, I think, should say it. 'Cause that's what keeps the relationship going.

Q: What makes you *un*satisfied with your life with Fela?

A: I suppose you want an honest answer but I don't talk about my deeper emotions.

Q: Why?

A: I don't want to. Actually, I'm an emotional person. I don't think I could ever . . . I mean, anything can set me being dissatisfied, you know. I don't know if you know what I really mean?

Q: No, I don't. That isn't clear.

A: [*Laughter.*] If I thought he was trying to treat someone better than me, which has happened on occasions, that makes me dissatisfied. But Fela always tries or thinks he's being fair. So I can't really say I ever blame him. Sometimes I misjudge him. A lot of the time, I would say. And he himself, not being very patient, wouldn't take time to talk to me about it.

Q: Well, you being Fela's senior wife and his first wife, I would expect you to have the deepest knowledge of Fela. I have noticed that Fela treats you differently from his other wives. You even talk to him differently from the way the other wives talk to him. There's a different type of relationship. I see that you wield much more authority in your relationship with Fela than the others. In other words, there is a paternal attitude that Fela has towards his other wives that he doesn't have towards you.

A: I don't think I talk to him any differently. He may have a paternal. . . . He had that for me before. Most of them are younger. I would say he doesn't treat me any differently. He treats each person how he sees them. I feel he treats us the same. Like Lamiley, she's a senior wife too. I think we are all treated individually. I don't think we're classed, like this is Remi, she is up and they are down or anything like that. And if I talk to him differently, it's because I'm more or less his same age and I've lived with him longer, so I know him more.

Q: What is it you like the most in Fela?

A: There are a lot of things. Fela being Fela. I don't think I've ever seen or met anybody like him, so I think he's everything you'd want. I would say first his looks attracted me, but not now. Just being who he is.

Q: But there must be a way in which you can explain your feelings of attachment because you've been with this man for twenty years.

A: Twenty-one!

Q: Twenty-one years! There must be something which keeps you tied to this man in spite of all the upheavals and tumultuous living.

A: Most likely because I know he's honest and he's really doing what he believes. You know, he's trying for humans. It's mainly those two; plus, of course, deeper feelings.

Q: What are those deeper feelings?

A: I can't say love. He doesn't believe in love. But I would say love.

Q: But do you believe in love?
A: Yeah, I do.

Q: So you love him?
A: Yes.

Q: That's very important. I want you to tell me something now about your critical views of Fela, those things that irk you, that rub you the wrong way.
A: His generosity is the first. This was in the past and sometimes now. And I think sometimes his humanity is misguided. I can be pretty hard with people. You hurt me, I can't accept anything else from you. He's made me change that a bit and I don't like that change, 'cause if somebody does something to me I don't want to talk to them again. But through Fela I've had to learn to subdue that feeling. So that's one thing that annoys me. Sometimes I may think he's unfair about something but usually it turns out he's right anyway.

Q: Is Fela always right then?
A: No.

Q: And when he's not right, do you tell him he's not right?
A: Not always. Sometimes I tell him. He may later come and say I was right but at the time he'll not often accept it.

Q: But Fela isn't the type of man who accepts that he's wrong on the spot? Is that correct?
A: I think it depends on *who's* doing the telling.

Q: Well, *who* can tell him?
A: [*Laughter.*] His mother could. His brothers. His senior brother.

Q: But not you?
A: I can't remember if I've ever had to be proved on that. I can't remember.

Q: What have been your major disagreements with Fela?
A: The schooling of my children. That's about all.

Q: What's his line on this?

A: What his line was then, I didn't understand it and he didn't explain it to me. So, of course, we disagreed. I thought he just didn't want them to go to school because he didn't want them to learn. But then I learnt it's because of the system of education. I now agree with him on that, but I didn't at the very moment he said it.

Q: So that was your major disagreement with Fela?

A: We don't really have major disagreements. I've only had, I think, few big quarrels with Fela. Three times, I think.

Q: In twenty-one years?

A: Yeah. We have spats, of course.

Q: But what are the things you consider negative in Fela? Things you don't like; things you would like him to change?

A: Being overgenerous to people who don't deserve it.

Q: But Fela is also very authoritarian. How do you accommodate to his authoritarianism?

A: That's how I think a husband should be. [*Laughter.*] I don't believe in women's lib at all. I mean I don't believe a man should tell me I'm lower than him, but I don't believe in me going to drive a bus. That's left to a man, you know. Just that type of thing. These women in Europe, I don't agree with at all.

Q: How did you feel when Fela married his twenty-seven wives?

A: That didn't worry me. It was that he didn't come and tell me himself.

Q: He didn't consult you before?

A: No, he told my children. Although he told them two weeks earlier, they didn't tell me. That didn't worry me because the girls had always been there, even more than what he married. So there wasn't any problem over that.

Q: But why didn't he consult you?

A: I sometimes feel Fela's a little bit afraid of me. I really do. [*Laughter.*] He may never show it or admit it, but I feel it.

173

Q: So that gives you a certain leverage over him, doesn't it?

A: I don't think so. I don't class it as anything other than that he knows me so well and he's giving me extra respect for being what I am. I don't think he gives me authority or power.

Q: How do you find life in Nigeria, not being a Nigerian by birth or culture?

A: By culture, not by birth. I think I've always felt at home there. There are things I don't like which every Nigerian doesn't like. But I like it. I've always wanted to come back. I had always wanted to. Of course, sometimes, you know. . . . Somebody asked me the other day, "How did I adapt to no lights, no water?" But when I got there, there were all those things. So, of course, I'm just treated like every other Nigerian. You grow up with it. It was a gradual thing, the lights and that. So I don't say I've had to adapt to it anyway.

Fela's oldest son, Femi, alto saxophonist with Egypt 80
Photo: Chico

Fela with oldest daughter, Yeni
and son Kunle
Photo: André Bernabé

:la's younger daughter, Sola

Lamiley
Photo: Raymond Sardaby

NAA LAMILEY

"You Must See Inside Fire
No Matter How Hot"

Tall, lean, languid, Naa Lamiley has the grace of the older assured woman. She's constantly moving. Often caught slouching, hands in pockets, this only adds charm and youthfulness to her normally assured composure. Her slow, easy gait matches her deep sensuous voice. Lively, elegant, she likes telling stories which she vividly animates. A woman who likes to enjoy herself and for whom life is interesting. Dominant without appearing dominating, she has the inner strength of a woman who takes all things in her stride.

Born in Accra, Ghana, on 12 September 1949, to the Ga ethnic group, Naa Lamiley Lamptey was brought up in a strict Christian household. Although beaten severely by her mother, her father who "doesn't beat anybody" didn't care "about what you do provided you are happy doing it". From a polygamous family, she is one of nine children born to her father's two wives. After finishing secondary school up to Fifth Form, Naa Lamiley began working as museum technician for the Accra Museum. In 1973 she was granted a UNESCO fellowship to study museum techniques in Jos, Nigeria. The first of Fela's two Ghanaian wives, she met Fela in Accra in 1971 and is thus considered one of the senior wives. Lamiley works as a disc-jockey at the Shrine.

Q: So you've known Fela since 1971? How did you meet him?

A: I met Fela in Accra while he was there on a trip. He came to play. Very fortunately we were one day standing at the gate by our house, near the street and the next thing we saw was this taxi that came and stopped. And I saw Fela inside with one other friend,

177

Raymond Aziz, who I knew in Ghana very well.

Q: Did he talk to you?
A: He just say hello to everybody; greeted everybody.

Q: Had you ever heard his music before?
A: Yes. Well, I wasn't familiar with the music at that time, at all. I just hear the music; and knew it was Fela's music and that was all. It was when I went to Lagos that I started liking the music.

Q: OK. Now, seeing the man for the first time, what did you feel?
A: About him? I didn't feel anything about him. I just saw him as any other man.

Q: When did you see him again?
A: It was after he left, that this boy who was friend to him, told me, "Fela says he likes you." Then Fela invited us to where he was playing. We didn't go, so he came to our house the next day again. So from there he keep coming to our house.

Q: Did he tell you he liked you?
A: [*Laughter.*] He has already told somebody. So when he keeps coming I believe the boy. I keep seeing him any time he comes to Accra. Any time. Whether on holiday, private visit, or if he comes to play.

Q: And you started liking him?
A: Yes. Because I didn't meet him playing. When I met him, I met him as any other man. Then he keeps coming. Then one time, he invited me to come to stay in Lagos before 1975. But at that time, I was working and I didn't know anything and I didn't know how I can be on my own in another country.

Q: And what did Fela tell you?
A: He didn't tell me anything.

Q: But, finally, you just decided to leave?
A: Until then, I stayed with him for about three to four years. '71 I knew him. '72 he has been home. '73 he has been coming. Then in '73 I had a fellowship from UNESCO to go to Jos to do museum techniques. So when I went, on my way to Jos, Fela picked me up at the airport in Ikeja. I had to leave the next day, so I

left for Jos the next day.

Q: You spent the night with Fela?

A: Yes. We were at the Shrine and everything together. So I left him then in the morning to Jos. Then I kept coming from Jos whenever we are on holidays.

Q: You kept coming to see him?

A: To Lagos. He sends me a ticket to come to Lagos for a few days and go back after. So, during that time – coming from Jos to Lagos to meet him – I got close to him. So after I finished the course I stayed with him for about two weeks again in Lagos.

Q: By this time were you in love with him?

A: Yes. I'd got so close to him.

Q: What made you fall in love with him?

A: I just like him as any other man. I didn't like him because of the music, because I didn't understand his music at that time. He was speaking Yoruba, singing Yoruba music and *pidgin*. I didn't understand *pidgin* at that time. So I just like him as any other man. Which means, if hadn't been a musician, a popular man, anything he was, I would have still liked him.

Q: What is there so special about Fela, that makes him different from other men, for you?

A: Something special about him? There's nothing special about him.

Q: Well, why do you stay with him then? Why are you his wife?

A: I like him as a man. Just like anybody who see a man and like him. If he is the type of man you like, you will be with him.

Q: When did you start living with Fela at Kalakuta?

A: I wasn't living at Kalakuta. I was in the Crossroad Guest House, Ikorodu Road, a few yards from Kalakuta until the house was burnt down. After the house burnt down they came to live with me in my guest house. It was big enough for the whole group.

Q: So what did your parents think about you going to live with Fela?

179

A: Well, I didn't tell my parents I was coming to stay. I always come whenever I have my annual leave, and go back. So I had my annual leave in September. When they knew I was staying with Fela, they disapproved. . . .

Q: What is it you don't like in Fela?

A: There is only one thing I don't like about him. When two of the wives are quarrelling, when you just support one, but not the other.

Q: What would you like him to do?

A: What I want him to do is just to look at the whole thing – whatever anybody tell anybody. If you have mouth to answer, you answer. That's all. But if it comes to case – that is regulation in the house – you can't say this to this one and that to that one. We can go to him for judgment. But when we are in that *yabbis* (or whatever they call it) exchanging words, he must just stay back and look at both of us. But at times, you say something and Fela will come back and tell you, "You are directing your speech to *me,* not to the person you were arguing with!" Whereas in your own mind you think, "In my own mind, I am directing the speech to his other wife and not him."

Q: Has Fela ever beaten you?

A: Three times he's slapped me on my face. The first time was in Italy. It was nothing. Yes, twice in Lagos, once in Italy.

Q: Did you like the slapping?

A: No, I don't like beating at all. How can I like that?

Q: Do you ever feel that Fela discriminates you as being Ghanaian from the other queens?

A: AT ALL!!! NEVER, EVER!!! To me, he even care about the Ghanaians more than the Nigerians.

Q: OK. Well, what is it you like most about Fela?

A: I just like him as a man who I want to marry and love.

Q: Well, you are already married to him. Do you want to give him babies?

A: If the baby comes, it's good. If it doesn't come, I can't do anything. And he can't do anything about it either. [*Smiles.*]

Q: Tell me something now, what is it that you want most in life? What would make you happy in life?

A: Happy in life? As I am now, I am happy. Because I am married to the person I want to be with.

Q: So you don't want or need anything else?

A: I don't want anything else. Anything that comes our way I take. What do I need? I don't need anything? I have all I want.

Aduni
Photo: Bernard Matussière

ADUNI

"Sweet Thing Good to Own"

True to her name, Aduni has a disarming smile that sets off her almond-shaped eyes and high cheek-bones. An unusual and pleasant combination of features. Sometimes lively. Sometimes sullen and withdrawn, Aduni expresses either mood quite unexpectedly. But generally, she is both friendly and warm, and enjoys making friendships. Of medium height and a round slimness, she moves with the grace that befits her role as one of Fela's four dancers.

Yoruba in origin, Aduni Idowu was born to a business-man father and a trader mother in Lagos, Nigeria. From a polygamous family, her father has two wives and two children. Completing her primary education in Kano, Northern Nigeria, and speaking Hausa as well as Yoruba, she was unable to continue any secondary education because of the Biafra war. She confesses that although she "don't have brain for book", she does have an exceptional talent for dancing. In 1971 she met Fela.

Q: How did you meet Fela?

A: I and my friends, you know, they come to me that we should go to Fela's club. You know, to go and watch him. So we go there to watch the show and we see Fela. Then we like Fela now. Then Fela take us to his house with his Range-Rover at that time. So since that night I like Fela and since then I am with him.

Q: You made love to him that night, you mean?

A: No. I don't make love with him. I said since that time I like him and I am staying in his house.

Q: Did he tell you to come and stay, or did you ask him to stay?

183

A: I just like to stay there because Fela don't drive anybody.

Q: You went on your own?
A: Yes.

Q: Did your parents agree?
A: They agree.

Q: Why did you like him?
A: I just like his person. I like him, you know.

Q: What don't you like about Fela?
A: That question is difficult for me. You say what?

Q: You know, the thing you no go like for Fela? No dey like for him, beat you, something?
A: I can't say it's only one time he beat me. Not only once-o. Many times.

Q: But you like it when he beats you?
A: I don't like it-o.

Q: What else don't you like?
A: [*Laughing.*] I don't like Fela to beat me, but I like him. When he beat me I don't like the beating. But I like him as my husband.

Q: How do you get along with the other wives?
A: I don't fight with them. Something can bring our quarrel. We yab ourselves. Finish.

Q: Remi is 1961. You and Lamiley are 1971. That makes you the second or third oldest queen.
A: Yes, ending '71, I enter Fela's house.

Q: Are you a happy woman?
A: [*Laughs.*] Yes. But I want baby. Baby is number one.

Q: And what else do you want in life?
A: Many things. Good, good things, you know. Anything in this world that's good.

Q: Like what?
A: I want many people to know me. And I want to have money in my hand. You know, to do anything I want to do for myself. To enjoy myself, you know. To live in life.

184

Q: What are your ambitions?

A: Ah-ah! Me, I no agree for that thing-o! Me I no dey do horrors for nobody. . . .

Q: I don't mean that. I didn't say you were "ambitious".

A: Me, I only hear *oyinbo* language small-small-o!

Q: Well, what I meant was, what do you want in life?

A: Oooooooh, me?

Q: Yes, *you.*

A: I want be great woman. Dancer!

Q: Eh? You say you want to be a great woman?

A: Yes. I want many people to know me in this world.

Q: Why?

A: Why? I like people. I like meeting people. So I want many people to know me in this world.

Q: You want to be powerful?

A: Yes?

Q: A powerful woman? And how can you? As a famous dancer?

A: Ahuh. Yeah. They will know me. Everybody will know me, you know. I'm Fela's dancer, so many people will know me in this world. Because when Fela travel I am with him, you know. Where Fela go, I go with him, you know. So I meet many people in this world. So I want to meet some more people.

Q: And if one day a man come up to you and say: "Here is plenty money. You are a good dancer. Come away from Fela. I will give you money for you to dance." What would you say?

A: I can't go because of money. Because I like Fela personally. That's why I stay with him. And nobody can come and tell me that one. I won't agree.

Q: You love Fela, then?

A: Yes.

Kevwe
Photo: Bernard Matussière

KEVWE

"Graciousness"

Only an inkling of her former vivacious and outgoing personality remains. Kevwe's shattering and brutal experience at the hands of the soldiers who raided and set fire to Kalakuta in 1977 has indelibly left its mark. Three years ago, the breakdown came and she tried committing suicide. Fela had her attended to by herbalists. When that failed, she was sent back to her family where she stayed one year for treatment before rejoining Fela's household again.

Usually keeping to herself now, her perpetually sad eyes stare into space. Occasionally she smiles . . . begins to sing with her soft, broken voice. Still one of Fela's singers, she now lives on the fringes, isolated by the others who consider her "crazy". It is not unusual that she will suddenly disappear from the household for days and weeks on end, only to return. What she wants most is "to be a housewife, a singer and just to take care of my family, my children", for she would very much like having children with Fela.

Ethnically Itsekiri, Kevwe Oghomienor was born on 29 May 1956, in Jese, Sapele, Nigeria, to a polygamous family. Her father has two wives and seven children in all. Her parents, both teachers and of Christian belief, raised Kevwe strictly. Very young, she learned to play the piano in a religious context. When the family moved to Lagos in 1960, Kevwe continued her schooling up to Form Five. Desirous of becoming an artist, she left school, meeting Fela in 1972.

Q: Where did you meet Fela in 1972? In Lagos?
A: Yes.

Q: You went down to club?
A: No! I went down to his house with a girlfriend.

187

Q: He liked you or you liked him?
A: I liked him!

Q: And what did he say?
A: He decided to look after me.

Q: You told him, "I want to stay."
A: Yes, I told him that. And I gave him a wrong name.

Q: Why?
A: I wanted to bear that name. I didn't fool him because at that time my parents were coming after me then.

Q: They were coming to take you back?
A: Yes, but I refused. They brought police but police didn't find me. Then police came back again. I was hiding in house. So they did not find me.

Q: So, then you stayed on? Your parents gave up?
A: They gave up.

Q: Were you at Kalakuta when it was attacked?
A: Yes, I was there.

Q: What did they do to you?
A: They blind my eyes with gun. At first they came and shot house. I was bending down in the toilet, so as I heard the gunshot I just flew out in their midst. Then they give it to me. They beat me up, then they tear my pants. They took me. . . . Two soldiers, with heavy sticks . . . took me to room . . . put stick. . . . That's when I started shouting, "Mama! Mama!" Then I fainted. They kept me between them. . . . My nose was bleeding. I fainted and then I couldn't remember anything. When I woke up I saw myself on the floor with a girl called Kehinde. So I called her, "What's going on?" She said, "Everything is. . . . They're taking me to hospital." I'm gonna be in hospital too. In a minute's time they took her and she beside me. I was the last person they took. So they got stretcher and then they took me in ambulance.

Q: Fela told me that because of all that you fell very ill and he tried curing you with herbs. . . .
A: Yeah. But it didn't help. I was still very sick. So he go send me to my mama's.

Q: And what did your family do?

A: They take care of me altogether, all of them. They brought this woman doctor, a sort of herbalist, something like that. She taught me how to open my eyes. My eyes were closed completely. She was giving me herbs. She started curing me. For one year I couldn't see. . . . Then I go back to Fela's.

Q: What do you want to be in life?

A: I want to be a singer. [*Starts to sing.*] "There is a new world somewhere they call the Promised Land and I'll be there someday if you hold my hand. . . ." I like singing. Before I was the favourite, but now it's Funmilayo.

Q: So it is Funmi, the dancer, the one who's expecting a baby who is favoured?

A: Yes.

Q: But you used to be a favourite before?

A: Yes, before. But not again. Now I'm a favourite of Fela.

Q: So it's you and Funmi?

A: And Alake, Najite. And Fehintola.

Q: That means that there are five favourites. Do the others get jealous?

A: Yes.

Q: What happens when you fight among yourselves?

A: When we fight, hit someone, we pay 10 naira. For abuse, we get punishment, like wash house.

Q: You take turns in your sleeping arrangements with Fela. How does that work?

A: We take turns. My day is Monday. Kike too is on Monday. Aduni and Najite are on Tuesday. On Wednesday Ihase and Funmilayo. Adeola and Lamiley on Thursday. Remi and Aduni on Friday. Lamiley and Alake go again on Saturday. On Sunday, Kike and Najite who go sleep with him.

Q: So there are four who sleep with him twice a week and six once a week. What about the other five.

A: Yes. He calls the others any time he likes. 'Cause

189

when we are on tour, he calls them . It's he who calls them.

Q: If he doesn't call you for a week, ten days, do you have to wait?
A: Yes.

Q: What do you like about Fela?
A: I like his eyes.

Q: What do his eyes say to you?
A: The eyes say love. And I like his hands too, even when he beats me. His hands have something very, very beautiful. I like watching him when he eats. I watch him a lot.

Q: What don't you like about Fela?
A: I don't like his girls. I don't like his way of working; he works too much.

Q: You say, you don't like his girls?
A: I don't like them because they don't realize we're their sisters. They don't realize our friendly ways to them.

Q: You mean Fela's daughters?
A: Yes.

Q: You mean they don't get along with the queens?
A: Yes.

Q: You think he favours his daughters?
A: Yeah.

Q: What is he to you, a husband, a brother, or what?
A: He's a brother to me.

FUNMILAYO

"Give Me Happiness"

Funmilayo has a proud, unapproachable bearing. Dark brown in complexion. Large, melancholic eyes and high cheekbones. Her cool, rather haughty attitude detracts from her softly-sculptured face. Not often found in the company of the other queens, Funmilayo is the first of those who married Fela in 1978 to bear him a child.* She is one of Fela's dancers.

Funmilayo Onilere was born in Lagos, Nigeria, on 28 August 1956, of Yoruba parentage. Her father is a business-man in the shipping and forwarding line, while her mother is a clothes trader, both of them from Ikorodu, Lagos. Sent to a secondary boarding-school, where she completed her studies up to Form Three, she left school around 1971 and returned home. Unable to get her into a day school, her parents wanted her to go into trading with her mother, but she refused and left home. Not long afterwards she met Fela.

Q: Where did you go when you left home?
A: I went to a friend's house and from there we went to Fela's house. That was in 1972.

Q: How did you know about Fela?
A: I know about Fela before, but I didn't know if I can stay in his house.

Q: But why did you go to Fela's house?
A: 'Cause that my friend, she was living there, before me. She was living with Fela.

---

* Six-months pregnant at the time of this interview, Funmilayo gave birth in August 1981 to a boy, Olikoye, who died suddenly in April 1982.

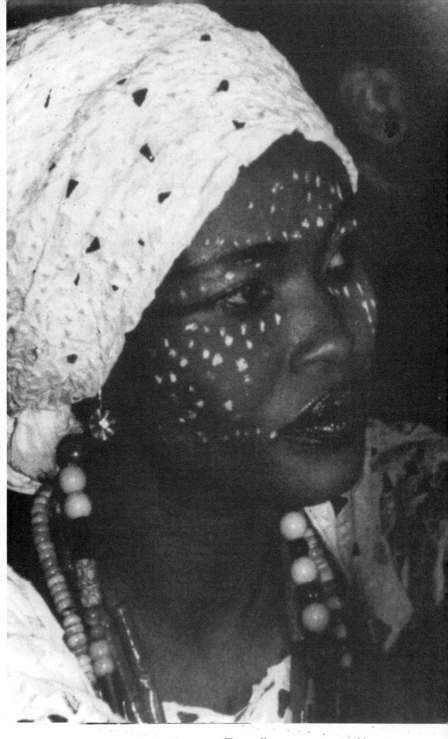

Funmilayo
Photo: André Bernabé

Q: Is she still with Fela?
A: No. She left Fela when the house burnt. Her name is Lady Ranco.

Q: And when you went up to see Fela for the first time, what did you tell him? "I want to come and live with you?"
A: Yes. So he asked me some questions. He asked me which job I want to do. So for some years I didn't do anything. I was just a disc-jockey. Playing music in the house. Then after I joined the dancers.

Q: But when he asked you what work you wanted to do, what did you answer?
A: I didn't tell him anything 'cause I didn't know how to dance.

Q: Did you love him then?
A: I wasn't really talking to him. I was just living in his house.

Q: When did you start loving him?
A: Around '74, '75. [*She looks bored.*]

Q: Yet, between '72 and '75 you used to make love to him. Not so?
A: Yes, but. . . . [*Answer inaudible.*]

Q: You didn't love him particularly? Is that what you said?
A: I love him, apart from making love. Since I've been in his house, I love him.

Q: Were you at Kalakuta when they attacked the house? Did the soldiers beat you? Did they wound you?
A: Yes. On my head. I had my hands broken. And they naked me. Then they took us to their barracks. We are the first people they took. Because when Fela left the house we are still inside the house. The house got fire in front of us.

Q: How long did the attack last?
A: About two hours. For two hours they were attacking, beating us 'cause they couldn't find Fela.

Q: Where was he?
A: He was in the other house. The Lebanese house. I

didn't see him, or some queens and some boys. I didn't see them throughout the attack. They all scattered.

Q: Were you taken to Kiri-Kiri, or to hospital?

A: Myself, I didn't go to Kiri-Kiri. I was in the hospital 'cause I was still not well. I was wounded for my head and my hands. [*Looking sad.*] I like to stay with him. . . . Maybe, I don't know, if they didn't burn Kalakuta, I could have gone. . . . [*Looking down.*] Gone. I don't know. Maybe I could have left too.

Q: But why is it that you stay because they burnt Kalakuta? I don't understand.

A: 'Cause some of us have left. We used to be many more than this. So some left. Maybe, they thought Fela has finished. But not me. I stay with Fela because I like his music, his ways, and I like moving with people.

Q: Moving with people? You like to live in a group? Is that it?

A: Yes. [*Looking very sad.*]

Q: But what are the things you don't like about Fela?

A: About Fela? . . . [*Long pause without answer.*]

Q: You have told me what you like with Fela. Now can you tell me what you don't like?

A: I don't like the way he is cheating me. [*Breaks down crying.*]

Q: Cheating you? He cheats you? How?

A: Like this morning when I went for the box. . . . [*Sobbing.*] Since yesterday he say I should collect the money from him; but I couldn't see Fela. Then he sent me to his senior wife. And me, I don't know, as we all have got married to him at same time I don't know how to talk to his senior wife. But Fela say I should collect money from her.

Q: You have problems with the senior wife?

A: All of us is like that. Sometimes she gets annoyed. Sometimes, she is cruel with us. As for me I don't know anybody. . . . [*Weeping.*]

Q: So you have problems with the senior wife?

194

A: Not actually; but I don't like Fela to be sending me to her. I like Fela to solve the problem himself.

Q: You are the first one of all the queens to be pregnant with Fela's baby. How do you feel about that?

A: I feel happy. But they don't make me feel happy. [*Weeping.*]

Q: But it doesn't make you happy?

A: THEY! . . . [*Sobbing, unable to talk.*]

Q: Oh, you mean the queens? You mean they are all jealous of you? You feel it really, eh? Why do you think they are jealous?

A: They show it. . . . [*Starting to cry again.*] They don't like me. . . .

Q: They are jealous that you are pregnant with baby for Fela, not them?

A: [*Silence. No answer. Deep sobbing.*] . . . Yes!

Alake
Photo: André Bernabé

ALAKE

"Chosen to Be Taken Care Of"

The perfect hostess. Warm, friendly and generous. She will make you feel at home at any time. Lively, affable, Alake loves recounting stories. Quite obviously, she enjoys life to the maximum. Graceful and self-assured, she projects elegance and stylishness. Above medium-height and fleshily round, her deep velvet brown is offset by sparkling, expressive eyes which shine even more when she smiles. And it is rare that she isn't either smiling, or laughing with that deep, husky voice which makes her one of the five talented singers of Fela's group. At present she studies astrology in her free time.

Born on 14 June 1956, in Ibadan, Olubokola Alake Adedipe is of Yoruba parentage. From a polygamous family, her father has five wives, with there being fourteen children in all. At the time of her birth, Alake's father (originally from Ijebu) was a lawyer but later became a High Court judge in Lagos. Her mother was a nurse's assistant who later went to London to become a registered nurse, then returned to Ibadan in 1971 to continue her nursing career. With this background, Alake attended elementary school in Lagos and secondary school at New Era up to Form Five. She was to continue her education in Lagos, but this did not materialize nor did she take the West African School Certificate exam. Consequently, Alake left school when she was seventeen years old, meeting Fela in 1973.

Q: And what happened then? Why did you leave school?
A: When I came to Lagos to study there was no boarding house, so I used to go from house to house. Then Yeni, Fela's first daughter, was in my school, Form One. Before then, you know Fela is popular in Lagos, the youth love his music; he was a bit ideological then.

It was my half-brother who first took me to Fela's nightclub where Fela was playing. Then I started liking the music, making my family buy me the records, and I'd listen to the records and everything. So when I was in New Era I used to go with my friends to Fela's club.

Q: You started going to Fela's club in 1973?
A: Yes. I was still in school. Friday and Saturday I would go to Fela's gig then.

Q: So you meet Fela in the club?
A: Yes. I like his music. I like his ideology. From then I used to come to his house, but my father didn't know about me going to Fela's gig and coming to his house. My father knew through my junior brother. You know he revealed the thing in the house. That day I'd been in Fela's house so before I came back to the house they'd planned for me that I choose Fela or I choose my father. [*Laughter.*] My father is very strict. Then in Nigeria they didn't like colonial children going to Fela's; they think that Fela corrupts the youth and all sorts of things. People going there smoking hemp. In Fela's house they rape girls, all sorts of untrue rumours, untrue things. My father is judge then. So we start to make discussion that either I take Fela or I take him. He told me he would stop paying my school fees.

Q: And what did you decide?
A: You know . . . me . . . in my family, I'm so different from all the other children because all of them are so colonial. It's only me, you know, that don't behave like them. All my friends they just got married. I don't move as these children, my brothers, their friends, they move around in the bourgeoisie, but me I love all the people because I don't like the way they (the bourgeois) treat the workers, the common people. I don't like it. But I can't do anything about it. Like in my family, the driver, the servants, they treat them badly. Even the way my stepmother treats our house, I don't like it. You should see it. You know I don't believe in that kind of thing, so I told my father that unless he explains why he doesn't like Fela – 'cause I like him – and if he doesn't want me to stay in his house I can choose where I'll stay. He didn't want for

198

me to leave the house and he didn't want me to go to Fela's house. There was nothing he could do then about my movements.

Q: So what did you do?
A: So I packed out of the house. I came to tell Fela that my father had sent me out of his house and I don't know where I will stay.

Q: And what did Fela say?
A: Fela asked: "Do you really want to leave your father, or shouldn't you go and talk to your father or find some of your relatives to talk to him?" I said I would do that later, but that that night I should have some place to stay. So Fela sent me to J.K.'s house.

Q: Oh, he didn't keep you in his house?
A: No.

Q: Had you made love to Fela by then?
A: [*Very long silence.*] Yes. [*Whispered.*]

Q: So he sent you to J.K.'s house?
A: Yes. So I packed all my things to J.K.'s house. So I was staying in J.K.'s house and fom there I used to go to school.

Q: Oh, you kept going to school?
A: Yes, I was still going to school. They paid already for that term so I was still going to school. When I started going to school my father planned. . . . You know, my father is working for the government, so he had some CID on me, coming to school to watch me. You know, sometimes I'd just be in class and I'd hear my name, the principal wants me. They were just giving me all sorts of troubles, so I went to see my uncle. I told my uncle everything. You know, my uncle is on my father's side. He said he wasn't the one who borned me and the only thing he can tell me is to go back to house and keep away from Fela. And I told him I can't keep away from Fela. If they don't want to take Fela, me I've taken him.

Q: You're still living at J.K.'s house?
A: Yes, I was.

Q: You were in love with Fela then?
A: Yes, I was.

199

Q: So you had made your choice?
A: I'd made my choice.

Q: And when did you move to Fela's house?
A: During then, I used to come to Fela's house; sometimes I'd sleep there. But I'd packed all my things to J.K.'s house.

Q: Had you started singing or dancing?
A: No, I was just there with some other girls.

Q: And when did you start living there?
A: The same year. About a month later. Because J.K.'s house is sometimes so boring. You know, there's just his wife in the house and me. So when the boys left the house it was boring, you know. I'd just eat alone.

Q: Then you started living in Fela's house in 1973? So you were one of his girls up to '77. You went through the horrible thing in February 1977?
A: Yes, I was there for everything.

Q: How was that attack?
A: Ooooooh.

Q: Fela told me that several of the girls were raped.
A: I wasn't among those who were raped, but it was true. And I even saw one being raped.

Q: You saw them being raped?
A: They stripped me too, naked! They removed all my pubic hair. They were messing us. You know, we were the last batch to be taken. I was with Fela. . . . When they came, they started burning the house, so we had to move to the second house, the Lebanese house behind our house. We were there when soldiers rushed upstairs and took us one by one. They stripped the women naked then; they would just tear your clothes off, your pants, start messing around with you.

Q: The soldiers?
A: Yeh, they did all that. They broke my head too. They did many things. They even. . . .

Q: They cut your head?
A: Yes [angry]. They knocked my eye out!! I saw the man who did it!! And anywhere I meet the man I'll recognize this man. I knew there were many but two

200

of them messed much with me, because one . . . [*deep laugh of pessimism*] . . . started sucking my breasts. Anywhere I see the man I will recognize him. There were two of them.

Q: Did any of your sisters get raped?
A: I saw one of them. But there were many it happen to. Many. Some of them have left. Many of the soldiers were drunk. You know when you cock a gun . . . . that's what iron they used in some women's vaginas. YES! Iron and bottles [*screaming*]!!

Q: You've been with Fela since 1973. What attaches you to him?
A: I don't even really know . . . so many things! You know, the kind of life I'm living with Fela is so different from the kind of life I've been living with my family. In my family they're very, very colonial. No freedom of speech. No freedom of movements.

Q: Would you say Fela is your new father?
A: Yes! Just father, husband, everything, everything you can think of. Because in his house I have my freedom. I'm free to do what I like. He has never forced me to do anything with him or with anybody. It's just like . . . you know, the kind of home I've been hoping to have and I've got it.

Q: What do you want in life?
A: To have a child for Fela. Then to go with child to village for a year or more to rest. For in the village is where I can learn about the African traditions which are being lost.

Adejonwo
Photo: André Bernabé

ADEJONWO

"We Are All Looking Up to the Crown"

With large, deep, warm eyes that are in perfect harmony with her highly pronounced cheekbones, Adejonwo's softly chiselled features make for a striking appearance. Of medium height and slight build, she has that kind of self-assured, slow and swaying gait of someone who enjoys living at her own pace. Of consistent disposition, she projects an inner calm and is always ready to engage you with a frank, warm smile.

Adejonwo Iyabode Oguntiro was born on 14 August 1955, in Port Harcourt, Rivers State, of Yoruba parentage. Her father is a retired Postmaster-General and her mother a seamstress and clothes trader. She attended secondary school up to early Form Four, and it was when she left to begin making her own living that she met Fela.

Q: How did you meet Fela?

A: I have been hearing of him for long. So, one day I was with about three others, going to work. I saw them (Fela and his group). They were going to court. So he sent somebody to say that he likes me.

Q: How did he see you?

A: We passed his house. He was in his house coming out. We were going to work. I didn't go in that very day. I decided to go after he had forgotten my face; forgotten everything. So I decided not to go into his house that day.

Q: But you really liked the man?

A: I like him. Yeh!

Q: Because he sent for you?

A: Not only that. I'd been hearing of him from school.

Q: Did you live around where he used to live?
A: Not very far. So, one day I went to his house with my friends. He entertained us. From there we went to his Shrine. Since then I decided going there with my friends. From there, he said he liked me.

Q: He told you that in Shrine?
A: No, in his house.

Q: Oh, you start going to house now?
A: Yes. I did not fall in love immediately, like that. It was about three or four days before I fell finally for him. So, then I started to like him.

Q: And that was what year?
A: 1974.

Q: And since then you have been with him?
A: Yes.

Q: When you told your parents you wanted to go and live with Fela, what did they say?
A: I did not really tell my parents I was going to stay with Fela. I use to go there for about four years. I use to go and come. I would go to his house.

Q: Go stay overnight?
A: Yes. Then go back home.

Q: Yes, but how did you tell your parents?
A: My mother knows quite all right. She knew I was at Fela's. Yeh!

Q: But what would you tell your father?
A: My father. I told him, "I like the man, I like his music. . . ."

Q: No! Where did you tell your father that you stayed overnight? With friends?
A: No. I use to tell him, "I am going to Fela." And I would stay there till morning.

Q: He didn't mind?
A: My mother?

Q: Your father?
A: I wasn't staying with my father then. I was staying with my mother only.

Q: Oh, so your mother didn't mind?
A: She mind, but she can't do nothing because I told her I like the man. You see what I mean?

Q: Then you started living with Fela in '74?
A: I'm not staying with him in '74. I started living with him in '78 when he was ready to marry us.

Q: So you were not at Kalakuta when they burned it down?
A: I was there.

Q: You were there when they attacked?
A: I was the one that slept in Fela's room that day.

Q: So the army abused you?
A: They beat me seriously. All my head, my eyes, this hand was broken. Look at this burn. My eyes, my head, everywhere was swollen.

Q: Tell me something, why are you with Fela?
A: Because he's the type of man I like. Secondly, he satisfies me. Before I got married to him he use to give me anything I want. The things he use to give to me when I was working, I don't use to have. I didn't use to have the amounts of money he gives to me. And he satisfies me.

Q: What is he to you? Father? Brother? Or husband?
A: Fela is a husband to me. I can't have my husband as my father. No way!

Najite
Photo: André Bernabé

NAJITE

"I Am Satisfied"

Small and thin with a creamy, light-brown complexion, Najite's classically sculptured Fulani-like face is often softened by broad smiles and a flashing of even white teeth. The impression she gives of being unabashedly imbued with her own importance tends to mar the force of her otherwise imposing looks. Frank, provocative eyes project a mischievous temperament. No one can deny, however, the impressive charm of her supple, willowy body as one of Fela's dancers.

Najite Mokoro was born 5 February 1960, in a village called Bacca, near Warri in Bendel State, Nigeria. Urobho ethnically, from a family of nine children, Najite was raised by her father – a trader – and his second wife after the death of her own mother when she was ten years old. In 1974 she left the place of her birth to go to Lagos and live with Fela.

Q: When did you meet Fela?
A: I meet Fela at Lagos in '74. . . . I was just passing Fela's house with a friend, and my friend showed me his house. After about three days I came to the area, so I saw Fela's Shrine. I saw the whole group and I feel to join. So I went in. When I got there, I like the way Fela do with all the women, there, all the boys there. He does not know me, but Fela give me short money. Anybody enter, Fela have to give everybody short money. So me myself I like the organization, so I join.

Q: You ask Fela, "I want to join?"
A: No. I don't tell Fela I want to join. I enter the house so Fela saw me and like me.

207

Q: And made love to you. *No be so?* (Isn't that so?)
A: Yes. [*Laughter.*] It was very fine-o.

Q: That's what makes you like the man? Or is it his political ideas?
A: I like the ideas and I like the ideology.

Q: Yes, but this "thing" came first?
A: I love that "thing" so much. And since then that's what turned my mind [*roaring with laughter*].

Q: Fela told me you were the first woman to be dragged outside when they attacked Kalakuta.
A: I am the first woman they take out of the house the day when they come and burn the house.

Q: Did they beat you?
A: Too much. [*Sad flash in her eyes.*]

Q: Did you bleed?
A: All my head they sew it with needle. . . . All my neck was broke. They plaster all over my neck. All my body. Sure, everything they broke in my body [*fighting back tears*]. . . . They rape some of our people too. Not me but some of our girls. The soldiers they take bottle . . . I saw it.

Q: And how long were you in Kiri-Kiri?
A: Me, my own very serious, I don't go to Kiri-Kiri then. They put me in the hospital. Yes, after there they take me for Lion Building* and then they come and bail me out.

Q: Najite, tell me, why are you with Fela?
A: Because I like him. I understand him. He fights for African freedom and I like him for that too. All of that again. He use to do for me very much, and no how, I don't know, I can't leave him. I just like him. I don't know why. Because what Fela can do for me my father can't do it for me, and my mother too can't do it for me.

Q: Is Fela your father to you? Your mother? Your brother?
A: He look like father to me and mother and brother to me too. He look like husband too to me, especially.

* Police Headquarters of Lagos State.

ADEOLA

"Crown of Wealth"

In contrast with her reserved disposition, Adeola is generous with her wide smile that radiates with refreshing frequency. Of average height and plumply slender, her broad, round face is studded with large, sensitive eyes and an expression of alert awareness.

Of Yoruba parentage but born in Accra, Ghana, on 23 May 1958, Adeola attended primary school in Ghana. Brought up in a polygamous family of twelve children, her father – a businessman – has two wives, her mother being a trader. Leaving Ghana with her family at the age of eleven she attended secondary school in Oyo State, Nigeria. A few years later she was to meet Fela.

Q: How did you meet Fela?
A: I met him in 1974. See, I'm staying with my sister, so in our house we use to play Fela music, so one day we just play Fela's latest, "Jeun Ko'ku". So, when I hear the music I just like the music. So I say, "Ah! By all means I must join this man's group."

Q: You were there when they raided Kalakuta?
A: Yeah. Kalakuta raid, 18 February, I was there!

Q: Did they hit you?
A: They hit me a bit. . . . [*Reluctant to continue.*] I was among the girls they. . . . [*Saddened.*] There were about four soldiers. . . . [*Looks away.*]

Q: Four!
A: They want, you know. . . . Two of them hold a bottle of whisky. They broke the bottle on my head, 'cause I don't want to agree with them to do it. So they want to

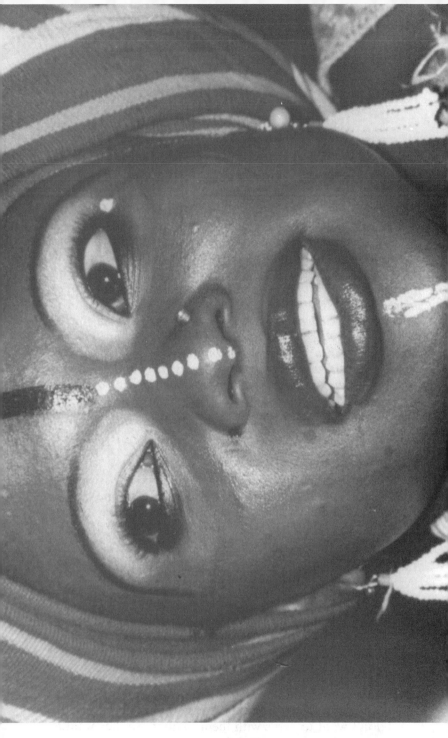

Adeola
Photo: André Bernabé

open my legs. . . . So one of their *oga* [bosses], you know, he just came round. So he asked them: "What are you doing?" So they said they didn't do anything. They say they don't want to do anything with me. So they stop everything. They just leave me. And they carry everybody go. So, I hide under the bed until everything go down; then I move to one man house near ours. The man is our tailor. So, I move to his house and I stay there until the next day.

Q: Hmm. Tell me something: How is your life in Kalakuta? Are you satisfied?

A: Of course I am satisfied with Fela now. Since I know that Fela is satisfying me. Everything I would like him to do he will do it for me. So I am satisfied with him.

Q: What is he for you? Father? Brother? Husband?

A: Fela is a husband to me. . . . Just husband. [*Smiles.*]

Q: How do you get along with the other wives?

A: Most, some. . . . [*Pauses.*] Some of the wives we move together. We eat together, you know. We do the same things.

Q: You get along with them?

A: Yeah.

Q: You have arguments once in a while?

A: Yes, we have arguments once in a while. Sometimes over Fela, or some other matter. . . . Sometimes we argue about clothes, or about what we want to eat, you know.

Q: About who should cook, things like that?

A: Yes, something like that. We would have our quarrels. [*Smiles.*]

Q: What do you want to do in life?

A: I want to be an artist.

Q: Is that what you always wanted to be?

A: Yes, I want to be an artist. I want to go to a school of music to learn how to play music and how to be an actress, too. Like my husband. . . . If I don't get to be a musician, I just want to be an actress. That's what I want.

Kikelomo
Photo: Raymond Sardaby

KIKELOMO

"Babies Are Precious"

Dark brown-hued, with a pear-shaped face, Kike's elongated eyes reveal a cool, distant temperament. The charm of her wide, bright smile is all too rarely seen. Perched atop spiky heels, she looks even taller and tinier than she actually is. Not one for conversing, hers is one of the two shortest interviews. At present, she is one of Fela's disc-jockeys.

Born in Ikeja, Lagos, Nigeria, on 30 June 1959, Kikelomo Oseyni is of Yoruba parentage. Sparse with any additional details on her childhood and family, Kike met Fela in 1974.

Q: Why did you join Fela in 1974?
A: Because I like his music.

Q: You didn't join him because you like him as a man?
A: Yes, I did because I like him.

Q: Were you in love with him?
A: Yes.

Q: In 1974, did you run away from home? What did your parents say when you left to live with Fela?
A: No, I didn't run away. I didn't tell my parents until later. . . . They agreed with me.

Q: Were you in Kalakuta when they attacked the house?
A: Yes. They broke my head. They beat me up and naked me. They pulled my private thing. Many things.

Q: What do you want to do in life?
A: I don't know yet.

Q: So you have no ambitions in life?
A: I just like to be Fela's wife.

213

Ihase
Photo: André Bernabé

IHASE

"The Ifà Oracle Should Be Respected"

Tiny and thin to a point of fragility, Ihase's strength rests in her quiet assuredness. Although youthful in appearance, she has a maturity greater than her years. Never imposing but always kind, soft-spoken and quick to smile. Oval-faced and mango-tinted brown, she spends much time on her appearance, but always in a natural, unaffected manner. She is a young girl who knows what she is about, whether on stage as one of Fela's singers, or off. She is presently studying traditional medicine.

Born on 26 August 1960, near Benin in Bendel State, Ihase Osayemeri Obotu is ethnically an Ejor. Her father has four wives and there are eleven children in all. According to Ihase, her father – a teacher – has "a real colonial" mentality, but her mother – a trader – is "an authentic African woman". Attending secondary school up to Form Three, Ihase quit her studies and went to Lagos in 1975, heading straight for Fela's house.

Q: Why did you quit? You weren't satisfied with life at home?

A: Yes, because when I wanted to go out with my boy-friends or play with my friends or go to pictures, enjoy myself, I don't have the chance. Until I had Fela and his music. . . . You know, I wanted to quit, go somewhere else, maybe stay with my friends before. . . . When I listened to his music and went to his show I was really put in 'cause I wanted to be with him.

Q: When did you meet Fela?

A: The first time was when he came to Benin to play. 1973. I went to his show. . . . Before then, I learnt that girls stayed in Fela's house, that he kept girls in his house. So, after watching the show that night I wanted to go with him to Lagos. Right straight from the stadium I wanted to go with him to Lagos. But I couldn't have the chance because my brothers wouldn't allow me to go that night. I was still in school then, '73, '74, '75, Class Three then. So something just happened that really made me fed up. So I took 28 naira from my father's pocket and ran to Lagos.

Q: You went to Fela's house? What did he say?
A: I told him I liked his group and I wanted to be part of it. He said OK and he took me.

Q: He took you into his house? Then what happened?
A: I stayed there and the next day I became his singer, just the next day. At first I didn't like him. I just took him as a father or as a person older who would take care of me. Then later, he sent for me that I should come to him. I didn't understand what he meant by that. So, I went to him and he said I should love him. Just like that, that I should love him. I haven't really understood that. He told me to sit down on the bed and he asked me if I'd like to drink. I said I didn't drink. Then he asked me to remove my dress and at that point I knew what he would do with me, that he likes me. So we made love to each other. It was after making love that I started liking him.

Q: Were you at Kalakuta when it was burnt?
A: Yes. I'd come in 1975.

Q: Were you one of those who were raped?
A: No, but I saw one being raped. I saw that one and saw it was going to be my turn. They were beating everybody. They break my head. You know, my cunt here they pull on it like this and then they break my head. Oh! My inner testine was bleeding.

Q: You were bleeding from the mouth?
A: No. From my private parts, because of the damages I had in my stomach. I was bleeding 'cause they wounded me there with stone.They shook me with stone, then they were beating my stomach, and I had some injury in my stomach. So after beating me I had

so many wounds on my head, they took me to Lion Building. After, they burn the house.

Q: How long were you all in prison, you girls?
A: We went there on Monday, five days in Kiri-Kiri.

Q: But tell me something, what is it you like about Fela?
A: Many things: one, the main thing is that I really like him now.

Q: You love him?
A: Yes. And secondly, his ideas. Before I didn't really know what I am. I looked up to white man as the master of everything. His ideas really make me like him too. And the love I have for him.

Q: The love you have for him, what type of love is it?
A: Many things. Love is many things, like giving him food, or the way he sleeps with me, or what he does for me. Those ones, these are the loves I have for him.

Q: Tell me, you have a special day for sleeping with Fela.
A: Every nine days, nine days. That is my time. Alake is every week, like today, Tuesday. . . .

Q: Why Alake more often?
A: You know, it depends on what you do, because Alake was in the house first. But Fela does not sleep with us by seniority. He sleeps with us according to what you do, because we have to make our husband satisfied.

Q: So, if you do something wrong he doesn't sleep with you. How do you call that punishment?
A: I have served the punishment.

Q: Yes, but they have a name for it?
A: Yes, edit. Like a week, two weeks. [*Laughing.*]

Q: Two weeks without fuck, that's heavy punishment.
A: That's heavy punishment, man. That's just a new punishment. That one really hooks us. If we mess around, two weeks, one month. . . . So we be careful.

Omowunmi
Photo: André Bernabé

OMOWUNMI

"I Like Children"

Quiet and reserved, with a girlish-type simplicity, there is nothing flashy about Omowunmi. She adds only a few touches of make-up to her deep-brown complexion. Rarely does she appear in public without an elaborate headwrap, the kind which best emphasizes her soft, full and very round face. Of medium height, small-boned but fleshy all the same. Often keeping to herself, Omowunmi is a shy, young girl, who of all the queens was the most intimidated by this interview.

Born in Lagos, Nigeria, in 1961, to parents of the Beni ethnic group, originally from Bendel State, Omowunmi Afesnay completed her primary schooling and part of her secondary studies in Lagos. It wasn't long before she met Fela.

Q: Omowunmi, where were you born?
A: I was born in Africa-o.

Q: I know that one. I want to know where.
A: Ah, I don't want to talk this thing.

Q: It is Fela who has said that I should come and. . . .
A: No! Not everybody. 'Cause I don't be ready for this-o. [*Long pause.*]

Q: Look, me I don't care-o! It's your husband who said I must talk to all the queens, or none at all.
A: OK. Go ahead. . . .

Q: When did you meet Fela? What year?
A: '75.

Q: Did you run away from your family's house?
A: No. How can I run?

Q: To go to live in Kalakuta. That's what I mean.
A: Why? I no have to run.

Q: Your family agreed, then?
A: Yes.

Q: They said it was all right?
A: Yes. . . . [*Looks away.*]

Q: Were you at Kalakuta when the army attacked?
A: I was not in the house. [*Long pause.*]

Q: Tell me, why did you marry Fela?
A: Because I like him.

Q: What do you like? The music? The man? His ideas?
A: Everything with the organization I like.

Q: What is your ambition in life?
A: [*Long pause and no answer.*]

Q: What do you want to become? An actress, a musician, a dancer?
A: I am a dancer. [*She gets up, ready to leave.*]

OMOLARA

"Child of the People"

With a tallness accentuated by her slender, angular torso and long-leggedness, Lara has a sort of boyish lankishness. She's ebony-hued, with short-cropped Afro, large round eyes, a warm, open smile and a deep, husky voice. Withdrawn at times, Omolara alternates between sombre moodiness and carefree joviality. She is happiest when performing on stage, for dancing is what she enjoys most.

Born in Ijebu, Nigeria, to Yoruba parents, Omolara Shosanya comes from a polygamous family. Her father (now deceased) had two wives and six children with both. Attending primary school in Ijebu as well as secondary up to Form Two, Omolara quit her studies at that time since, as she says, "I don't like book too much," and, "I wanted to be free and enjoy myself." Not long thereafter she met Fela.

Q: So, when you quit school you came to Fela?
A: Yeah.

Q: Why?
A: I hear with Fela you can live free.

Q: Your friends told you that?
A: No. I hear Fela's songs.

Q: Oh, and you like it.
A: Yeah. That's why I came.

Q: To Lagos?
A: No. I get sister from Lagos. When I leave Ijebu, I go to my sister's house. I stayed with my sister for about three years. So, '76 I come Fela house.

Q: Oh, in '76? That's before Kalakuta thing?
A: Yeah.

Omolara
Photo: André Bernabé

Q: You come and start living there? What did you tell him when you come? "Fela, I want to live with you?"
A: I tell him I want to come live with him, and he said: "All right, you can."

Q: And you started just like that?
A: Yeah! Just like that.

Q: And you just started making love to the man immediately?
A: Yes. Just like that.

Q: Was it good?
A: Very good, very nice. Too nice. [Laughs.]

Q: So you liked it, and that's why you stayed?
A: Yeah. That's it.

Q: Any other reason?
A: I stay because I like his way. The way he talks.

Q: What do you like in Fela most? The man? His mind? His sex?
A: I like his mind.

Q: That's what you like the most?
A: Yeah. And I like his prick. [Laughter.]

Q: Mama mia! Is "it" special?
A: Yes. It be good-o. Na sweeter than sugar-o.

Q: Oh, my God! Let's go on to something else. Tell me, when the army attacked Kalakuta, were you there?
A: I'm there, man.

Q: Did they attack you?
A: They shook me under here. . . . [Points to her sex.] I get one private wound. When they take me outside – 'cause all of us are rushing. When the army enter like this . . . [gesticulating violently] . . . me and some of the queens are inside Fela's room. So the army attack Fela room. They open and they catch all of us. When [nervous laugh] they catch me, they put me outside. They beat me, open my legs and shook my private thing with bottle. And one man says, "No, no, no! Leave that girl alone!" And they leave me. They beat me, beat me, beat, beat, beat! . . .

223

Q: Did you see any of the queens raped?
A: I don't see any rape. They raped some queens, but I don't see. Me myself, I hear that one later, but I don't see with my two eyes.

Q: Tell me something, what things don't you like about Fela?
A: I like everything.

Q: OK. What are the things you don't like with the other queens, then. Because sometimes you have fights among you?
A: That one doesn't mean anything. We can fight anytime, we can talk anytime.

Q: But do you fight with fist? Do you hit each other sometimes?
A: Oh, it can happen. I don't hit anybody. We fight sometimes; and we can quarrel anytime. We talk anytime.

Q: What do you want in life?
A: Ah, I want pregnant. I want to born pikin* that's for Fela. That's what I want in my own life.

Q: And what else?
A: I want something else. [*Pensive.*]

Q: What?
A: To enjoy my life, if I can before I die.

Q: Are you afraid of death?
A: Ahh! Anytime I can die. That is why I am here now, to enjoy my life 'cause I can die any time.

* Pidgin meaning child.

FEHINTOLA

"Resting on Wealth"

Long, lanky and roundly thin, Fehintola has a slow, unperturbed, and rather lofty gait. Hers is not an outgoing personality, though when she smiles one would never know, for her deep-ebony, pear-shaped face becomes warmly radiant. Reservedly off to herself, and of an impassive temperament, she is usually seen attending to her appearance. Fehintola is one of Fela's singers.

Of Yoruba parentage, Fehintola Kayode was born on 25 October 1959, in Ipoti-Ekiti village in Ondo State, to a large polygamous family. Her father, a retired colonial soldier who now does trading, has nine wives, and some thirty children. Educated in her village, she finished primary school and did three years of secondary. Upon leaving her village in 1976, Fehintola went straight to Fela's house.

Q: How did you meet Fela?
A: One day I just decided to join any musician that has name and get the sense of music.

Q: So you joined Fela because you liked music?
A: Yeah.

Q: Not because of Fela?
A: Ah, it is because of Fela. Because I like Fela and I like the music.

Q: And were you living in Lagos?
A: No, in my village.

Q: So you ran away from your village?
A: No, I didn't run. I just tell my parents that I can't stay with them any more and I left the house in '76. I come straight to Fela's house. I told him I wanted to stay with him.

Fehintola
Photo: André Bernabé

Q: And what did he say?

A: And he told me that whether I can stay, I say I will stay. He say OK, I should stay. And I stayed.

Q: And you made love to him that day?

A: No. After about two weeks.

Q: And then what happened?

A: Nothing happened, I enjoyed everything and I satisfy and I stay.

Q: OK, that was 1976. So that means you were there when Kalakuta was attacked and burnt.

A: Yes, they beat me, shook me and abused me with bottle and knife. When they take me to the hospital people don't know that there is bottle inside my body and they saw the bottle and knife on my body so they carry me to Kiri-Kiri. . . . The knife was in my body; they sew it together.

Q: They put knife in your body?

A: Yes, and some bottle like this. They sewed on my body. So afterwards at police station they took us to court. After court we went to Kiri-Kiri. That is where the prison yard is.

Q: How long were you in prison?

A: About one week, let's say five days. After I left the hospital they took me to hospital again to go and do operation for me, remove the bottle in my body.

Q: But tell me something, you have suffered in your life with Fela. What makes you stay with Fela?

A: First because I believe in what Fela is doing.

Q: So that means that you believe in him politically.

A: Yes. I believe in what Fela is doing and I believe in his political. . . .

Q: How would you consider him? As a husband? A brother? Or as a father? How do you see him?

A: I see him as my father, as my husband, as my mother because he takes care of anything in life.

Sewaa
Photo: Raymond Sardaby

SEWAA

"The Beautiful One"

Feline-featured and velvet brown, Sewaa is often off to herself and quiet, her large doe-like eyes absorbing everything around her. She is generous with her smile, her youthful laughter accentuating the softness of her expression. Voluptuous and of medium height, with an agility that makes her an excellent dancer, she is kind and sensitive in character, always pleasant whatever the occasion.

Born to a polygamous Ashanti family on 1 June 1960, near Abisua, Ghana, Sewaa comes from a family of nine children. She grew up helping her grandmother in her shop in Accra before meeting Fela there in 1977, Sewaa is Fela's second Ghanaian wife.

Q: When did you meet Fela for the first time?
A: I met Fela in '77. In Accra when he had a concert.

Q: Did you know his music before? Did you like it?
A: Yes. And my grandmother too like the music.

Q: She likes it?
A: For me, I don't know Fela before, but we just hear the music. So if my grandmother want to do party for house, they go like some slow music. Then one day she say she want to go party with Acheampong, the president before. So she go buy new record of Fela.

Q: Was your grandmother a friend of Acheampong?
A: Yes.

Q: And she went to a party of Acheampong?
A: And she took Fela record. I didn't go the party that day. Fela music she like. Because the sound, the beat; they take dance. We be playing Fela's records every

day for house. My brothers they buy any record because they like to hear music sometimes.

Q: How did you meet Fela?
A: One of my friend, a girl – her name now Elizabeth, Lizzy. So she come to tell me, say she go get one new boyfriend name Nabayo. The boy plays. So my friend, the girl, we go get the boy and reach where Fela dey stay for the hotel. We go upstairs and sit down there. When I go there, Fela there. I think Fela is asleep. I just see one man sit down with pants. With pants. Fela! I didn't know him before.

Q: OK. And what did he say to you?
A: So the boy just come and him say Fela say he want go see me.

Q: But you're talking too fast. Talk slower.
A: That's how I de talk. [*Laughing.*]

Q: OK.
A: He said Fela say he want to see me at night, that day. Then I tell him I can't go stay 'cos I go fear 'am.

Q: You were afraid of him?
A: Yes.

Q: Why?
A: Because everybody talk about Fela. Smoking hemp.

Q: And you'd never smoked hemp before?
A: No. So they talk bad about Fela. The next day we go Fela club. We go dance. And there be one man they call Abajungwo, they come meet me. They say Fela say after he finish the show he wants to see me.

Q: And what did Fela say to you?
A: Then I go. He say make I come meet 'am for hotel the next day. Next day I bring my grandmother motor there. They wait for me with the driver. Me and that friend, Lizzy, go to the hotel. Then he give us food. We eat. Then he tell Abajungwo to go take me to any club, make I go drink anything what I want. Then in the night me and Abajungwo we go club. I just meet him another day again. So for night, he tell me saying they go, the morning, the next day.

230

Q: Fela was leaving?

A: Yes. So he say if I want to go with them. I say I feel for 'em go, but my mama she dey for Accra. If he feel I go, I say make I go, less my mother travel.

Q: Did he tell you he liked you?

A: Yes. No. I don't know. I can't say, because when a man say he want to get something, it mean he likes you.

Q: That means he liked you. But did you like him then?

A: Yes. [*Laughing.*]

Q: When did you leave Accra and come to Lagos?

A: March '78. When I come my mother died.

Q: OK. So you started living with Fela in Kalakuta. How was life at the beginning? Did you have problems with the other queens?

A: Oh, we go fight with ourselves, but we can fight anytime and we can settle anytime.

Q: And you have problems of jealousy among the queens?

A: Some are jealous. I don't know whether some (others) are jealous. We do fight.

Q: So when you fight what happens? Who separates you? Is it Fela?

A: Sometimes. No, only one day I fight with one queen. because when the two women they fight, Fela go leave us to fight ourselves, but Fela sometimes he wants put himself inside. So when me and one girl fight, Fela come and stand with the girl. He come there and *yab* me for the girl.

Q: Has he ever beat you?

A: He beat me three times.

Q: Three times?

A: He beat me six one time. Bang! Bang! Bang! Six. The next one he give me three. Another time he just give me one bang on my back, because I say I no go do practice. No be saying because of another woman. Because I say I no go do my work. Me, I don't want to have pain in my life.

231

Q: Tell me, what don't you like with Fela?
A: When him beat me. That be the only one I don't like. Finish. Everything else I like.

Q: What do you like the most with Fela?
A: [*Laughing.*] I just like Fela because sometimes he no get money or he get trouble. So sometimes when somebody get problem, he come tell Fela, then Fela go settle for the person, or he would give the person money. And that too why I like 'am.

Q: OK. But what is it in the man that you like the most? Why do you love him?
A: [*Laughing*] I don't know. Me, I just like 'am. I like the ideology. The way he do. The way he pity for another person. The way one person get trouble he help 'am for trouble. The way he deal with the people, 'cos no be only Nigerians Fela like. Fela like and I be Ghana and he be a Nigerian man. So he make me like 'am.

Q: Good. What is he for you? A father? A brother? A husband?
A: A husband. He's my husband and we be friends – a brother.

Q: Do you get everything you want in life?
A: Yes.

Q: So you're happy?
A: YES! When I see Fela, he say I get anything I want.

Q: What do you want to be in life?
A: I want to be a millionaire. I want to get like all the houses. Make them be my own. Me, if I get two thousand houses I don't mind. And if I be rich, I go help sickness people; those people ill in paralysis, I can help them.

Q: What do you do now at Kalakuta?
A: I'm a dancer.

Fela in concert with his queens

Photo: Chico

20

What Woman is to Me

*"Mattress", "Lady"**

What I think about women in general is a subject which calls for a colloquium. Women? Mmmmmm! You see, before I used to be afraid of them. That's how it started. After that, fear changed into understanding. What do I understand about women? First, that they like to be slept with. They like you to make them do things for you. They're like Satan in that stupid book, the Bible: they like to test you, so that they can get away with something. If you let them get away with it once, you're in trouble. But if you stop them from getting away with it, then they'll stop.

What else? If a woman really likes a man, she doesn't really mind sharing him with other women. Yeh, I understand many things about women. Women isn't anything you should be afraid to talk to. But they're not on the same level with men. Men and women are on two different levels. You can say different wavelengths. Man. Woman. Two points that can never meet. Women have different feelings than men. It's as simple as that. You can't compare them. Equality between male and female? No! Never! Impossible! Can never be! It seems the man must dominate. I don't want to say so, but it seems so. Why?

Well, let's put it another way. What can a woman do to rule the world? You see, to rule the world you have to do very heavy work, like agriculture, etc. Understand? You have to build houses. Understand? You *have to* build. And building is hard work. It's a man's job. Producing babies is

---

* Two of Fela's big hits, which sum up his ideas about women. "Mattress": the woman's function in life is to serve as a mattress for man who lies on top for . . . rest! "Lady": a satirical attack on "modern" African woman (who refuses to cook and insists on eating at the same table as men); while praising the virtues of the traditional African woman (passivity, submissiveness, obedience, etc.).

woman's job. It's more tender. The more vigorous job is man's. The tenderer one is woman's.

The position of women? Do I see man as being naturally superior to women? Naturally. Why? Well, I wouldn't say superior. I'd say *dominant*. Yes, dominant. Dominant is the word I want, not superior. Dominant means that there must be a master. Men are the masters, not women. When you say the "master of the house", you mean the head of the household: the father, not the woman, man. That's life, man. Natural life. Life is based on nature. The nature we don't see now. You can't ask me "Which nature?" 'cause you can't see nature. You understand?

What I'm saying is that there's a natural order which says that man must be dominant. Yeah! The advantage is that one has more strength, can carry heavy loads. He can even carry the woman when she is tired. More strength. But the woman is more subtle. She is more passive and that is the way it's supposed to be, 'cause that enables her to take care of the house. You can't have two dominances. One must be dominant and the other passive. Then you have a smooth life. There must always be a leader. Even among spiritis, there's a head spirit!

It's part of the natural order for women to be submissive to man. Yeah. Africans know that one. We don't have to argue about that one. 'Cause let women come and carry heavy load and you'll see. They call men to do the heavy things they can't do. So what's all this women lib about? Let them come and do exactly what men are doing, man. Let them come and start to build roads. What's the matter with them? Are dey craze, or what? When they can do man's job, then we can talk about women's lib, if you want. Not before!

What's the woman's role? To keep the home smooth, the children happy, the husband happy. To make the husband happy, that's a woman's job. Women got no other work than making the man happy. 'Cause when the man is happy, he can move mountains. That's all. Women today are not making men happy, man. They are constantly confusing the man's mind. So there's no happiness. There's too much deceit, too much confusion going on. The Christian woman and the Muslim woman – oh, yes, too much bullshit, man! The non-Christian African woman is much more together. Well, I mean they don't argue in the house. To

235

them, the man is always right. That's the point: the man is always right; they don't argue. 'Cause when the man is wrong, he will repair his wrongness by himself. He will apologize by himself. If he makes his decision, and he's wrong, he will always repair it. 'Cause it's better for a man to make the decisions and learn for himself, from his mistakes.

If he's the right man anyway he won't want anything bad for his family. That must be clear. No man wants anything bad for his family. The woman must understand that. When a man decides something, he must have his reasons. And if the woman disagrees she must let him do it anyway. 'Cause if he makes mistakes he'll be apologizing. He'll always come back to apologize, 'cause he's the man of the house.

That thing they call women's lib is against the natural order of the world. It comes from European religions. Their religions didn't teach them properly. They teach that man and woman are equal in the house, for better and for worse. No, man, that's bullshit! There's no *for better and for worse*. Nobody can force a woman to stay with a man she don't want. Nobody can force a man to stay with a woman he don't want.

If a woman don't like a man, she should leave and go find another man. That's why polygamy is fantastic! Monogamy was imposed by religion. It's against the natural order. Unless all mankind can tell me they don't fuck any other woman but their wife. It's unnatural, man. 'Cause men just have to go for other women. Why? You explain it! Nobody can explain it. It's just a natural phenomenon. But it's been proven that a woman can stay with one man if she likes him enough. A man with many wives is natural. A woman with many men is not. Yeah. The woman can be satisfied with one man. Besides, women can stay without sex. They can do it but men can't. Why? Go ask nature, man! Different sexual structures, that's all.

Sex! It's beautiful, man! But there are taboos on sex in all societies. People search for sex in porno books, magazines, films, press. That's 'cause they don't have sex in bed. If you're fucking well like you should, you won't go looking for sex in a book or in a film. What for? Take my marriage, for example. Why do you think so many journalists showed up? They just wanted sexual sensationalism, man! Because of the taboos on sex. Why has sex been made into something shameful? Fucking religion, man. That's why. Christianity and Islam made sex immoral. What's sex, anyway?

Sex is a gift of nature. So why do men make laws to check it? A law deciding whan a woman's ready to fuck. Another law saying where to fuck. And soon one to tell you which day to fuck. When a woman's ready, she'll tell you, man. Not some law. Some women are ready when they're nine; some when they're thirty. What's natural can't be *illegal*. The only kind of sexuality that's against nature is homosexuality. 'Cause it don't create life. When I told Nigerian students at the University of Ife that in Holland they allow men to marry men in churches, they were shocked. They couldn't believe it. "Impossible!" They said I was lying. I told them: "How can I, Fela, lie to you? After all these years, why would I start lying to you now?" No. That thing isn't natural. The cause? It's caused by them, man. Pollution. Environment, man. Religion. The law that says: "Don't fuck until you're sixteen," turns men into homosexuals and women into lesbians. Yeah, I think it's caused by the food they eat, their diet. Too many chemical foods. Not enough natural foods. Pollution, religion, and food. Those, I think, are the causes of homosexuality.

You see, if you study the human body properly, nothing gives pleasure but sex. Nothing else. Your leg doesn't give you pleasure. It makes you walk. No orgasms, man. Your hand makes you carry weight, touch things. No orgasms either. Your eyes make you see violence, see things that you don't want to see, man. But no orgasm. So the only thing that gives pleasure in the body is sex. Why should it be immoral? Why should sex organs be "dirty" and feared? They should be worshipped. They should be worshipped every day. It should be seen as something positive, not negative. Sex should be something people participate in properly, with joyfulness and happiness. OK, maybe people have to hide to do it, yes. But not hide *shamefully* to fuck. Shame and privacy are not the same. Having sex must be a proud and joyful thing. People should be proud to say: "Last night I had a fantastic fuck!" Not a thing to whisper: "I'm having sex-o, but I'm sad." Sex *is* clean. But by bringing human laws into it, it's made "dirty". Sex is life-giving. Sex is joy! Pleasure! Happiness! To fuck! That's one of the most important things in life, man.

237

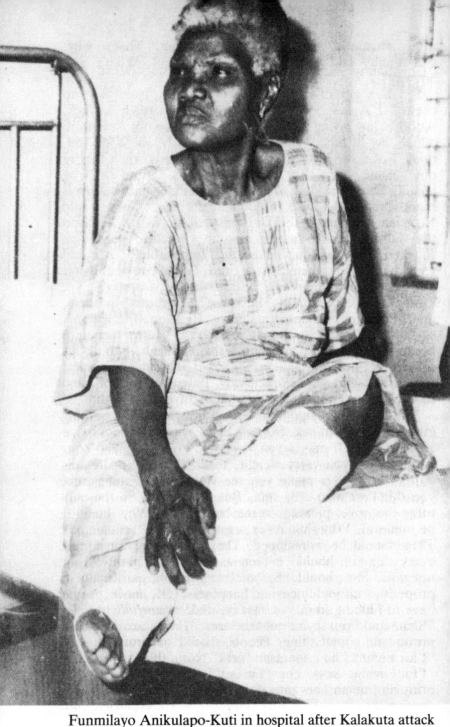

Funmilayo Anikulapo-Kuti in hospital after Kalakuta attack
From album cover of *Unknown Soldier*

21

My Mother's Death

"Coffin for Head of State"*

I've rarely been happy in my life. But marrying my twenty-seven women made me feel happy. The few times I've felt happiness, it's always been followed by something terrible. This time was no exception. Two months after my marriage, my mother's condition worsened. You see, she'd never recovered from the wounds and the shock she suffered during the attack on Kalakuta. Since that time she was always sick. I couldn't stand seeing her sick. I just had to feel that my mother was happy every minute of the day. Whenever I'd hear that my mother was sick or unhappy, it would fuck me up completely. Completely, man. All my brothers know it, so they don't even tell me what's happening when it comes to my mother. "Fela musn't know," they'd say. 'Cause I get mad at everybody, man. I get really mad. Oh, yes. One day she was sick and my brother was jiving me: "Yes, she can come for treatment *tomorrow*." I said, "No! TODAY!" I couldn't stand that. But her death did not really make me completely sad, 'cause I had been sad with her since she couldn't operate. You understand?

When my mother died, the sadness at that point was nothing. I had been sad with her since her silence. The sadness started when I started my film. When I went to film my house in Abeokuta, that's when my sadness started. That was in '76. You see, I was coming back to my home. My mother was in that home. She was sitting in the same house where I'd always known her. The house of all my

* "Coffin for Head of State", Fela's composition and album title, relates the day when he took his mother's coffin in broad daylight to lay it at the front gate of President Olusegun Obasanjo's residence, the day before the latter left power.

childhood memories. It was there I'd seen her operating, running about the country with other women, agitating in the streets, talking, travelling everywhere. . . . And I see me now believing in the same things she believed in then, even on higher things, me working on the things she believed in. And I see how she was there in the same old house. . . . I could feel she doesn't like the conditions she's in. 'Cause I can read it in her! And I see that she's sad. And I see that the home is not the same home any more. That's when I became so very sad, man. I'd never felt that sadness before. That was the first time. Since then it has been in the back of my head. So I'll have to spend all my life with that. That sadness killed everything I had.

This peaceful woman. She looked so. . . . So I go take her. I had to bring her to Lagos to stay with me, man. I did everything, man. Brought her over to Lagos where I thought she'd be happy and safe. And for a while she was really happy and safe here. She loved the company of all the women in the house, the noisiness, the children, the street life. . . . Oh, it made her really lively. Brought smiles to her face. Getting involved in the house was bringing back a new life to her that she had missed before. It was beautiful. Then the soldiers came. . . .

I got very sad again when I was writing her from Ghana in '77. She had to be walking long distances. Once she fell down, man. I couldn't stand it. So I was sad before she died, man. She didn't speak to anybody on her deathbed, when she was sick for two weeks. She didn't utter one word for two weeks. Not one word-o! Not even "Good" or "Ahhhhh". She didn't say a word. She'd just open her eyes to greet everybody. Smiling, nodding her head to say "yes" or "no". That's all. She knew she could operate more if she died. Talking would just bring more confusion in our minds.

Once I went to ask her: "Say, Mummy, you're not talking to anybody. Are you annoyed with us?" I had to ask that question. It was getting too much. She was just smiling, not talking. I knew she hadn't lost her voice, man. Ahah, I got so worried. I had to ask her that. It took courage to ask that question, man. Everybody wanted to ask it, but everybody was afraid to ask that question, in case she said, "Yes." But me, I HAD TO ask. She just nodded her head to say, "No, I'm not annoyed with you."

Now I understand that those two weeks of silence were for her a sacrifice. If she'd spoken, there would have been great confusion in the family. Later on, I would understand why.

Came Thursday 13 April 1978. My mother died! When she died I experienced something fantastic. That day I had gone to see her in hospital. I was on my way from hospital. I was going to sleep in house of my first wife. I got there round midnight. Then around 5.30–5.45 a.m. there was a big blast, like the commotion on the day they'd come to burn my house. That's what woke me up. I woke up and I saw a bright, yellowish light near the wall in front of me. My first wife was getting up to get water and she fell down. When I asked her why she fell down, she didn't know why. But I didn't think about it any more. I didn't think of my mother either. I went home about 8.30 a.m. I was in my room with another of my wives, Alake, when they came and told me my mother was dead. Later that same day, in the afternoon, when we got to the family meeting with my brothers, I asked them what time my mother had died. I was thinking of the noise I'd heard. They said around 5.30 a.m. or quarter to six. I *knew* then my mother had told me when she died.

But let me get back to that actual morning. I was in bed with Alake when Lara and one boy called Bayo came and knocked at my window. They said, "Fela, your mother is dead." What did I do? I can't remember. Oh, yes. I buried my head in my hands. I stood up, I dressed and went to hospital. You see, my mother made her death easy for all her children. She had actually died before her death. We were already crying in our minds since she had stopped speaking. So when she died it was like how she was two weeks before. I said to myself: "This woman finally died. My mother's died. . . ."

At hospital. There was her corpse. My mother had died at General Hospital. People were standing. Some government officials were there. I raised my fist to some people and they all shouted, "Hey-o." I didn't cry then. They wanted to put the corpse inside the ambulance to take her to Luth Hospital. I wasn't crying then. It was when I got into my bus to drive that tears started to fall from my eyes, man. I don't know what made me cry. Maybe, it was jus' that I would never see my mother again as a human being. I

Original album cover of *Coffin for Head of State*
Design: Babatunde O. Banjoko
Photo: Femi Osunla

would never see my mother again, full stop! 'Cause at that time I didn't even think of any possible future contact. It was the idea of never seeing her again that really made me cry. I wanted to see her. It finally dawned on me: fuck, I will never see this woman again. She'd gone, man! Gone! And when I think that I'll never see her again! Ever! Ever! Ever AGAAAIIIIIIIIIIIN!!!

Abeokuta. The burial. It was so sunny on that day. It was fuckin hot. Everybody was suffering from the hot sun. We'd been walking three, four miles. We were sweating and hot. We were about 50,000 people. Long lines. You could see people in the streets, far, far. All under the hot sun. I was in front with my brothers. The coffin was in the back of us. My sister was walking behind the coffin. When we got to the house, my sister and the coffin go to the front of our house. Then, exactly at that time there's a heavy rainfall. Everybody wanted the rain. So when it started to rain, everybody was so happy for the rain, man. We wanted the rain. But it was raining so hard that when I went to carry the coffin, the rain broke it! Can you imagine that? Rain is normal, true. But what happened that day was not normal, man. I knew then that my mother was going to use rain to communicate with me in some way. Since then rain has become a *sign* in my life.

On 1 October 1979, Nigerian Independence Day, Shehu Shagari was due to assume power, ending thirteen years of fuckin military rule. So Obasanjo was gonna go just like that, and with honours. I just couldn't let him get away like that, man. *Obasanjo's soldiers had killed my mother.* This wonderful, good and peaceful woman! That man will have to answer to that one-o! At any rate, I let everybody know that on the very last day of his rule, I would take my mother's coffin to his residence at Dodan Barracks, and place it in front of his gate. I told everybody. At Shrine. In the streets. To the press. To everybody! I knew I might get killed trying to do it. But I *knew* I would do it. That's the least I could do for my mama, man! So I said, "Fuck it!"

We're now September 30th. The night before we had worked till late at Shrine. Everyone was tired. I almost overslept, man. I woke up in a hurry and got my people together. And we enter bus. Vrrrrrooooooooom! We were off for Lagos. Coffin was inside bus, man. But, oh-oh! Look for front-o! Roadblocks! The army had set up roadblocks at every point leading into Lagos island! Man, I said, "Fuck!" and I stepped on the gas. Full speed, past the armed soldiers. They recognized my vehicle and started making frantic signs for me to stop. Then they came towards the bus and opened fire. Bam! Bam! Bam! Bullets hit bus, but none of us, the queens and my boys, were injured. So they started giving us chase. But we got away and headed straight to Dodan Barracks. Man, I don't know how they didn't kill us that day. Anyway, we arrived at Dodan Barracks.

"Get back or we'll shoot!" It was a young officer. We'd taken out the coffin and were still same way from the gate. I told my boys to stay back. Only me and my wives were to carry coffin up to the gate.

"Back, I said!" the officer shouted.

We continued walking up to the gate. Slowly. Oh, my wives, those women are courageous-o! The sentries lifted their machine guns and rifles.

"We'll shoot! Get back!"

We stopped. I told them:

"My brothers, will you also shoot my women?"

And we continued. . . . They lowered their weapons. We arrived at gate. We lowered coffin to ground. We turned round. And we left. At that same moment it began to rain. Heavily! Oh, that rain-o!

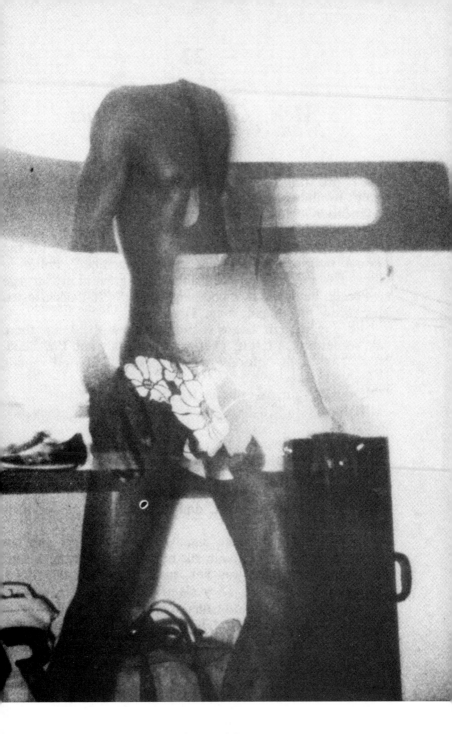

Fela's Spirit
Photo: Donald Cox

22

Men, Gods and Spirits

There are things that are difficult for ordinary human beings to understand, unless you're metaphysically inclined. My mother is dead. Yet I communicate with her. The first time she spoke to me since her death was when I was in Italy. That was in September '80. I'd gone to play for the annual ball of *Unita,* in Milano. Remember? Police in Lagos had made one American girl put grass in my luggage so I could be charged of peddling drugs. So Italians arrested and threw me in jail, man. Five days.

The day we left Lagos it rained heavy-o! I knew there was something. I felt it. Then we get to Italy and I'm jailed. Now, the night before I was released, it started raining heavily. I asked:

"Does it rain like this in Italy?"

"It hasn't rained like this in Italy for years," they told me.

It was while I was in prison in Italy that I saw my mother in a dream for the first time. She said to me:

"Fela, never give up the struggle!"

Oh!! Then I asked her: "This rain, what is it?"

She answered: "Ehhhh, don't ask me that. Everybody does this thing up here."

Now I know what she meant. That's the first and last time I saw her in a dream till now. What did she mean? She meant the rain was her, man. The next day I was released from prison. They cleared me of all the charges against me. So what she meant was that I would always know she would manifest herself to me by other means. Now I know. You know why? Listen, man. I'm gonna tell you some heavy shit-o that I've never told anybody!

Tuesday, 16 June '81 was Femi's* birthday. He became nineteen. That afternoon there was a big thunderstorm.

---

* Femi Anikulapo-Kuti, Fela's oldest son.

246

Lightning struck the Shrine and smoke came out of the ground. That's when the whole thing started. The rituals started then. You see, for you to understand I have to go back. After we left Paris in March '81 and got back to Lagos, my son Femi had an experience. He found eight marks on his left hand when he woke up in the morning after our return. We sent him to the *Ifà* priest, who said it was a manifestation of something, but he didn't want to tell Femi what. The priest knew Femi didn't understand Yoruba properly, so he told the guy who had taken Femi to see him.

Just before his birthday, Femi started having fever, a funny fever. We gave him all the medicine but it wouldn't cure it. When you have malaria, you take medicine once and it goes, man. But not his! It refused to go, man. During this fever, he told me he saw my mother's image. I thought it was malaria 'cause when you get malaria, the high fevers make you delirious. We were giving him so much fuckin' herbs, man. No cure. I said: "Shit! What kind of malaria is this?" Only he had this "malaria". Nobody else . . . yet. It was a bad day. He didn't sleep.

The second day Femi was telling me that the spirit's in him; that the spirit was gonna come and take over him. He kept saying: "He's comin'. . . . He's comin'. . . ." I said, "What is comin', motherfucker? What is comin'?" I thought he was mad. Then he said he's got to have some of his friends with him. Then he went to this room and locked himself up. This is when the spirit went into him. Femi's very psychic, you know. And it was in that room that he saw my mother. He saw her first before the whole thing of rituals started.

Then, after Femi, his friends got this fever too. None of them boys had "malaria" before. Femi started the whole thing. All the boys who had this fever fell into trances, like Femi. It was the beginning of the rituals. All these boys, Femi and the others, were being taken over. They were getting the spirit in their bodies, man. One of the boys, Femi Osula, from Arigidi near Ife, got caught by the spirit. He's the one who gave me the sign that I should always use my left hand for punishment and my right hand for justice.

I was in the midst of all this, man. I couldn't sleep. I was going through the same ritual myself. Those ten days were fantastic. We would sleep for something like one hour a

247

day, at the most three hours a day. When I would wake up I'd never feel tired. What did the spirit say? It said that the dead people of Africa weren't being taken care of. And that I was supposed to start teaching others to care for their dead. It said that there is no Africa left. That only Kalakuta was Africa. Many things, man. Many. Me, I was jus' watching these things going on. Then came Thursday.

It had all started on Tuesday of the week before. Now it's Thursday morning, second week, tenth day. Femi came and knocked on my window.

"Fela, they're comin' today."

"Come, come! How do you come and tell me that in morning? Who tell you? How you get this information?"

I was in bed in my room with Adejonwo, one of my queens. Then something started happening. I want to try to remember it. . . . Yes, I was with Adejonwo. I was fucking her-o. My prick was still hard in her cunt-o.Suddenly, she said she won't have nothing to do with me.

"Hey, Fela," she said. "Mama is here. Look! Mama! Fela, see Mama!"

I began wondering. "Where is she? Show me. Show me."

"There!"

I looked. I started to feel my head swirl. You know the feeling? It goes swirling. *Brrrrrrrrrrrrhhhhh*. . . .!

Adejonwo pushed me away and said: "Mama say I shouldn't have anything to do with you at this moment."

Shaaaaaaaaaah! Then suddenly she started to speak to me like my mother.

"So you want to travel, eh? . . . You want to travel tomorrow. . . . Where you go? . . . We are not going anywhere! . . . You want to get yourself killed? . . ."

Then, just like that, she said: "Abiola, get out of this room!"

I didn't see who she was talking to. (I didn't want to tell you these ones before. I am telling you this one because the spirit has said I can tell you. I have to tell you.) She said:

"Abiola is there."

Oh, the speed when this woman got up to go to the door. I was so scared. I had to hold her 'cause I had read in books that you have to hold people when they're in trances. I was trying to hold this woman down. I could not. Her strength was too much, man. Then she said:

"Leave me! Leave me, Fela! I know what I am doing,

248

now leave me!"

It was the voice of my mother. I let go of her.

Then she started to kick the door, like in voodoo rituals, man. The spirit took her over. She became as strong as ten men-o. And she gave my door one of the baddest kicks anybody can give a door. I was thinking: "How can a woman kick a door like this?" She went on kicking and saying all the while:

"Abiola, get out of here! Obasanjo out! Open the door! Slap them out!" *Blrrrrrrrhhhhhhh*! . . .

Adejonwo went running outta my room-o. She didn't even care about her nakedness. All her *nyash* was showing. But she went anyway all through the house like that, calling the other queens. At this point I went berserk.

It was me now running 'bout the house. I couldn't follow Adejonwo any more. I got confused. Then, suddenly, I felt something enter my body. Ohhhhhhhhh, my brother! I didn't know what I was doing-o. I lost control of myself. Oh, wow. I was moving all over the house, man. Up, down. Then I saw my mother. I saw Femi. Femi was really the one who was trying to cool me down. But I could not do what he told me 'cause I couldn't remember his role. Everybody saw what I was doing, but I couldn't remember Femi's role in the whole thing. I saw his face everywhere. I saw his face popping at me, you know. Then I did my ritual. It went on for about two hours. Yeah, man. The spirit was in my body for about two hours.

That ritual took me to Egypt, to Ife. I saw Egypt-o. I saw Ife. Egypt, Ife. They're telling me that that's where man started. That's where humanity started.* And the spirit took me forward and it took me back. Ooooooh, it was like a film. It took me back to what I was. What I am. What I'm gonna do in this world. What I'm supposed to be doing. How we have to do it. It went on and on and on and on and on. Everybody in the house thought I was mad. They couldn't understand that it was a trance. During the ritual I was told that there was danger for me in Europe. . . . There was death for me in Europe. . . . I saw everything. . . . After the ritual, man, I was so weak. . . . I wasn't even able

---

* It was after this experience that Fela changed the name of his organization from Africa 70 to Egypt 80.

to fuck that first day after the ritual. . . . I was like a baby, man . . . a child!

I believe in spirits now, man! I've seen them enter my wives, my son Femi, my close friends . . . and *me!* Spirits descended on us, man. It really happened and we saw it. I didn't believe these things till I saw. All along I've been hearing 'bout this and I've wanted to see. I've seen now. I've been part of it. So nobody can come and jive me any more that these things don't exist. I can categorically say spirits *do exist!* Don't nobody jive with this boy again-o! I've seen these "people" sitting with me for two days! I was completely in shock.

What is this world really about? We people, we just walk over this world and we don't know shit. We don't know shit-o. It really baffles me-o; really baffles me! How did it all start? The whole thing seems to have been falling into place for the last ten years. What really baffles me are the many "coincidences" in the whole thing: J.K.'s uncle coming to my house; how I met Lamiley in Ghana; how Sandra showed me the road to play; how during this whole period I went through experiences of complete changes in my life. . . . This J.K.'s uncle – J.K., my friend since childhood – was the first one who really told me many, many things. Just three days before the ritual, he started to bring out some salient facts that make it so difficult for me to live in this world. Facts that revealed if I had done things as today's human beings normally would do them, I would have failed the rest.

Anyway, J.K.'s uncle knew what he had to do to me at a particular time. You see, he called me about six years ago and said:

"Fela, you've got to put something in your head, you know." So he said he'd do something for my head. I asked:

"What is it?"

"It's good for you. If you believe in African liberation you must do it."

I started thinking, "If you believe, you have to do it! . . ." Then he started talking to me:

"Fela, if you do it, witches will want to see you, but will not. They will not touch you."

I didn't want this kind of juju. I said: "I want juju to disappear, to hold fire."

But he didn't want me to have that power. He said:

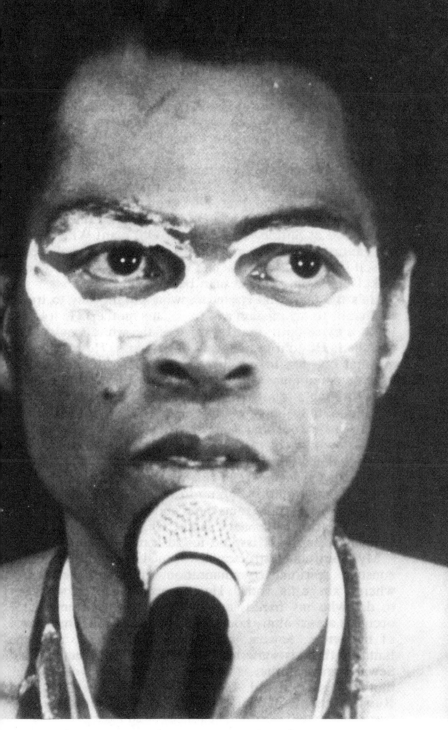

Fela with white spiritual powder around his eyes
Photo: André Bernabé

"Look, before you get those ones you have to start some-where. Try this one. Anyway, Fela, you have to trust me. Let me give you something that's good for you."

"OK," I said. "Give me."

J.K.'s uncle made incisions in the centre of my head. Some time went by. Then, one day, a man from Ghana, a so-called magician, came to see me. He brought me a letter from a friend of mine in Ghana. This man wanted to perform at Shrine. In the letter I was told this man had the power to "kill and wake". I said to myself, half-believing it, "If this guy can do that I'll announce it to the whole world!" So we put him up in our house. And that night he performed at Shrine. Three shows. Oh, man! What he did was fantastic! It was incredible!!! I wouldn't have believed it myself if I hadn't seen that shit with my own eyes. "Kill and wake!" Bringing a dead man back to life!!

He's the man who started showing me the way to truth, to myself, to my mission and to . . . my mother! He told me I was a twice-born; that I'd rejected the white man's name and died. He told me a lot, a lot of things. He revealed to me that one has to put this white spiritual powder on the face to communicate with spirits. He spoke of the three stars forming a triangle last year, in 1980. You see, that star formation only happens once every two thousand years. We'd seen it too, that same star triangle, the year before. You know what it meant? That the Age of Good was at hand; that the times of Evil were about to end. I also found that Africa was the *centre* of the world, the place from where Good would spring up to embrace the rest of man-kind. Just as the first men came about in Africa, man, and went to settle all the other lands. Oh, that man taught me so many things. At last I'd found a real Teacher!

My spiritual instructor lives in Ghana. But I'm in constant spiritual communication with him, no matter where I am in the world. He tells me what to do, what not to do, who my friends are and who are my enemies. He occupies a part of my house. And speaks to me through one of my wives, Sewaa, who's also from Ghana. And the fantastic thing is something I only found out recently: that Sewaa's grandmother, a woman called Akosia Ade, was my mother's good friend. I swear. She's been to China and Russia with my mother. I didn't believe Sewaa when she first came to tell me that. Then she showed me a photo: her grandmother along with my mother, together in China! The woman is still alive-o! And it's Sewaa my mother enters to talk to me! Do you see that, man?? It's like it was all planned for all of us to meet.

When I want to speak to my spiritual instructor, I call him. When I call him, he gives me a name to call him. Then I wait. Then he enters Sewaa and she starts shaking in convulsions. It's he who then puts me in touch with my mother. So my Teacher calls my mother. When she comes, the one's she entered falls into convulsions and then gets quiet. Oh, man! That first conversation with my mother!

My first conversation with my mother since her death. She calls me "Fela". I jus' call her "Mummy". She said to me:

"Fela, you're travelling tomorrow, eh? You're not going anywhere. You're not travelling anywhere.* JUST STAY!!! Want to get yourself killed? . . ."

That was the first thing she told me. Then other things you might misunderstand which I won't say.

"Mummy, you have to go. Go 'way."

She insisted. "Do you have to go get yourself killed?"

That was the sort of argument for the first five minutes and it went on for two hours, man. My Teacher was holding on to the queen; he was accompanying the queen, to direct her. My mother told me how she was. She said that when she died she went for treatment for two years. And that that was why she'd been delayed till now. And then she told me she had died from poisoning! Yes, poisoning! She told me everything. So I know now.

---

* Fela was about to leave on a concert tour in Europe (end-June, early July 1981). At the last minute it was cancelled by the concert promoters.

Fela preaching Blackism and PanAfrikanism: "The struggle must stop!"
Photo: Chico

23

This Motherfucking Life

Who am I? I know it now. It was revealed to me in a trance. The spirit told me who I was. And what I am about. But that one I will not say to anybody. Never! Maybe a time will come when I will have to reveal it. Maybe. But all I can say now is: I know exactly who I am and what I am here to do. When it comes to forces that aren't human forces, you must be careful. These things must manifest themselves in their own time. What has happened to me will make me reveal a lot of bad things going on in *this* world. But I cannot say it yet. I've got a lot of facts in my head. But they are not enough for me to say anything yet. I still need some time to put my thoughts together. OK?

What am I pursuing in this life? Greatness! That's what I'm after, man. I want to be a great man. Great Man! I want to stand on an equal footing with the other races. 'Cause when you're walking on the road with other races you are not branded. That is greatness. I want to achieve that individually, first. The other races must come to recognize me as an equal partner. That's my own philosophy I'm saying. And if other Africans have this same approach and want to be great, well, that's fine. To have a great nation, you need great men. And to be a great man you need a great nation. You just can't be a great man by yourself, man. *You have to have a great nation first.* That's why I say *Africa* – not Nigeria, Togo or Senegal – must become a great nation for all of the peoples that live there!

But in this corrupt world of ours, "greatness" is seen as the ability to . . . *destroy*! The more you fuck up nature to build highways and airports; the more wars you make; the more shit you invent to make life more miserable for the four billion of us, the more you're said to be great! Look America! Look Russia! England! France! Japan! China! What they call 'em? Na *Great Powers*-o! Rich mother-fuckers are *great*. Government leaders dey be *great*. Generals dey be *great*. . . . All of the massacrists of the

255

world, the *killers*, man, those na be *great* people! But the little motherfucking musician, the artist, who is trying to bring some colour, hope and happiness into this world, what is he? Now *dem go say he dey craze*, man! Yeah, they'll say he's crazy! *No be so? "He dey craze!"* dem say. He-he! So the one *wey dey create* na crazy one. But the one *wey dey destroy*, na him be great! Now what kind of a criminal shit logic is that? *Please, I beg, explain dat one fo' me-o!*

So when people say America, Russia, China are great powers, I say: "No!" They're not. They are *destructive*, not great powers. The man they called "Alexander the Great" was not *great*; he was a destroyer. Oppressors, destroyers, massacrists can never be *great* people. Oh, people are so brainwashed, man! *Creativity*, not destruction, should be the yardstick of greatness. If you cannot create anything that will make your own life, or that of your fellow human, happier, then get out of the way. Split! Disappear! And give others a chance. That's my advice to these so-called *great* people and *great powers!*

I've known for a long time, since I was a child in school, that I would be *great*. I started to realize this after I had found myself always in trouble. I kept asking myself: "Why am I in this trouble? Why am I so uncompromising? Why am I so demagoguing?" And I knew there must be a reason. 'Cause it's not natural for me to keep on, keep on, when everybody keeps telling me I can't do it, that I should stop. Nobody's ever told me: "Fela, it's good for you to be like you are." It's always: "Fela, why don't you cool down, cool down? What you're doing there, that's not done." Everybody around me said: "Be careful. One day you're gonna get yourself killed." So I saw a clear *mission*. I wouldn't say *mission*; that's not the right word. Let's say *class struggle*. That's the term.

I arrived at that conclusion one day when I asked myself: "Why do they call me stubborn? Why do they always attach a negative name to me when I really know that I am honest?" So I started to search myself. Then I found out that there was a child born in my family before who died. That one was me. So I came *twice*, man. I asked my spiritual teachers and he says it's true. Otherwise, how do I explain my uncompromising stand? You see, I had come purposely to give a message. That's why I split when the

256

white man gave me name. And that's why I was born the second time. So I don't like people giving me names, man! Like "radical", "agitator", "hooligan", or shit like that! My name is Fela Anikulapo-Kuti. Black President or Chief Priest of Shrine, if you want. But no other names, I beg!

Do I want to leave an imprint on the world? No. Not at all. You know what I want? *I want the world to change.* I don't want to be remembered. I just want to do my part and leave. If remembering is part of the world's thing, that's their problem. I'll do my part. I have to do my part. And everybody has to do his. Not for what they're going to remember you for, but for what you believe in as a man. That's what everybody should be about. If you want to do things because you want to be remembered, you are doing it for personal reasons only. Just do things 'cause you believe in them. A human being should be like that.

A human being should appreciate power. A human being should have knowledge. Power corrupts? I don't want to say power corrupts. It's when a man is powerful and *un*knowledgeable that he misuses power. But if he is knowledgeable he can never misuse power. It's impossible. What is power? Control of your mind, man! Control your mind, don't let your mind control you. Then you have power. Power is not government, you see. It's a question of mind.

Is there anything I regret in life? Something I would have done another way if I had the chance to do it again? No. Everything I did wrongly was for experience. That's how I see it. Once a man is looking for a better knowledge and he tries to be honest and truthful in all his endeavours, then his life is just an experience. It cannot be a regret. But the one thing I do not forgive: leaders who exploit! I can forgive a man who steals, a man who lies. . . . But I cannot forgive a leader who is corrupt. A man who kills? Well, it depends on what he did, of course. To kill is a different matter. I can forgive killing too. It depends on the circumstances. But not wanton killing. Not that one. Self-defence I can understand. But in principle I don't agree with killing.

I'd just like to see happiness in people. That's all. I hate to see brutality. I hate to compromise with wrongdoing. Whether you're Black or White, what is bad is bad. A Black man must know what is bad. There's no favouritism in this thing, you know. There are rights. There are wrongs.

Fela singing
Photo: Raymond Sardaby

258

So what I believe in is: what is bad is bad, and what is good is good. The only thing I hate is injustice? I cannot stand that one. I cannot favour someone 'cause he's Black. If I do this, I'm starting the struggle in life on a wrong footing. What is right is right. What is wrong is wrong. That applies to everybody.

Hatred. Do I hate anybody? No. *Nobody!* Anybody who is honest must have trouble in life. You cannot afford to hate, man. You know what hate does to you? When you hate you don't think, you don't eat. You're too busy thinking of *what you're going to do to him.* So all the time you're wasting, you're going down. You don't achieve nothing by hating, man. You just waste precious time. Go and do what you have to do. Then when you're ready to deal with him, then remember him.

Obasanjo? No, I don't hate him. If I saw Obasanjo I would deal with him though. I can slap him. I can really kick his ass. But killing him, no! Or anybody else. Not killing, man. If I kicked Obasanjo's ass, it wouldn't even be because I hate him. I would kick his ass so people would know that bad people who are *great* can get their ass kicked too when the time is ripe. If their ass couldn't be kicked when they were doing the bad things, it can be kicked afterwards. When am I going to have the chance to kick his ass? I don't know, but I'd love to. 'Cause he's a man who loved to kick other people's asses. That's why I would love to kick his ass. If I ever meet him on the road, I will kick his ass. . . . You know where he's staying now? Obasanjo is staying in a zoo, in a forest reserve: Yankari zoo. He's already getting his punishment. When you can't stay with humans you stay with animals and you speak animal language.

Since June '81, when my mother revealed to me that she had been poisoned, I've been thinking about that. She didn't ask for revenge. What for? She didn't need to. It was revealed. That's all. Now it's up to me to do my own thing as a human being. And if I didn't know before, I know now. So I do what I can do about it. If I didn't do something about somebody who killed my mother, then I must be a bastard. I must get justice. . . .

Sadness. Since a child, up till now, I've always been both happy and sad. What makes me sad today is to see people pushed around in life by other human beings. Selfishness by

259

human beings also makes me sad. And the work that has to be done in Africa for Africans to progress. . . . To think of all this makes me sad. To think of how many Africans are so unaware, how they suffer in oblivion. That makes me sad. What makes me happy? When I play music. When I stay with my women. When I sit down with my people, discussing, chatting, laughing. . . . But my state of mind and feeling is shared between happiness and sadness. I want peace. Happiness. Not only for myself. For everybody. If I get it for myself I can't have peace. When everybody has peace then I will have peace. Because if just me has peace and police don't have peace, they will come and fuck my thing up. So I want peace for them too.

Despite my sadness I create joyful rhythms. Yeah, I am sad. I am an artist. I have my reasons for being sad. I want to change sadness. I want people to be happy. And I can do it by playing happy music. And through happy music I tell them about the sadness of others. So that they will come to realize that, "Oh, we *can* be happy!" With my music I create a change. I see it. So really I am using my music as a weapon. I play music as a weapon. The music is not coming from me as a subconscious thing. It's conscious. I'm consciously doing what I am doing. What I mean is that whatever I want to do is in my mind. Man can have complete control of his mind. That's what *knowledge* is about. To be able to control one's mind.

Creativity. How to define that? You see, when you're sitting down as a musician, you have different sounds coming into your head, man. You hear so many things! Then you have to pick what is best from your own mind. That's your own decision. So to decide which sounds are the best, that's a development of the mind. 'Cause your mind can also pick what is not good, what will *not* appeal to the people. So the mind is in control all the time. Yeah, spontaneity exists 'cause different sounds come to you like that. But then you must know in your mind which of those sounds to pick, which are best to use. So there's no mystery in creation, man. The only mystery in creation is being gifted. That's the only mystery. If you're gifted, you just have to know how to use your gift the best way. Nature has given it to you. If you are not gifted and you want to play music you will fail. As I said, everybody has a purpose in life. You have to know your purpose. And if you don't

Fela on saxophone
Photo: Raymond Sardaby

Fela on piano
Photo: Chico

know it, then you have to find it out by yourself.

Education today doesn't allow people to know their purpose. It is meant to stifle that purpose. That's why I am against the education the white man has brought to Africa. In Africa they make the child want to be doctor, lawyer, or engineer by force, you know. People are just not allowed to choose and go their own way. The white man's way stifles creativity, man. See what I mean?

My favourite instruments? I love all instruments, man. I wish I could play all of them. But I'm still finding out the horn, man. I haven't got that horn together yet. People say, "Oh, yeah, Fela plays horn," but I don't got it yet, man. When I get that horn together you will know, man. You will fucking well know! The piano? OK, fair enough. I play the piano. I'm using it right now for solo work. So you can only judge my piano as solo work; to do free line to the arrangements of rhythms. How do I define my music? People continue to call it Afro-beat. I call it *African music*. . . . But African music is so extensive. . . . Let's call it African music by Fela, then. Finish!

Time. What's that? Nine o'clock? . . . Ten o'clock? . . . That kind of thing? No, man. I don't deal with that. Time is *moment*. Not hour. Let me give you my experience. Everytime I go and play or give a lecture some place, people say: "You're always late." One day I told them:

"How can you say I'm late? Just because of the watch you're wearing on your wrist?"

Then I explained. "For instance, let's say you're expecting me at 5 o'clock and I'm coming from Abeokuta to Ibadan for this lecture. At 5 o'clock you don't see me. At 6 o'clock you don't see me. You're annoyed. You say, 'Fela is late.' The next morning you hear I'm dead in an accident. Now, how about that annoyance you felt about my being late? How do you forgive yourself?" So don't get annoyed when I'm late. Time is not the wristwatch, man. Time is the importance of an event, a moment. Say you're expecting someone to come. He must be important enough for you not to get annoyed if he keeps you waiting. You must *feel* the importance of the guy. Time is understanding of what is important. Time is not a mind-disturbing matter. Happiness is the essence of this world.

When we see our children growing up, we see ourselves getting old. That's not time. That's experience. Man must

Fela reflective
Photo: Donald Cox

grow old to prove that this is not a world of spirits. If you look back again to your youth, it will be like yesterday. It's not far. The mind dictates time really. The mind makes you feel what time is about.

Dreams. Before, I never knew what dreams were about. But now I believe dreams are the soul in the body that travels. If you can co-ordinate and control the dream, then you can go astral travelling. This is what I experienced one day. I dreamt I was on top of a tower. A tall tower. I was surrounded by soldiers, police and people who wanted to harm me. They had guns, every sort of instruments. I was at the peak of this tower and they were around the edge, surrounding me. There was no means of escape. I realized in the dream that I was dreaming. And I said to myself: "It's a dream anyway. I can jump. Nothing will happen." So I jumped, man. And I started waking up in bed as if I was dropping from a height into my body. And I *dropped into my body* and I woke up. I felt fine, rested. I felt a beautiful sensation after that. And I've tried getting that control since, but I've not been able to.

If one can remember a dream, I think you can start controlling it from there. Dreams are uncontrolled travels of the soul. We go to places. We can see the future in our dreams. We can go backwards and forwards. For instance, I dream many dreams. I found out that many dreams I dream are *opposites* of the future. If I dream about something successful, it's a failure; and if I dream about failure, I'm always successful. Any time I remember a dream, it always comes to pass. I always forget my dreams, but any dream I remember always comes to pass. Dream is an experience the body cannot feel, only the soul. The body cannot pass through a wall. In a dream it can. In a dream you are given the opportunity to see, to feel the future. What you *will be*.

What is life? Osiris said it. Amenhotep solved it too. "Life is eat, drink and enjoy yourself because tomorrow you may die." That is life. What is death? A transition into spirits. Death is a beautiful thing. Don't fear it. You become a spirit. You leave this material body. This body's a cell. It keeps you. It doesn't let you go. It's a jail. But man must not seek release as such from his existence. Release will come. All men must die whether they're worth the release or not. That's a point. But not all men go to the same place when they die. Why must man die? Because he

265

cannot really exist in this body. The ultimate is the spirit, I think. I guess. I'm not sure myself. I think the essence of life is: "Eat, drink and enjoy yourself for tomorrow you may die." That is what one must do first. But before you can eat, drink and enjoy yourself, you must be *happy*. And before you are a happy man, you must make other people happy. You see, I don't believe those people who say 'cause they have money they're happy. That's not happiness, man!

Happiness. That's the essence of true life. The mind is the source of happiness. Good health, a clear mind. Finish. To be happy is not easy. Loneliness. Yeah, that makes people unhappy. But it is man who makes himself lonely. Take Africa. Africans always had what Europeans call the extended family. You stay in the compound together: sisters, brothers, uncles. . . . Everybody lives all together in the family house. Loneliness is absent in that culture. But in a culture where you live with your wife and children alone, loneliness will crop up inevitably. Loneliness is inevitable in European culture. So human beings brought on loneliness for themselves by making the wrong cultures. That's why I think Africa is the pacesetter for culture.

My future? Oooooooooh! That's a big one, man. You see, man is here against his will. Where do we come from? What was before us? I was born twice, so let me tell you what I think. Sometimes when I think to myself, I say: "I don't want to be part of this world." I sit down and meditate and I say: "I don't want any part of this world. I don't want any part of this shit, man!" When I see a policeman beating up somebody, a government man committing wrongdoings and shit like that which I can't stop. . . . Ohhhhhhh, I feel so bad! I really don't want to be a part of this world. What I mean is . . . I do not want to exist. Not wanting to exist means I'm not here. I don't feel. I don't see. I don't know. I'm just nothing. I just don't BE, don't BE! But here I am. I'm existing. I say to myself: "How can I cancel my existence?" 'Cause I don't want to be any more. You understand? I think about that one a lot. *I want to cancel my existence*. . . . Commit suicide . . . kill myself . . . take poison . . . do something. Then I think about all I've learnt in books, that when you think you die, you're not dead. It's a *transition*. So I don't really cancel my existence. I still see. I still feel. I still be. So man cannot

The Black President and Chief Priest of Shrine: Fela
Anikulapo-Kuti ("The One Who Emanates Greatness,
Who Carries Death in His Quiver and Who Cannot Be
Killed by Human Entity")

Photo: Raymond Sardaby

cancel his existence after all. That's why I say men are here against their will. This world is not just a world of accident. We're not just born. Everything has to be done properly, naturally, as it's supposed to be. That's what I think about life. Human beings have a purpose in this world. And if you do not do what you're supposed to do, you will die young and come back again.

Death? Death doesn't worry me, man! When my mother died it was because she'd finished her time on earth. I know that when I die I'll see her again. So how could I fear death? But I don't want to die too fast. . . . Let me stop now because my mind is not working like I want it to. . . . I don't know why. . . . You see, I don't want to exist. . . . I want to put a stop to my life. . . . But I cannot take my life. . . . You see, when my mother and father wanted a baby, they didn't want *me*. . . . They wanted a baby, any fuckin' baby, man! Well, here I am now. I came. So what is this motherfuckin' world about? . . . I believe there is a plan. . . . I believe there is no accident in our lives. . . . What I am experiencing today completely vindicates the African religions. . . . I will do my part. . . . Then I'll just go, man. . . . Just go!

Epilogue: Rebel with a Cause

Carlos Moore

The Turning Point

In 1982, when *Fela, Fela: This Bitch of a Life* originally appeared, Fela Kuti was at a political crossroads and in the midst of an existential crisis. Twelve years of relentless, single-handed confrontation with Nigeria's political and civilian establishments were chronicled in the scars he bore all over his body, testimony to the brutal price he had paid for championing the cause of society's underdogs. But the Nigerian masses—in whose name he had suffered broken legs and arms, a fractured skull, repeated imprisonment, and unabated harassment—gave no sign of being ready to defy their oppressors head-on. Much to the contrary, they voted en masse in 1979 to elect as president Alhaji Shehu Shagari, a man Fela had described as a "weak and dangerous" politician.

Fela therefore faced an awful dilemma.

Disappointed and distressed in his personal life, too, Fela was mired in confusion, at times bordering on chaos, as he inconsolably mourned his mother's death. There were moments when he seemed to be suffering from depression and would express his wish to "cancel my existence"; increasingly he gave signs of paranoid delusions. But the end of his agonies was not yet in sight. For another fifteen years he would be flung from one jail to another, enduring a string of horrors likely to have broken any other human. Yet, remaining remarkably true to himself, Africa's premier rebel clung to his political beliefs and lifestyle until felled in 1997 by an apolitical enemy whose existence he had steadfastly refused to acknowledge—AIDS.

The tumultuous final itinerary of one of the twentieth century's most inspired and flamboyant artists may not be captured in a few pages. But to approximate an understanding of the crucial events that marked Fela's last fifteen years of life, one has to backtrack to that watershed period in the early 1980s when he underwent his second epiphany, a transformation that threatened his artistic career, reshaped his music, and nearly claimed his sanity.

The Spiritual Saga

Until his last breath, Fela was a proud thorn in the flesh of every military or civilian despot that occupied the revolving presidential chair in Nigeria, a distinction that made his position nearly untenable. How did he manage to stay alive during that fifteen-year stretch? Some believe that he found salvation through conversion, in 1981, to a bewildering esoteric mysticism that he called his "spiritual saga." If so, that flight into the world of spirits proved costly, for it gradually eroded the political coherence of the movement he had fought so hard to build. Ultimately, it sowed chaos among those around him.

Convinced that he was a marked man, the rebel musician desperately sought spiritual protection and began to explore ways to "seal his body"; more than ever, he resorted to traditional herbs and potions to ward off "bad spirits" and consulted traditional soothsayers to help him plan his life and actions. Thus, in the early 1980s, the Afrobeat king was fully engrossed a process of spiritual transformation designed to make himself invulnerable to death. This implied a return to ancestral worship systems, which Fela's creative mind laced with his own ad hoc rituals.

It would appear that the more the Nigerian military establishment came after him with its trademark ferocity, the more the rebel retreated into a metaphysical quest that would help him to deal with his powerful adversaries. The truth is that the extreme mysticism Fela began to exhibit in the early 1980s had been building for years; it was part of his own idiosyncrasy. Like most people, he strongly believed in life after death and resurrection. Like most Africans, he practiced ancestor worship. And like many, he upheld the existence of UFOs, besides being someone very superstitious.

I recall that in 1977, I accompanied the Senegalese historian and Egyptologist Cheikh Anta Diop to Nigeria, which was then under the rule of a nationalist and populist regime headed by Murtala Ramat Muhammad, whose politics, for once, coincided with Fela's own Pan-Africanism. Knowing of Fela's admiration for Diop, I scheduled an encounter between them in our hotel.

Uncharacteristically, Fela showed up on the dot of the appointed hour, with a retinue of some thirty persons, including several of his wives. After a half hour of listening intently to the professor, Fela began an assault of inquiries.

"Professor, how did the ancient Egyptians built the pyramids?"

Diop responded that the technology used to build those massive structures still baffled modern engineers and scientists.

"Sir, I have the answer," Fela said. He went on to tell Diop that the ancient pyramids were built through mental telepathy and levitation!

"Professor, sir, *dat be why* nobody can say *wey dey* build the pyramids," Fela said.

He further informed Diop that the ancient Egyptians had spacecraft that traveled to other galaxies and returned with extraterrestrial scientific knowledge. Instead of conventional fuel, these spacecrafts were propelled by mental energy.

Diop fell silent.

The Quest to Conquer Death

Fela's die-hard belief in what he termed "black magic" and his quest for ways to deflect death set the stage for the arrival of a character who would trigger one of the weirdest chapters in his already troubled life. A Ghanaian and a mystic by trade, Kwaku Addai—popularly known as Professor Hindu—claimed powers that allowed him to communicate directly with the spirit world and resurrect the dead. Addai conflated traditional African beliefs, the Hindu idea of reincarnation, and the Christian faith in resurrection, professing thereby to be at the forefront of a new "science."

At one stage, informed that in a certain village a medicine man was reputed to have created bulletproof spiritual vests that could stop the most powerful projectiles, Fela paid handsomely for one. On discovering it was a hoax, he broke down in tears. Therefore, when rumors reached him that there was a magician in nearby Ghana who *truly* had supernatural powers, he was ecstatic; his enthusiasm being fueled, additionally, by Hindu's reputation for curing sterility. His collective marriage in 1978 had so far sired only one child—Kunle—and Fela was self-admittedly sterile.

In 1981 Professor Hindu was brought to Nigeria at Fela's expense. On that first visit, Hindu remained for some days, performing rituals designed to protect Fela and his household from attack and treating his infertility with a special diet. Enchanted with the magician, during performance intermissions Fela presented him to the crowds as the only human being with the power to "kill and wake." Hindu became a regular attraction at the Afrika Shrine club, nightly entertaining a wide-eyed public with the most extravagant stunts and extraordinary tales.

In no time, Fela would elevate Hindu to the status of spiritual adviser, eclipsing all the members of his entourage—wives and children, childhood buddy J. K. Braimah, and trusted political aides—who now saw themselves relegated to the background. But no sooner did Hindu assume his new function as Fela's guru than truly bizarre happenings began to occur. First, several of Fela's wives experienced states of trance that made them prophesy untold events, mostly cataclysmic and threatening to Fela. Second, Fela himself began to have visions, hear voices, and feel strange presences in the household— *spirits*! Soon the entire household was taken over by what appeared to be collective hysteria. One of Fela's aides, ID, explains the scene:

"Spirit" men and women started to spring up within the organisation, most of them claim[ing] to have been possessed by Hindu's "spirit" or that of Fela's late mother. Randomly, people were falling into all kinds of "spiritual trance" and making outrageous "prophecies." With these came personal witch-hunting and vendettas. If you had any bones to pick with someone, all you needed to do was fall into a "trance" and you could accuse the person of anything from being a spy to practicing witchcraft. Outrageous claims of clandestine involvement became the order of the day. Suddenly, people were claiming to have been sent to the organization for various clandestine reasons; some of them even claimed to work for America's CIA. . . . [T]hus, the "spirit" saga gained more legitimacy and those who did not believe had to leave the organization or join in the game.[1]

The growing phenomenon made Fela grow ever more paranoid. He threw aggressive tantrums and conducted himself in an increasingly bizarre manner that made many suspect he was suffering from a psychological disorder. He exerted undue influence on his entourage to embrace his flight into the irrational and thereby legitimize it. Under pressure, one after another of his wives, assistants, and hangers-on began to report falling into a trance, experiencing sightings of spirits about the house, or testifying to having heard the voice of Fela's mother. At one point he accused two of his wives of attempting to harm him with witchcraft.[2] As it happened, he woke up one morning with an upset stomach, and one of his wives, Sewaa—known as the Spirit Woman—accused two other cowives (most likely rivals) of employing witchcraft on his food. The problem is that Fela believed it and almost went berserk. At the time, this particular wife had empowered herself by "claiming she was spiritually possessed by Hindu to continue the spiritual vigil while the Ghanaian was absent."[3]

It was in such circumstances that in the spring of 1981 a French promoter hastily put together what would be Fela's second European tour. Everyone agreed that Fela needed to relaunch a career that was badly floundering. Years of confronting ruthless governments, their armies, and police, had left him financially broke and politically boxed in. Emotionally and physically bruised, Fela welcomed a respite that would allow him to breathe some fresh air away from the foul politics of Nigeria.

But here, too, Professor Hindu's influence would be felt; no sooner was the tour announced than some of his wives began to prophesy all manner of doom scenarios for the trip. "As expected in an atmosphere filled with superstition," ID recalls, "all kinds of prophecies were being foretold, especially regarding the outcome of the tour." Adejonwo, one of the cowives, began to report "visions" and claimed that during a trance she had seen "an international conspiracy to assassinate Fela" during the tour. Therefore, "chickens were slaughtered to appease the gods to give Fela victory over his alleged enemies."[4]

Fela's European tour took place in the midst of such tensions. And even though prior to departure sacrifices had been made to the appropriate spirits, while in Europe Fela and his entourage were on a constant lookout to ward off the prophesized attempt on the musician's life. On airplanes, at airports, in the hotel, and even onstage, Fela and his entourage were on the watch for an assassin. Anyone who came into contact with them—especially journalists—was suspect.

Throughout the tour, Fela reported having visions and hearing voices. He was convinced that these unsettling events were induced by his dead mother's attempts to communicate with him. As a consequence, his musicianship suffered. "For the first time I saw Fela perform without the precision and the particular attention he gave to the presentation of his shows," remarked ID. "Members of the organization who had nothing to do on stage were standing there in the name of protecting him from an alleged assassin's bullet. On the final leg of the tour we had a week's stay in Paris to record the album *Original Suffer-Head* for Arista Records in England. Despite all the 'prophecies' there was no attempt on Fela's life."[5]

From his Paris hotel, Fela anxiously phoned his former girlfriend and confidante, Sandra, in California. "He felt that they were trying to kill him," she later recounted. "I just jumped on a plane. I went to Paris for three days. The scene at that hotel was unreal. He had some heavy, wicked people around him at that point. I don't know how he could have remained sane in such an insane environment."[6] In an attempt to bring some levelheadedness into play, ID sought out Fela's first wife, Remi, who had accompanied Fela on the tour along with their two daughters, Yeni and Sola. But ID was faced with a dilemma, as Fela had begun to suspect the mother of his children of being an undercover agent of the CIA. "I would have to tell Remi what Fela whispered in my ear in Lagos airport," he recounted. "How could I tell a woman that her husband for twenty-one years thought she was a CIA agent?"[7]

The disclosure shook Remi, who decided, forthwith, to return to Lagos with her daughters. Her mind was made up to leave Fela. When he returned to Nigeria and found that Remi had moved out of the house, it was a huge blow. Remi had always been the anchor of his life, the objective link with reality; now that, too, was gone. The musician turned his fury on ID. "I felt he considered my [having divulged] the CIA accusation pushed Remi to finally leave him. He held me responsible for her departure," he explained.[8] The episode introduced an unbridgeable chasm between ID and Fela. Ultimately, in 1983, the loyal ID, too, would quit the organization.

In the commune was a season of madness, with "evil spirits" threatening Fela's well-being, "ghosts" tormenting his sleep, and his dead mother's "spirit" advising him—through Professor Hindu—on how to deal with both. Fela would uncover "spies" and "agents" all over the place, sometimes accusing members of his entourage, or even some of his spouses, of plots against him. As the deleterious effects of the spiritual saga raged like a brushfire, it began consuming the political tissue of his organization. Fela himself seemed to have lost his ability to think rationally. Only a few people—such as his trusted friend J. K. Braimah, ID, or bandleader Lekan Animashaun—seemed to escape the wild phenomenon, but none enjoyed the authority to intervene. Braimah, in particular, was alarmed. "I don't know what's really going on," he told me gravely in 1982. "I've never seen Fela acting that way!" In 1984, after Fela was jailed, Braimah, like ID, would separate himself from the organization.

As intimate friends who loved him dearly and respected him, but who knew there was something wrong, were singled out as being CIA agents, Fela began to lose once-loyal supporters. (Jamaican-born novelist Lindsay Barrett, who'd already distanced himself over an earlier incident, in 1979, was one of them.) Wives who had exposed their lives and suffered for him now separated from him, and several of his best musicians fled. It is only thanks to Fela's own creative genius and the rare loyalty of bandleader Animashaun that Fela's band rebounded over and again to rise from its ashes.

Rumors that Fela was losing it began to spread, but the artist reacted by becoming even more detached. His younger brother, Beko Ransome-Kuti, a medical doctor, became alarmed. Reportedly, he tried to no avail to convince his famous brother to seek professional assistance—outside Nigeria, if need be. The artist was highly distrustful of Western medicine, which he regularly denounced as "chemical poison." Moreover, he insisted that there was nothing wrong with him; he was simply following the voice of the spirits and obeying the commands of his deceased mother.

But something was indeed sorely wrong; Professor Hindu, the magician who supposedly held the keys to life beyond death, had taken over control of Fela. "He's the man who started showing me the way to truth, to myself, to my mission and to . . . my mother!" the artist would explain. "He tells me what to do, what not to do, who my friends are and who are my enemies."[9] Suffice it to say, during the long period Fela spent under the spell of his spiritual adviser, his career came perilously near to ending. Indeed, Fela now insisted on having the magician along on his international tours, and presenting him to audiences otherwise ill acquainted with black magic. As a result, his third European tour, in 1983 to 1984 was an unmitigated public relations disaster.

Prophet Unarmed

In power since 1979, Alhaji Shehu Shagari was Nigeria's first civilian ruler since 1966, and he sought to convey an image of statesmanship and civility. For the first time in ten years, Fela enjoyed a spell of immunity from government assault. But he had not been duped; Shagari's administration was tainted by the same corruption and inefficiency as its predecessors. In 1983, Nigeria was indeed in the midst of a grave financial crisis, and unemployment was hitting new heights. Even the middle classes were feeling the economic pinch. The stage was set for a triumphant return of the men in khaki, who indeed struck on New Year's Eve 1983, catapulting to power a dull, dour despot— General Muhammadu Buhari.

The operation was the typical cosmetic transfer of power that Fela immortalized in "Army Arrangement," a hard-chopping tune released in 1985; for Fela, it was back to square one. Again he was politically encircled, but this time his own libertarian commune was traversing its gravest crisis ever at a moment when a big door of opportunity had opened up. The recording moguls were in search of a charismatic successor to Bob Marley, dead since 1981, and the Nigerian rebel fit the bill.

Marley's antiestablishment reggae had tapped a worldwide market while Fela's equally defiant Afrobeat remained cloistered in the steamy slums of Lagos. Marley's stardom epitomized the triumph of the message of Jamaica's ghettoized Rastafarian underdogs; Fela's continued marginalization thereby seemed an anomaly. A frustrated Fela came to view the Jamaican's global success as the result of his having sold out and, in tune with that view, continued to refuse a compromise with the musical cartels.

In the mid-1980s, the musician again attempted to relaunch his embattled artistic career through a number of foreign tours. The first was to have been in America where he would coproduce an album; the artist had not set foot in the United States since his ten-month stint there in 1969, which had opened his eyes to Pan-Africanism. But on September 4, 1984, as the artist and his forty-piece band were about to board their plane, he was detained under the accusation of "foreign currency violation," and his passport was seized. The charge carried a sentence of up to ten years' imprisonment.

Dragged before a court that handed him a stinging five-year sentence, he was interned in the maximum-security prison at Kirikiri, Lagos, then moved far away to the Maiduguri penitentiary in the Muslim North, totally cut off from his relatives and friends. In Fela's absence, his Shrine nightclub continued to put on its regular shows to support the large commune comprising Fela's household, his musicians, their dependents, and the numerous hangers-on that drifted ceaselessly into Kalakuta Republic. Fela's son Femi, who was asserting himself as a saxophonist, took charge of the band and also tried to reorganize the commune away from the esotericism into which it had fallen.

This time the victimization of the maverick musician caught Amnesty International's attention, which began to campaign for his release. Fela's worldwide fans swung into action; "Free Fela" benefit concerts and rallies were staged internationally, and Nigerian embassies in Europe's principal capitals were besieged by demonstrators demanding the artist's release. In frustration, the Nigerian police again raided the rebel's home in January 1985; soon after, the landlord had the entire Fela household evicted.

The prospect of Fela's long-term imprisonment threw his family into disarray; there seemed to be no end in sight to their suffering. After years of being harassed and demeaned for their loyalty to Nigeria's Public Enemy Number One, some of the cowives were understandably weary. They had withstood three major attacks on the compound, during which the soldiery had sexually assaulted many of them. With Fela locked into a long prison sentence and no obvious hope for his early release, some of his wives looked for individual solutions to their dilemma.

Fela's amazing luck would again save him. Ironically, this time it came in the shape of yet another military coup, which in July 1985 ushered in Major General Ibrahim Babangida. He accused his predecessor of the same ills that General Buhari himself invoked to depose the civilian Shagari: incompetence, corruption, inefficiency, the breakdown of law and order. This time, however, the military appointed Dr. Koye Ransome Kuti—Fela's own brother—as minister of health. (He retained the portfolio until 1993.) The regime change would therefore force a review of Fela's case.

Fela had already served twenty months of his five-year jail term for crimes he had not committed, when, in April 1986, a popular local magazine revealed that the judge who had sentenced him to jail paid the rebel a secret visit and confessed to having acted under duress. This sensational revelation, heightened by the international commotion over Fela's imprisonment, prompted the Babangida regime to grudgingly review the case. Still, the musician would be kept in prison for yet another ten months.

No sooner was Fela free than he publicly distanced himself from his brother's participation in the new regime, which he vowed to continue fighting. "I won't thank government for releasing me but I thank all Nigerians, Africans, Europeans, Asians and Americans who have in one way or the other called for my release," he told the press. "To all of you, I thank from something more deep than the bottom of my heart."[10] His politics were as defiant as ever.

If anything, the long spell in jail further entrenched Fela's belief in black magic and African witchcraft. He claimed having emerged from his prison experience stronger and wiser. He was now "half Spirit and half Man" and, accordingly, began to designate himself as the Ebami Eda (the One Touched by Divine Hand), which his awed followers loosely translated as "the Weird One."

Fela's communal compound was sacralized, for, as he claimed, "Kalakuta is not an ordinary place, it is the center of the world."[11] The Afrika Shrine was also turned into a sort of spiritual heartland, where complex rituals and sacrifices to ancestral spirits were performed before each performance. Now permanently "possessed" by spirits, Fela began experiencing states of trance in which he believed he could see into the future. During one such trance, he reported having seen the future of the entire world:

> [I]n that trance I saw the tide will change, that this whole earth was going to change into something different, into what people call today the Age of Aquarius. I saw that . . . [it] was going to be the age of goodness where music was going to be the final expression of the human race and musicians were going to be

very important in the development of the human society. And that musicians would probably be presidents of different countries. The artists will be the dictators of society. The mind will be freer, less complicated institutions; the revelations to less complicated technology, all these things I saw in the trance.[12]

Simply, Fela had now placed responsibility for Africa's renaissance squarely into the hands of spirits, for whom he was merely an emissary. However, an important shift had taken place in his own household, which bore no relation to spirits. While in jail, Fela had been assailed by rumors that several of his wives had taken lovers, and some were even reportedly pregnant. On his release, he found the rumors to be accurate. These women were young and eager to be mothers. Their famed husband was suspected to be sterile as a result, some believed, of blows to his groin sustained during the brutal sack and burning of his commune in 1977.[13]

In an uncharacteristic move for someone who upheld many patriarchal views but totally to the credit of his sense of fairness, Fela refrained from accusing his wives for having "strayed."[14] On the contrary, he said he understood them; in prison he had come to the realization that marriage was both dysfunctional and an aberration. "Marriage is an institution [and] I condemn the institution of marriage," he said.[15] Marriage fostered sentiments of possessiveness that limited the options of the partner and thus created tensions. "Marriage brings jealousy and selfishness. . . . I just don't agree to possess a woman. I just don't want to say: 'This woman is mine, so she shouldn't go out with other men.'" He therefore concluded that

The marriage institution for the progress of the mind is evil. I learned that from prison. Why do people marry? Is it to be together? Is it to have children? People marry because they are jealous. People marry because they are possessive. People marry because they are selfish. All this comes to the very ugly fact that people want to own and control other people's bodies. I think the mind of human beings should develop to the point where that jealous feeling should be completely eradicated.[16]

In tune with this, Fela announced his decision to end his collective marriage. The divorce was as simple as had been the collective marriage to those twenty-seven women eight years earlier. Without acrimony, he thanked them for having stood alongside him throughout those harrowing years. Those who chose to remain could do so and would be free to conduct their individual lives as they chose (half a

278

dozen took that option). As remarked by LaRay Denzer, that entire episode pointed to a key characteristic of Fela's otherwise patriarchal worldview:

> One important thing about Fela in his relationship with women was his absolute honesty. Almost every woman in his life commented on it as a reason for their falling in love with him in the first place and for remaining friends when a relationship was transformed. He did not pledge fidelity. He did not demand total subservience. Despite his pronouncement about "mattresses," he allowed the women in his life—wives and ex-wives, mistresses and girlfriends, daughters and employees—plenty latitude to develop their talent and lives.[17]

On the heels of his divorce, Fela faced yet another traumatic crisis—the break with his would-be-heir musician son, Femi, who had kept the organization from falling apart during his father's imprisonment. A composer in his own right, the budding musician was on his personal journey of creative self-affirmation; father and son no longer saw eye to eye on the most basic front—music. Moreover, Femi had introduced housecleaning changes in the commune that Fela swiftly discarded. As Femi would recall later, "By the time he came out [of prison], he had so many yes-men and the household was very crazy at this time. So . . . I decided to leave. . . . I was tired of agreeing with everything I saw. So I said, '*This is enough.*'"[18] In 1986, Femi walked away from his ten-year membership in Fela's band and set up his own Positive Force; father and son would remain estranged for five years.

Fela reacted to the shrinking of his commune by withdrawing even farther into himself and becoming ever more immersed in his invasive mysticism. In the process, his music was metamorphosing from the joyous, bouncy, infectious tunes of the 1970s to slower, somber compositions more in line with the spiritualism he now professed. He even came to reject the term "Afrobeat" and began describing his compositions as African classical music. The shift was more than metaphoric; it indicated a change in the way Fela had come to regard and harness his own creativity. The term "Afrobeat" denoted irreverent slackness, whereas "African classical music"—besides placing his creativity on a par with Europe's well-recognized musical traditions—was more in tune with his new, more subdued mood.

Fela continued to work at a furious pace during the second half of the 1980s. In 1986, he undertook successful tours of the United States and Europe, where his music seemed to be catching on, performing in Giants Stadium in New Jersey for an Amnesty International event and touring in several U.S. cities. But the fact that Africa's most prolific musical revolutionary still had to share the stage with others highlighted the long road still ahead for Fela.

The following year, in October 1987, the rebel musician's creeping sense of isolation was heightened by another personal blow. In Burkina Faso the revolutionary leader Captain Thomas Sankara—the only African ruler to have publicly embraced Fela and his music—was assassinated in a coup d'état apparently orchestrated by the West. A revolutionary, Sankara had seized power in a bloodless coup in 1983 at the age of thirty-three; since then he had attempted to pry his landlocked country away from French imperial control. Some months before the assassination, the leader had personally hosted Fela in Burkina Faso. "Underground System"—one of Fela's most beautiful compositions of the period—was a tribute to the fallen Pan-Africanist hero. According to the song, Africa had fallen under the control of a complex network of subterranean, transnational institutions whose aim was to perpetuate the subjection of its peoples; Sankara had been felled by this gargantuan, imperialistic cobweb. The tune was a big hit when released in 1992.

Sankara's murder most likely increased Fela's awareness of the hovering threat to his own life, but his trip to Burkina Faso had its own tragic personal resonance: in the middle of his sojourn, lesions erupted over the musician's body, causing him to cut the trip short and rush back home to consult soothsayers and herbalists. It would take nearly a decade to become dramatically clear that the unsightly breakout was the first sign of AIDS. Fela, however, was induced to interpret the mysterious lesions as concrete signs of his ongoing "spiritual transformation." He was merely "changing skin," he would later explain to the press.[19]

Coming from someone as well read as Fela, such gullibility may seem, today, incomprehensible. However, it must be viewed with an understanding of two elements—the fluid ideological framework within which Fela operated to form his political opinions and the wholesale ignorance about the AIDS pandemic that was preponderant at the time. In the 1980s, AIDS was still a mysterious phenomenon unknown to most people, including heads of states and governments. Fela, consequently, denied its existence, claiming that the purported disease was an "invention of the white man." Later on, he would also argue that, "Africans cannot get AIDS—[because] Africans eat fresh meat and vegetables; most of our food are all fresh, as a result we have natural immunity against those white man diseases."[20]

As a principle, Fela thoroughly rejected the use of any form of birth control by Africans as politically irresponsible, because he believed that the West and Asia were seeking outlets for their own population overflow. He surmised that these hegemonic regions wanted to scare Africans into adopting practices of sexual abstinence and condom-protected sex that would in fact depopulate the continent, opening the way for their own settlement. He contended that Africa was already depopulated as a result of the Arab and European slave trade, and the West was now using the AIDS scare to deter Africans from having large families to repopulate the continent. Europe, China, and India, he suspected, wanted to impose a Malthusian solution on Africa in order to hoard the continent's resources and gain land to absorb their own demographic overflow.

Therefore, in 1991, when the AIDS alert began to be sounded throughout Africa, Fela had no qualms in composing what would be the most reckless song of his entire career, "Condom, Scaliwag, and Scatter," a tune in which the rebel musician roundly condemned the use of condoms by Africans and decried protected sex as "unnatural." It is clear that Fela tragically—as many people at the time—did not understand what AIDS really was.

The Light Dims

The glory days of the Kalakuta Republic were now clearly past; the "rascal republic" was crumbling. Fela was barely making ends meet, but he was known to grow in adversity and rebound from his defeats. He was a phoenix. His musical exigencies remained as demanding as before, and the new recruits to his loyal big band strained to follow the increasingly complex, solemn compositions of the master.

In the late 1980s he released "Teacher Don't Teach Me Nonsense," an unforgiving satirical assault on the colonial education that was fostering cultural alienation among the surging generations of Africans. He fired two still more powerful shots: "Beasts of No Nation" and "Overtake Don Overtake Overtake." These devastating commentaries delineated the emergent face of a new world order that a decade later would bear the name "globalization." The rulers of this "global village"—an environment without borders, not to promote the free transit of humans but to incite the unencumbered flow of capital—were simply "Beasts of No Nation," intent on pillage.

Fela's hit tunes of the late 1970s, "I.T.T." (International Thief, Thief), "V.I.P." (Vagabonds in Power), and "Authority Stealing," already betrayed a perceptive recognition of the local implications of an emergent transnational capitalism. In that new scheme, the ruling elites in Africa appeared as amoral and soulless comprador classes, devoid of any national interests or cultural moorings, people without any specific allegiance to nation, country, or continent. African despots, too, were beasts who belonged to no nation.

The Shrine was the only place where the anointed could listen to the new Fela music, so his enduring audience continued to pack the place, which was now declared to be a sort of spiritual mecca for all mankind, not solely for Africa. From just a nightclub the Shrine had evolved into the seat of a new religion, planted in the heart of one of Lagos's most squalid, disinherited areas. There, Fela performed inventive rituals that he believed would engender Africa's renaissance but that conformed to no particular traditional belief system. Even in that sense he was a creative innovator.

In 1989, 1990, and 1991 Fela and his Egypt 80 band made sporadic forays into Europe and the United States; twice he played at Harlem's famed Apollo Theater (the first time at a benefit concert for his musical mentor, James Brown, who was then in prison). Fela's continuing refusal to compromise with the demands of the international music cartels was a significant factor in preventing those tours from having global repercussions. Thus he was unfazed when, while on tour in the United States, eleven not-so-politically-inclined members of his band left him. He was simply not interested in compromising his artistic creativity for money, even turning down a multimillion-dollar offer from Motown "on advice from the spirits."[21] On the other hand, according to former Fela aide ID, the musician also "went through a lot of economic embargo—no record company wanted to sign him. For example, one record company executive thought the ten million dollars Fela asked for the sale of his back catalog was crazy."

Those who visited him in his shrinking commune or spoke to him during his foreign tours during the 1990s witnessed the unmistakable signs of battle fatigue and demoralization. "Fela told me there was nothing else to sing about, nothing else to talk about, because he'd said it all [and nothing had changed]. He was very sad," commented his longtime friend Sandra. "This was a man who had been [a] very jovial-type person. He became a recluse. Fela was caught in his own world of Kalakuta. He was the king there, and he surrounded himself with a bunch of 'yes-men.'"[22]

The "old Fela," whose fresh, boyish manners had charmed so many, whose iconoclastic lifestyle defied the stultifying neocolonial environment of the so-called New Africa, had repositioned himself as a spiritual guru. From the frolicking, energetic Fela of the 1970s and early 1980s, a somber, humorless, withdrawn, introspective Fela had emerged, who seldom left his commune. The "new Fela" was a tormented pessimist who, during his appearances at the Shrine, looked

282

tired and haggard. But he had not lost his capacity to pour scorn on Africa's neocolonial elites, as in his tune "Just Like That," one of his very last releases. Thereafter, although he continued to compose, he steadfastly refused to record. "Why even bother?" he said in an interview, in 1991. "I've said everything. It's all been said. It's all been done."[23]

But those who deduced that the rebel had copped out were unaware of another underlying reason for his less energetic performances and increasing penchant for seclusion. Unknown even to Fela, a lethal illness that had gained total control of his destiny was sapping his energies. Fela's performances at the Shrine became more infrequent and shorter than usual. He appeared frail and at times walked unsteadily; he was losing his sight and had developed a persistent cough, but he refused to see a doctor or to consider what he derided as "toxic" Western medication.

The symptoms of AIDS continued to show up as blotches that appeared on parts of his body and face. Since Fela habitually performed bare-chested, these lesions were all too evident. Naively, the musician continued to insist they were "spiritual marks," testimony to his ongoing spiritual transformation. Thus, he announced that on January 1, 1992, his entire body would be covered with "new skin." In an interview the following year, he even claimed immortality. "I will never die," he said, "my ancestors have told me so."[24] Fela had no idea whatsoever that he was the carrier of a fatal, undiagnosed illness.

The Final Round

The Babangida regime did not let up: in January 1993, when the police discovered a dead body near the rebel's compound, Fela was arrested and charged outright with murder although he had had no involvement in the crime. For the three hundred and fifty-sixth time in twenty-five years, the musician was in court. Sent to the sordid Ikoyi Prison, he spent two and a half months there before his lawyers could win his release. Fela would have no cause to celebrate, for in November 1993 Nigeria experienced yet another military takeover, this time by the country's most sanguinary leader to date—General Sani Abacha.

The new military tyrant wasted no time in showing that his rule would be more unabashedly lawless and bloody than all preceding regimes. The latter liberally relied on kangaroo courts to frame and imprison opponents. Abacha resorted to hired killers who gunned people down in broad daylight, in the streets or right in their homes before their very families. His trademark signature was visible when, within weeks of his takeover, unknown assailants sprayed Fela's compound with bullets.

The message to Fela and his followers became even clearer when the new dictator moved against the country's most prominent human rights advocate, the internationally known author Ken Saro-Wiwa. Despite a worldwide outcry against his imprisonment and secret trial, Saro-Wiwa and eight other human rights advocates were hung for treason in November 1995. As always, many Nigerians expected the people's rebel to confront the new dictator on their behalf, but rumors were spreading that the he was suffering from a serious illness, which most believed to be prostate cancer.

Generally, Fela now maintained a very low profile but continued using the Shrine as a forum for his veiled attacks on the brutish Abacha regime. In his testamentlike composition "Clear Road for Jagba Jagga," he called on Nigerians to rid themselves of immoral elites, corrupt politicians, and dictators, including the incumbent Abacha, whom he identified by name. So in February 1996 armed plainclothes policemen invaded his compound, arresting him and thirty members of his band on the charge of illegal possession of marijuana. After spending ten days in prison, the ailing Fela was released on bail, but he remained at the mercy of Abacha's courts.

In July 1996, the police sealed off the Shrine. Even more ominously, Fela's junior brother, Dr. Bekolalari Ransome-Kuti, a well-known civil rights advocate, was arrested along with others accused of plotting against the regime and swiftly sentenced to life imprisonment (commuted later to fifteen years). In April 1997, the regime ordered another raid on Fela's home. Along with several cowives and about one hundred followers, Fela was arrested and charged once more with illegal possession of marijuana. This time the seriously ill Fela was sentenced to ten years imprisonment and interned in the Kirikiri maximum-security prison in Lagos. The Abacha regime now closed down the Shrine for good.

In July 1997, the televised sight of an emaciated, visibly ill Fela being dragged in handcuffs before the courts provoked a public outcry. Released on bail, the unrepentant rebel had exactly one more month to live. For the following weeks Fela remained at home, depressed and refusing visits. In the final days of that month, in a state of paranoid delusion, he locked himself in his room, refusing any food or contact with the outside world. "[M]y sister Sola came back from tour and he let her in," recounted his son Femi. "She found him lying down, practically dead. At this point, he saw almost everyone around him as evil."[25]

On August 1, Fela slipped into a coma, and his immediate family to rushed him to hospital. The next day, he expired at the age of fifty-eight, still unconscious. Only then did Nigerians and the world discover the real cause of the iconic musician's death—complications associated with the AIDS virus. At the time of his death, thirteen self-identified wives were in the musician's household.

His older brother, the former minister Dr. Olikoye Ransome-Kuti, told the press that had Fela known of his illness, he would certainly have revealed it himself. Nonetheless, how Fela could have remained totally ignorant until the very end about the real nature of his illness, despite having two medical doctors as brothers—one the former minister of health and the country's most prominent AIDS-awareness activist—is cause for amazement. As for the women in his life, other than Fehintola—singer-artist Seun's mother, who died of AIDS in 2007—it is still unclear how many of Fela's wives became HIV positive or died as a consequence of AIDS.

As befit the choices he made throughout his life, Fela died a poor man. During his affluent years, the rebel was notorious for his habit of distributing weekly—in cash—a part of his wealth to the poor. Naive as such a gesture may seem, it underscored Fela's conviction that humans are responsible for their fellow humans. As Rikki Stein, Fela's manager, would say of him

> I saw him as a social engineer, concerned with issues of injustice, corruption, the abuses of power. He was ready to lay his life on the line in defense of such causes, which he did on countless occasions. For his trouble he was beaten with rifle butts, endlessly harassed, imprisoned, vilified by the authorities, despised by bourgeois society (whose sons and daughters were captivated by him). His house was once burned to the ground by a thousand soldiers after they had raped and beaten his followers, thrown his mother and brother from a window, both of whom suffered fractures (his mother was ultimately to die from her injuries). Each time they were to beat him, though, he always bounced back with a vengeance, stronger than ever. It is my view that the only thing that kept him alive and the ultimate source of his strength, was the love the people had for him.[26]

If there was any doubt about the special place that Fela Kuti held in the hearts of ordinary Africans, it was dispelled by the outpouring of grief that led one million Nigerians to file past the transparent casket displayed in the heart of Nigeria's capital. On August 12, multitudes lined the route to Fela's compound to bid good-bye to the man who gave voice to their silence. Their last image of their hero was that of an elegantly attired Fela, wearing one of his favorite many-colored shirts, with a large marijuana cigar defiantly held between his fingers, peace suffusing his emaciated face. Rikki Stein described the moment:

> A hundred and fifty thousand people or so gathered in Tafawa Balewa Square to pay their last respects. Bands played, people queued endlessly to file past his glass coffin. We then ran with the coffin to a hearse (there were still thirty thousand people queuing up) to make the 20 mile journey to the Shrine where Fela's children were to carry out a private ceremony for family and friends. In a cavalcade of vehicles we rode through Lagos City behind a band in the back of a pick-up truck playing Fela tunes. The road was thronged with tens of thousands of people, until we came to the brow of a hill. I looked down across the valley to the distant horizon. The road was filled with people from one side to the other and as far as the eye could see. A million people or more, and even more came as we passed through each neighborhood. Seven hours to cover 20 miles and the band never dropped a note.[27]

Fela was laid to rest at the compound that symbolized his twenty-seven years of running resistance against all that he perceived as wrong in society. At last, Kalakuta had truly become a sort of new mecca. Appropriately, in June 1998—eight months after the rebel musician's death—General Abacha, the tyrant, suddenly collapsed and died of a heart attack in office, leaving behind a reported personal loot of four billion U.S. dollars stashed in several foreign bank accounts. How much sharper could the contrast be?

The Ultimate Social Rebel

Fela: This Bitch of a Life lays bare the soul of an extraordinary man whose innovative, infectious, and inimitable Afrobeat rhythm was already influencing world music when it caught the ear of internationally celebrated musicians—Miles Davis, Hugh Masekela, Gilberto Gil, the Beatles, Bob Marley, Jimmy Cliff, James Brown, the list goes on and on. But Fela—more mythical than real—for most people remained an unknown quantity.

His lengthy compositions were danceable, hypnotic incantations that induced a trancelike state in rapturous audiences, but the words riding atop the earthy sounds were always rocks hurled at the ruling classes. The record moguls found it difficult to admit that this was no mere eccentric pop star but a passionate Pan-Africanist, a rebel with an eminently political cause whose protest resonated well beyond the borders of Nigeria and Africa. His repeated clashes with politically immoral and repressive military regimes made him a hero at home; his colorful, iconoclastic behavior and radical views caught the attention of antiestablishment rebels across the globe.

Throughout his career Fela released seventy-seven albums and wrote one hundred thirty-three songs, many of which he never lived to hear on disk. But he died broke and in isolation. A government-imposed ban on his music being played on the airwaves; the destruction of his communal compound and property after ceaseless raids; countless violations of his civil liberties that prevented him from engaging in tours; his own refusal to kowtow to the demands of the music industry—the government succeeded in holding him down and keeping him at bay.

At the height of his career, Fela was an anomaly even when compared with other iconic musical rebels, such as his contemporaries Bob Marley and James Brown. Brown and Marley were the only twentieth-century musicians to have electrified the world with explicitly anti-establishment and unapologetically ghetto-inspired black music. But the Godfather of Soul and the Pope of Reggae confined their subversive onslaught to metaphorical allusions. Marley's attacks on Babylon were couched in cryptic philosophical allusions. Brown's black power invocations were conveyed in a suggestive nonverbal language: earthy groans, unabashedly ethnic body movements, and suggestive, catchy phrases ("Say It Loud: I'm Black and I'm Proud").

Marley effectively used the hypnotic sounds of reggae laced with poetic lyrics to protest injustices, creating an entirely novel philosophical discourse through music. Brown's aggressive funk, which became the backbone of Fela's Afrobeat, placed the reviled, feared black body and features on the map of the world in a positive, sensuous light. But neither Brown nor Marley tried to organize popular resentment into a political *party*, as Fela did. Neither went as far as Fela in identifying in unmistakably graphic terms the elites that were responsible for the oppression of African peoples all over the world. Nor did Brown or Marley confound the recording industry multinationals with the barrage of ideologically motivated self-entitlements and demands that Fela did. Fela was notoriously "undiplomatic": he graphically explained to millions, in and out of Africa, how the multinationals were raping an entire continent with the active complicity of local tyrants whom were designated by their very names. These he attacked frontally as "Beasts of No Nation" while deriding their armies and police as "Zombies."

Throughout the 1970s and into the mid-1980s, the wind was at Fela's back; no other musician in Africa—a continent superlatively rich in musical traditions and trends—was as prolific, ingenious, and admired as he was. Along with the South African singer Miriam Makeba, Fela was the African artiste who did most to place Africa on the world map, internationalizing the political and social issues that the African peoples had to grapple with. Like Makeba, his career was compromised by a refusal to become the sort of celebrity who turns his or her back on the plight of Africa and its out-of-Africa descendants. As a consequence, the Nigerian government, its military, and its police smashed his promising career.

Fela was an anticelebrity celebrity. In today's market-driven global economy where a premium is placed on material excess and social status, his was an authentic nonconformism that stood in stark contrast to the image of the modern popular artist. Indeed, he could easily have made a fortune, living and creating abroad and basking in the adulation of a growing worldwide army of fans. Nevertheless, he refused exile. "No one will force me out of this country," he warned. "If it is not fit to live in, then our job is to make it fit." Instead, he chose a life on the margins that rejected all the material excesses of Africa's postindependence elites. He saw the Africa that he and his parents inherited as "not the real Africa." The Kalakuta Republic he set up in the heart of a large, sprawling ghetto was his attempt to reinvent and reimagine another Africa: a space of belonging for all, especially the dispossessed.[28]

In the early 1970s, when he abandoned a life of ease and took up residence in the heart of one of Africa's most sordid slums, sharing the hardships of the poor, whom he called "my brothers," Fela made perhaps the most powerful statement any social reformer could make in rejecting the very things that the postindependence elites stood for: material greed, individual selfishness, class snobbery, puritanical mores (both Christian and Muslim), and submission to the world standards laid down by the West. As aptly summed up by Michael Veal, Fela was "one of the most irrepressible and profusely creative African spirits of the late twentieth century."[29]

The mainstream international media, with a voyeuristic focus on what it regarded as Fela's "exotic" eccentricities, attempted to reduce him to the vacuous caricature of an erratic hedonist, frolicking polygamist, and dope-smoking misfit. The elite-dominated African press fantasized his commune as an orgiastic harem—a nihilistic refuge of thugs, drug addicts, and prostitutes. However, both symbolically and pragmatically, Fela's commune was a flicker of freedom in a society reduced to a minimalist concept of the survival of the fittest.

The man obviously had chinks in his armor; at times, these could lead him way off mark even by his own revolutionary standards. Perceptively, Fela sided with the secessionist Ibos in their attempt to set up an independent nation called Biafra, but he misguidedly supported the Ugandan dictator Idi Amin, a despot who paraded as a Pan-Africanist. Despite his refreshingly unconventional approach to life, he rejected nonheterosexual orientation and believed in supportive roles for the female gender. In that sense, he echoed both traditional African views and the patriarchal views still dominant worldwide. Yet he championed women's quests for authenticity in their own right and encouraged the fullest self-expression of the women who sided with his cause. Clearly, Fela too was hemmed in by his own idiosyncratic limitations.

But when everything is considered, Fela's was certainly one of the most remarkably courageous voices of libertarian protest heard on the African continent in the twentieth century. His message that solidarity was humankind's most precious achievement may be the reason why, in this century of global interconnections and concerns, his memory and music refuse to go away.

Notes

1. Mabinuori Kayode Idowu (aka ID), "Fela: Phenomenon and Legacy," 2006, pp.168–69. (Unpublished manuscript, graciously communicated to the author with permission to quote.)
2. ID to the author, August 12, 2008.
3. Ibid.
4. ID, "Fela," pp. 168–69.
5. Ibid.
6. Sandra Izsadore, quoted in Jay Babcock, "Fela: King of the Invisible Art," *Mean* (Oct./Nov., 1999).
7. ID, "Fela," pp. 168–69.
8. Ibid.
9. Fela, quoted in Babcock, "Fela," *Mean*.
10. Fela, quoted in ID, "Fela," p. 176.
11. Fela, quoted in Babcock, "Fela," *Mean*.
12. Fela, during interview with Roger Steffens, "Free at Last—Now That the Nightmare Is Over, Fela Has a Dream," *OPTION* (Sept./Oct. 1986).
13. Another version was that during his younger years Fela had become sterile as a result of repeated venereal infections. Nonetheless, Fela sired a total of seven legally recognized children, four born during the 1970s and 1980s. Paradoxically, in the

1990s, after having been infected with the AIDS virus, Fela sired three more children—Shalewa, Motun, and Seun. Seun became a singer-artist; her mother, Fehintola, died of AIDS a decade after Fela.

14. For a nuanced explanation of Fela's complex relationship with women, see LaRay Denzer, "Fela, Women, Wives," in Trevor Schoonmaker, ed., *Fela: From West Africa to West Broadway* (New York: Palgrave MacMillan, 2003), pp. 111–34.
15. Fela, quoted in Michael Veal, *Fela: The Life and Times of an African Musical Icon* (Philadelphia: Temple University Press, 2000), p. 207.
16. Fela, quoted in Carter Van Pelt, "Africaman Original," *Beat* 16, no. 5/6 (1997), pp. 52–59.
17. Denzer, "Fela," in Schoonmaker, ed., *Fela*, pp. 131–32.
18. Femi, quoted in Babcock, "Fela," *Mean.*
19. Ibid.
20. ID, "Fela," pp. 11–12.
21. Veal, *Fela,* p. 220.
22. Sandra, quoted in Babcock, "Fela," *Mean.*
23. Van Pelt, "Africaman," *Beat.*
24. Fela, quoted in Babcock, "Fela," *Mean.*
25. Femi, quoted in Vivien Goldman, "The Rascal Republic Takes on the World," in Trevor Schoonmaker, ed., *Black President: The Art and Legacy of Fela Anikulapo Kuti* (New York: New Museum of Contemporary Art, 2003).
26. Rikki Stein, "Fela Was Sweet" (March 5, 2008), on http://en.afrik.com/article12745.html. Accessed Aug. 18, 2008, and quoted with the author's permission.
27. Ibid.
28. This point is convincingly made by Sola Olorunyomi, *Fela and the Imagined Continent* (IFRA-Ibadan/Africa World Press, 2003).
29. Veal, *Fela,* p. 240.